MONSIGNOR WILLIAM BARRY MEMORIAL LIBRARY
BARRY UNIVERSITY

0 2211 0082129 9

DATE DUE

GAYLORD   PRINTED IN U.S.A.

D1205900

Twenty Months
in Captivity

Twenty Months in Captivity

Memoirs of a Union Officer in Confederate Prisons

Bernhard Domschcke

EDITED AND TRANSLATED BY
Frederic Trautmann

Rutherford • Madison • Teaneck
Fairleigh Dickinson University Press
London and Toronto: Associated University Presses

Barry University Library
Miami, Fla. 33161

Originally published as *Zwanzig Monate in Kriegs-Gefangenschaft: Erinnerungen* (Milwaukee: W. W. Coleman, 1865).

© 1987 by Associated University Presses, Inc.

Associated University Presses
440 Forsgate Drive
Cranbury, NJ 08512

Associated University Presses
25 Sicilian Avenue
London WC1A 2QH, England

Associated University Presses
2133 Royal Windsor Drive
Unit 1
Mississauga, Ontario
Canada L5J 1K5

The paper used in this publication meets the requirements of the American National Standard for Permanence of Paper for Printed Library materials Z39.48-1984.

Library of Congress Cataloging-in-Publication Data

Domschcke, Bernhard.
Twenty months in captivity.

Translation of: Zwanzig Monate in Kriegs-Gefangen-schaft.
Bibliography: p.
Includes index.
1. Domschcke, Bernhard.   2. United States—History—Civil War, 1861–1865—Prisoners and prisons.   3. United States—History—Civil War, 1861–1865—Personal narratives.   4. United States—History—Civil War, 1861–1865—German Americans.   5. Prisoners of war—United States—Biography.   6. Prisoners of war—Southern States—Biography.   I. Trautmann, Frederic.   II. Title.

E611.D6713   1987   973.7'71'0924 [B]   85-46015
ISBN 0–8386–3286–6 (alk. paper)

PRINTED IN THE UNITED STATES OF AMERICA

E
611
. D6713
1987

To Beth

Contents

Preface

The Civil War settled the issue of union amid a welter of nationalities and a babel of tongues. Mercenaries from abroad shouldered muskets for the Union and fired cannon for the Confederacy; immigrants marched cheek by jowl with Billy Yank and rode stirrup to stirrup with Johnny Reb; and ethnic Americans brandished swords and wielded bayonets for the North and the South. These speakers of foreign languages included the longtime citizen who used his ancestral speech after generations on these shores.[1] This outlandish talk baffled and irritated English speakers (so much gibberish to them); they may also have shuddered at the English of Scots and Irish under American arms. Yet up and down the ranks the alien words lilted and droned, flowed and jerked, as men of other countries and different origins conversed, wrote letters, took orders, sounded the alarm, screamed in pain, shouted for help, begged for mercy, and met their Maker or thanked Him for sparing them—in Swedish, Norwegian, Danish, Polish, Dutch, Italian, French, Spanish, Hungarian, Portuguese, Welsh, Turkish, several American Indian languages, the Hindi and Urdu of a few sepoys, perhaps Greek and Russian, probably others, and certainly German.

In absolute figures as well as relative to their proportion of the population, immigrant and American-born Germans outnumbered the war's other foreigners.[2] German accordingly took precedence over the other foreign languages and became as important in the War between the States as it was in the United States.[3] Indeed, during the eighteenth, nineteenth, and early twentieth centuries, in any ship or home or shop, at any crossroads, on any corner, off any beaten track, on Fifth Avenue and on Main Street, German might be seen or heard. It was taught in public schools. Books, magazines, pamphlets, circulars, broadsides, and newspapers issued from a German press vigorous since colonial times.[4] The *Wöchentliche Pennsylvanische Staatsbote* carried the first notice of the Declaration of Independence, 5 July 1776. On the ninth the *Staatsbote* featured the Declaration itself—in German, the second American language.[5]

When Bernhard Domschcke volunteered for Union service, he had been an editor of German newspapers in the most German of American cities,

Milwaukee. He had opposed slavery for years, like most Germans of the North and many in the South. He became a captain in the all-German Twenty-sixth Wisconsin infantry; a prisoner of war, captured at Gettysburg; and the author of a memoir of Confederate prisons—in German.

He joined the captives making the rounds of Southern prisons; he observed faithfully and noted with care the life and conditions behind bars in Danville, Macon, Savannah, Charleston, Columbia, and Richmond; and he produced a laudable account of captivity "on the officers' circuit" of Confederate imprisonment. A keen observer and a capable reporter, he probably exceeded in education, literary talent, and journalistic skill the many other prison memoirists. Therefore, his thorough, accurate, and authoritative work was not only informative but also stylistically first-rate: immediate, engaging, and colorful. He explained plots and intrigues, enumerated the everyday routine, depicted camps and trains, described people and events, and evaluated conditions and attitudes. Not merely did he record what prisoners ate; he discussed relations among prisoners, too, and between prisoners and guards, and commented on slavery, the Confederate soldier, the government of the Confederacy, and the nature and quality of Confederate society itself. Moreover, his twenty months, more than long enough to establish his credibility, occurred at an important time in the history of Civil War imprisonment. Confederate treatment of captives changed then, from kinder to harsher, and he evinces the shift. In sum, his document of historical merit and literary excellence is one of the most complete, most balanced, and most authoritative Union memoirs of Confederate prisons.

Yet for 125 years only readers of German could appreciate a book that deserved greater attention and wider praise. For that reason, I have tried to turn Domschcke's German into accurate and representative English for all Americans interested in their Civil War.

Accordingly, I have deleted nothing, rearranged a few small parts, inserted interpolations, and added annotations. In translating I have tried to be as literal as possible. But word-for-word and letter-for-letter, the well-intentioned but unrealistic *verbatim et literatim* of the old translators' maxim have been characteristically elusive here. At any rate, ideally "a translator does not photograph an original text, he re-creates it through art," obeying the "unwritten law" to " 'translate not the word itself, but the sense and the style.' "[6] And then, the "ambiguities and resonances [of German words], which might be of significance in understanding" the text, "can be wiped away through an accurate but inadequate choice of [an English] word or phrase."[7] Moreover, "a systematic conceptual development" may be distorted, and "a line of argument might [then] be obscured," in a mere exchange of English for German. "Strategies" must be "adopted in such cases," each to solve the particular problem of clarity or fidelity.[8] Thus a translation apt for its times can demand "cutting and mauling and chopping and slicing" and even "infinite drubbings."[9] Now, I have not cut, mauled, chopped, sliced, or drubbed. But in the interests of unity, coherence, emphasis, and faithful representation of Domschcke's German, I have departed from a literal rendition as follows:

• Paragraphing has been altered occasionally, and the sequence of sentences shifted once in a while. No sentence has been moved far, and never out of the chapter in which it originally occurred.

• In a few instances the English would be wrong in another context. "Billet" is not usually right for *Lager;* but when Domschcke has *Lager* to signify the situation of some prisoners in buildings and others in tents, "billet" has been chosen as the best alternative. Again, he often refers to fellow captives as *Offiziere* ("officers"), and they were all officers, but in context it has often been more sensible to say "prisoners." What might be translated as "enclosure" and "fence" have been made "pen" and "stockade," the words then used for those things.

• The English is sometimes put into a tense different from that of the German—present for past, say, or past for present—usually because the historical present is more agreeable in German than in English.

• Infrequently, for clarity, variety, and grace, dialogue has been supplied in English, to represent reports of speaking; but only if the reports are in the subjunctive in the original. In the context of reported speech, the German subjunctive is usually equivalent to direct discourse in English.

• When spellings—of town names, for example, or geographical features—are outdated or grossly incorrect, today's correct ones have been substituted.

• Original quotation marks have been retained when they enclosed German. When they enclosed English, they have been deleted, unless they were intended to signify transcription, such as a copy of the words of someone speaking.

• Words in English in the original, listed at the back of the book, have been retained in the text when better ones might have been substituted. Misspellings of English in the original have been corrected in the translation.

• Words, phrases, names, and an infrequent sentence have been interpolated [thus] as needed or desirable.

*   *   *

For generous aid and unfailing comfort, I am indebted to these splendid helpers:

Elizabeth Delano Whiteman, my best and most faithful reader;

Maxwell Whiteman, who believes in the printed word and the people who create it, and who thinks books without life are (almost) as bad as life without books;

Joe Zucca and the staff of the Inter-Library Loan Unit, Paley Library, Temple University: skilled and congenial keepers of keys that open locks to the libraries of the world;

Leonard Barrett, who helped more than I can say, and who probably would be surprised that he helped at all;

Lady Luck, the best of muses, who smiled again;

Beth Trautmann, who urged me to start, inspired me to finish, and sustained me in between—to her above all.

Frederic Trautmann

Twenty Months
in Captivity

Introduction

The Civil War slashed like a sword across American history. On rainy days in the national life, the scar aches like a bone broken, badly set, and imperfectly healed years ago—a reminder and an influence, especially in the South. A bumper sticker flaunts a Confederate flag and snarls: "Fergit, hell!" In the old Confederacy, *the war* signifies the War for Southern Independence, unless an inferior one is specified, such as Vietnam or Korea or a world war. In 1984 a British novelist discovered "that the Civil War occupies a major and potent place in the Southern folk memory . . . more alive than, say, memories of the 1940 blitz are to Londoners," as if the Civil War had occurred "only a decade ago. Sherman's march to the sea is still spoken of in terms of genuine outrage."[1] In 1985 a former White House press secretary said of the Yankee attitude toward the march, "Perhaps they would understand how it feels if a group of Georgians marched on New York, burned 30 Rockefeller Center to the ground and stole their pigs and silverware."[2]

A vast and horrific conflict, powerful enough to rend the United States, produced casualties in the hundreds of thousands, damage in the billions, and incalculable and enduring political, social, economic, and psychological effects. Excepting the Chinese Taipeng Rebellion (1850–64), the Civil War was the biggest between 1815 and 1914, the largest and costliest ever in the Western Hemisphere, a war such as the world had never seen but that prefigured and shaped wars that followed. Casualties at Waterloo (1815) numbered 62,000; at Gettysburg (1863), over 51,000. "Even the battle of the three emperors at Austerlitz [1805] and the duel of Napoleon and Wellington at Waterloo [seemed] pallid in contrast" to the "long rows of dead," the "lines of wounded," the "hospitals [outside which] rose gory heaps of amputated arms and legs," and Bloody Pond "half-filled with men and horses." They had groped to its shores "only to die" at Chickamauga, Georgia, in 1863.[3]

The once United States fought a war of firsts and showed the world what wars would be like. Steam-powered military transport, ironclads, and heavy naval ordnance were tested,[4] along with aerial reconnaissance, the telegraph, mines, grenades, rifles and rifled cannon, the machine gun, trenches, and wire entanglements. In other words, this war standardized the weapons of the Industrial Revolution.[5] As to medicine, a physician in this war, Konrad Söllheim, observed, "The conduct of subsequent wars shows that the lesson of the need for proper care of the wounded was not lost on our posterity."[6]

No less significant were the changes with regard to prisons and prisoners of war. The curtain of the future rose on scandal and suffering. The case of Captain Henri Wirz, commandant at Andersonville, foreshadowed the barbarism that culminated, one can only hope, at Nuremburg in 1945 and 1946. Tried and hanged, Wirz died as the first military man officially to pay the full price for crimes against prisoners of war.

He and his successors in atrocity took too seriously some of the goals of imprisonment. Whether within civil society in peacetime or between nations at war, these goals include punishment, vengeance, reformation, rehabilitation, and advantage to the captor. The one who imprisons expects to be protected from the prisoner and usually to wring benefit from him. Thus, in warfare, the enemy's military forces, and sometimes his civilians, who remain alive, are to be seized, detained, and held at the captor's pleasure. In all wars since records have been kept of wars, that fundamental has prevailed, and prisoners have been paroled, exchanged, tortured, killed (by violence, by starvation, and by neglect), ransomed, locked up (in idleness here, in forced labor there), and indoctrinated or brainwashed. Massacre, crucifixion, burning, and other savageries ancient and modern have been visited upon prisoners. In many ways, then, both cruel and kind attempts have been made to reach the goals of imprisonment as an aspect of war.

The prisoner of war, a feature of war since the start, has been as much a part of war as war has been of civilization—in other words, one of the oldest conditions in human experience. Rules of conduct to and for him have accordingly been recognized in custom and codified in law since ancient times. The Egyptians, Assyrians, Babylonians, Israelites, Greeks, Mayas, and Romans waged war and took prisoners. Meanwhile, institutionalized justice had begun, and laws were elaborated. Hammurabi (died 1750 B.C.), the best known of ancient legislators, holds an honored place in ancient annals. Soon there were laws of nations and laws of war, and the codes included provisions for prisoners of war. As early as the First and Second Punic Wars (between 264 and 201 B.C.), Roman and Carthaginian generals exchanged prisoners, and differences were made up by payment in gold.[7] Later, Islamic practices influenced Christian. Muhammad's successor, Caliph abu-Bakr (seventh century A.D.) urged that the helpless be spared in war and that "prisoners of war be treated with pity"; the Islamic nations ransomed and exchanged prisoners of war in ways that spread to the West.[8] By 1581 Balthazar Ayala, judge advocate to the Spanish army of the Netherlands, could devote a treatise of three books to the laws of war, strategy, and military discipline, which included extended discussions of prisoners. In general he urged justice and kindness, not the crucifixion, immolation, and strangulation of earlier, crueler times.[9] Alberico Gentili, an Italian who became a professor at Oxford in 1581, went further in *De jure belli* (1588–89), which was longer, more specific, and increasingly inclined to justice, fair play, and humanitarianism: prisoners are not to be killed or tormented but treated with at least a modicum of kindness.[10] Hugo Grotius, the Dutch diplomat, historian, and one of the greatest writers on international relations, in *De jure belli ac pacis* (1625), urged mercy and Christian charity toward the captive.[11]

Those ideas prevailed, at least in theory, into the nineteenth century— even gained credence and expanded during the French Revolution.[12] The political philosopher and social theorist Montesquieu, in the influential *Spirit of the Laws* (1748), said that war gave "no other right over prisoners than to disable them from doing any further harm by securing their persons." Presumably they were not to be mistreated and certainly not to be murdered "in cold blood."[13] Seeking to "humanize" war, Swiss jurist Emmerich von Vattel, in *The Law of Nations* (1758), wrote with the eighteenth century's emerging sense of war as gentlemanly, chivalrous, and even romantic, and he opposed, among other barbarous practices, the killing of prisoners.[14] He agreed with prior theorists and with the international law of his time that combatants should be made prisoners of war, that they be humanely treated, that they might be exchanged and ransomed, and that they be set free "by treaty of peace at the end of the war."[15] Similarly, Rousseau—following his predecessor in social and political theory, Montesquieu—said in the *Social Contract* (1762) that a state of war did not confer the right of the victor to kill the vanquished.[16]

But in the nineteenth century, wars began to lose that romantic aura and to become total: struggles for victory at all costs.[17] In that passion to win, the old cruelty was revived. And then, too, sophisticated technology and modern organization changed war to mechanized horror.[18] "It has often been said—and truly said—that the American Civil War was the last romantic war and the first modern war," romantic at the start, modern (hence ghastly) at the end.[19] No longer a gentleman's chess match with some blood here and there for color, war became what generals in the century's biggest and grisliest war called it. Robert E. Lee said, "It is well that war is so terrible or we would grow too fond of it." He was speaking to General James Longstreet at Fredericksburg, Virginia, on 13 December 1862, as Union troops were falling by the thousands on Marye's Heights. Longstreet answered, "Not a fleeing chicken could survive our rain of lead."[20]

Lee probably wanted to grow fond of the war of fine uniforms, polished boots, glittering buttons, epic figures on grand horses—himself, perhaps, on Traveller—and wives and sweethearts in hoopskirts and crinolines throwing flowers and blowing kisses to departing and conquering heroes. Those elements of romance have lingered, like *Gone with the Wind,* in popular fantasy, and they reappear in "novels for television" in the 1980s, even though contradicted by the facts of the war: human-wave attacks, fire bombs, gangrene, and generals who wore privates' tunics, chain-smoked cigars, drank rotgut, and cared nothing for horses except as tons of cannon fodder. Suffering increased for civilians and soldiers alike, as weapons dealt death and destruction as never before. The eight-inch Parrott gun, a rifled cannon designed by a Union ordnance officer, could hurl a two-hundred-pound projectile over four miles. Union forces placed it near Charleston, South Carolina, nicknamed it Swamp Angel, and shelled the city with incendiaries in the summer of 1863. At the Battle of Stone's River in 1862, fifty-eight pieces of Union artillery fired a hundred shots a minute at "the mass of men" and "mowed [them] down by the score. Confederates were pinioned to earth by falling branches."[21] At Shiloh in 1862, Ulysses S. Grant saw a field that could be crossed "in any direction [by] stepping on dead bodies, without a foot touching the ground."[22] After William T. Sherman's army shot and burned its way across the South, Sherman told the mayor of Atlanta, "War is cruelty and you cannot refine it."[23] War might look like glory, he said in 1880, "but, boys, it is all hell."[24]

Prisoners of war meanwhile languished and agonized in something else from the brains of military Frankensteins: the concentration camp. Andersonville was nefarious among many grim ones. Hindsight shows the horrors of World War II being prepared a century before in the Civil War's brutalized and magnified Black Holes of Calcutta.[25]

In the years preceding the Civil War, combat had already been growing so gruesome, for both soldiers and civilians, that the first Geneva Convention was called to draw up international agreements to regularize procedures for the amelioration of conditions that bordered on atrocity and holocaust. Jean Henri Dunant, eyewitness to the Battle of Solferino in the second War of Italian Independence (1859), saw 300,000 troops create 40,000 casualties.[26] He recoiled from the suffering of the wounded, many of whom later died of neglect, if they were not among those buried alive. He wrote a book describing what he had observed: *Un souvenir de Solferino* (1862). And he organized the convention. It met in his home city of Geneva, Switzerland, in 1864, created the Red Cross, and framed a program for the "humanization" of warfare, including the international protection of the wounded and of prisoners. Most of the Western powers ratified the convention by 1866. The United States, fearful of entangling alliances, did not ratify until 1882.[27] Meanwhile the United States fought a war with over 2,000,000 men under arms, and suffered 1,000,000 casualties, 500,000 prisoners, and destruction of the possessions and damage to the minds of a people. Never before had wartime statistics mounted to such enormity. Suffering and devastation raged, a monstrousness not surpassed in every respect in the subsequent world wars.[28]

Francis Lieber, a German-American intellectual of the time, learned war and saw its agony in Europe and the United States. He fought in the Battle of Waterloo and for the independence of Greece, then emigrated to America in the 1820s, where he became a social and political reformer, a professor, and (in the term he coined for himself) a "publicist."[29] He opposed slavery, advocated reform of civil and criminal law, and urged codification of international law. When the Civil War broke out, he "began to agitate for co-ordinated rules because he wished to see the Union army become a smooth-functioning, efficient military machine." He contemplated "a little book in the Law and Usages of War, affecting the Combatants," as "nothing of the sort" had "ever been written."[30] Chiefly through Lieber's influence with General in Chief Henry W. Halleck, Lieber's "little book," a code of regulations for armies, appeared under President Lincoln's imprimatur in 1863 as "General Orders No. 100: Instructions for the Government of Armies of the United States in the Field," and "published for the information of all concerned."[31] Though not binding and of little effect on the treatment of prisoners, the code did influence some aspects of both sides' conduct of the war and shaped behavior in subsequent wars fought in Europe as well as by the United States, through World War II.[32]

"General Orders No. 100" contains 157 articles, or regulations, in ten sections covering the principal elements of any army's manner to enemies, military and civilian, when not in combat. In other words, "General Orders" is not a manual of strategy and tactics, but a code of ethics; not a guide to fighting the enemy, but a credo of how to treat him when not fighting him. Forty-five articles pertain to prisoners. The term *prisoner* is defined, and the definition includes the difference between a prisoner and a hostage. Prisoners, though subject to confinement or detention, are to be treated humanely, in accord with rank and condition, and without regard to color or race; and their personal property, money, and valuables are to be respected. Prisoners may be shot in flight but not otherwise punished for attempting to escape, unless part of a conspiracy plotting general escape. Prisoners may be exchanged in a way provided for by cartel, and they may be paroled.[33]

Thus the humane treatment of prisoners of war had been creditably and consistently urged since ancient times. Yet both sides of the Civil War were cruel to prisoners. The South seems to have been worse than the North, but the North was by no means innocent. "Northern prisons killed far more than their share of Southern soldiers"; the death rate was 24 percent at Elmira Prison Camp in New York.[34] In the North, physical and mental illness due to exposure, poor diet, and overcrowding caused much suffering. In the South, the infamous Andersonville became synonymous with cruelty, the nineteenth century's Auschwitz or Bergen-Belsen. Andersonville's overcrowding, polluted water, vile food, lack of medicine, eager bloodhounds, and vicious guards produced tuberculosis, dysentery, scurvy, gangrene, yellow fever, and injury and death by beating, shooting, stabbing, and hanging. MacKinlay Kantor dramatized the shame. His novel, *Andersonville* (1955), is so long because there was so much to tell, so much savagery to describe, so much degradation to relate.[35] The many other prisons, North and South, did not match Andersonville but were more cruel than kind nonetheless.[36]

In the prison at Rock Island, Illinois, prisoners were forced to perform menial labor. "The severe climate, the insufficient clothing, food, and bedding, and the condition of their barracks all told most seriously"; and many "sickened and died," smallpox being an important killer.[37] In the prison for Confederate officers at Camp Chase, Ohio, gangrene erupted in wounds, dogs were eaten, and dead Confederates on the boat from Fort McHenry, Maryland, were tossed overboard: "More damned rebels that we won't have to fight."[38] According to an inmate of a Southern prison, "If you never have smelled a dog cooking you cannot know how good that smells. There wasn't enough dog to go around. We picked him clean, then we picked his bones and made toothpicks of them."[39] Even a mild account of Andersonville, which mentions neither Captain Wirz nor any act of deliberate cruelty, details "the many hardships to which the Union prisoners were subject."[40] In a typical account of Andersonville, the inmates "who had been held the longest [as of 25 July 1864] were worn down with want, sickness, and famine, with shrunken bodies, dishevelled hair, eyes deep set in their sockets, fingers long and bony, and emaciated looks. Turn which way you would, you were met with suffering and sorrow, while the air was impregnated with sickening odors of rank corruption and loathsome death."[41] Vermin multiplied at "a terrible rate," covering many of the sick "with the terrible pest."[42]

Why, in a purportedly civilized nation, did such horrors occur such a short time ago? Were that question asked about Nazi Germany, the answer might point to vicious leaders, resentment over twists of historical fate, social irritation, economic depression, and widespread, deep-seated, rabid anti-Semitism. But that answer, however true for Nazi Germany, fails to explain what happened in prisons in a war led by Abraham Lincoln and Jefferson Davis in a prosperous country with few historical scars, no tradition of official cruelty, and mild social unrest.

A better answer might begin with the sadists in authority in Civil War prisons, notably Wirz of Andersonville, tried and hanged for his crimes.[43] More important, as neither North nor South ratified the Geneva Convention, international law on prisoners did not exist here; captors could do as they pleased with captives. Besides, Lieber's code and "General Orders No. 100," not binding on Northern forces to whom they were issued for information, meant still less to the North's antagonist. And, even at its strongest, international law projects a pseudo-legal system founded, not on statutory maxims or constitutional precepts willingly acknowledged and peacefully obeyed by nations subject to it, but on multinational relationships that shift, dissolve, and regroup according to the locus and balance of power. Nations can and do flout the law when strong enough to benefit by flouting it.[44] Indeed, the South could have been expected even less to behave according to it, for the North refused to treat the South as sovereign and resisted agreements that would recognize the South de facto or so much as imply recognition. Hence the lack of agreements on prisoners.

Still "when governments do not make such agreements, opposite commanding generals, during a campaign, regulate mutual exchanges of prisoners, and also determine the allowances to be made to prisoners while they are in captivity."[45] Under such agreements, or cartels, Civil War prisoners were exchanged, but in small numbers. The generals, after all, favored military advantages to be gained, not humanitarian services to be rendered. The generals did not wage this war—as they do not wage any war—to play angels of mercy; such mollycoddling is left to the Clara Bartons. They waged war to *win,* and they were dour and dogged, especially Grant. His eyes and jaw asserted "determination and stern fighting power."[46] If, to triumph, one must be savage, one would be savage; he epitomized the resolve. Furthermore, in this war of ideology, one of the first of the kind, "passions [flamed] on both sides."[47] Ideological wars breed viciousness because the victor must both succeed on the field and subdue if not exterminate everybody who believes the opposing ideology. Thus Grant would have "no terms except an unconditional and immediate surrender."[48] Though his losses and the enemy's had been heavy, he said later, he proposed "to fight it out on this line if it takes all summer."[49] He ran the Army of the Potomac like "a battering ram, without consciousness and without feeling."[50] Sherman expected him to become the war's "typical hero."[51] He did become "Unconditional Surrender" Grant, such a hero that he won two terms as president despite politics as notable for incompetence as his generalship had been exceptional in brilliance.

Little mercy and less care for prisoners resulted from that miasma. The Dix-Hill cartel, signed on 22 July 1862, provided for parole and exchange, but violations and misunderstandings ended it by the summer of 1863. In December 1863, Butler and Ould renewed exchange and restored the hopes of Domschcke and thousands of others in Confederate prisons. But on 17 April 1864, Grant and Chief of Staff Halleck stopped exchange until February 1865.[52] They acted out of expediency, contradicting humanitarian concerns for Union prisoners. Halleck deplored the cruelty of leaving them to be "tortured to death. But I suppose there is no remedy at present."[53] Grant explained, "We have got to fight until the military power of the South is exhausted, and if we release or exchange prisoners captured [by us,] it simply becomes a war of extermination"; therefore neither "exchange nor release" on "any pretext whatever until the war closes."[54] Hence exchange dragged throughout the war and practically stopped as the end neared, and more and more prisoners crowded into smaller and smaller confines and under worsening conditions, especially in the South. Domschcke refers again and again to the hope for exchange—not to be realized, for him, until the war was nearly over.

In short, despite the time-honored and prevailing philosophy of humanitarianism, prisoners were held because a modern nation balked at a technicality, and prisoners were detained and mistreated because bull-headed generals wanted to win a vicious war of ideology—win it by any means whatsoever, so long as victory was total.

Technicalities mattered, and ideology must prevail regardless of cost. Hence—to finish explaining cruelty in Civil War prisons—regulations, bureaucracy, and rigidly formal organization became standard in the first modern war. "Behind the carefully planned array of corps, divisions, brigades, regiments, and batteries was a more and more elaborate network of agencies to provide everything the armed forces required, from tent pins to siege guns."[55] The institutionalized and depersonalized cruelty of modern times thus emerged. It would worsen until World War II featured concentration camps with gas chambers. In World War II's nadir of barbarity notably, as if impersonal forces were responsible, camp commandants and gas-chamber technicians disclaimed responsibility and even proclaimed ignorance; at most, they had only obeyed orders.

The Irish author Oscar Wilde, after months in prison brooding on the supposed injustice that put him there, had reflected hard enough and deep enough to produce his long and thoughtful *Ballad of Reading Gaol* (1898). Accounting for the newfangled horror of legal, public, and amoral cruelty, he denied "medieval passion" in people who deliberately inflict pain and get "a real madness of pleasure." Rather, what was "inhuman in modern life" was *officialism* or authority wielded through regulations and bureaucracy: the "Board, and the system that it carries out." Those "who uphold the system have excellent intentions. Those who carry it out are humane in intention also. Responsibility is shifted on to the disciplinary regulations. It is supposed that because a thing is the rule it is right."[56] Thus Captain Vere, Herman Melville's "good man doing his painful duty," convenes the court-martial, rejects mercy, affirms justice, and hangs Billy Budd to maintain order and uphold the law. And Billy approves, shouting before death, "God bless Captain Vere!"[57] Similarly the post–World War II German writer Gunther Grass saw the crimes of the gas chambers, not as "human bestiality, but in the fragmentation of responsibilities, the

subdivision of the human conscience into narrow networks, the bu-
reaucratization of moral values so that loyalty to superiors and the imple-
mentation of orders are elevated to the *imperium* of human virtue. His
vision of Hell is that of Kafka and Orwell—a world directed by bureaucratic machines whose many-layered structure of responsibilities
means no responsibility at all."[58]

The crime of bureaucracy and the evil of officialism, vile and sinister
aberrations of modernism, began in the transitional war that segued from
the old to the new, the Civil War: the first war to be run by civil-military-
industrial bureaucracies in the sense that they are understood now. Thus
Robert E. Lee, arguing that deserters should be arrested and tried, said, "I
think a rigid execution of the law is kindest in the end."[59] He pleaded
ignorance of cruelty to prisoners at the Libby, Belle Island, and other
Confederate prisons; he knew "nothing in the world" about prisoners. He
called it his business to send them "to the proper officer," but he "had no
control" over "their disposition afterwards." He "never gave an order
about it. It was entirely in the hands of the War Department."[60] Abraham
Lincoln himself, as part of what he called "the duty of every government,"
met cruelty with official and bureaucratic cruelty: "For every soldier of the
United States killed in violation of the laws of war," he ordered a rebel
soldier executed. "For every one enslaved by the enemy or sold into
slavery," he ordered a rebel soldier to "hard labor."[61]

Thus, the Civil War was not only pivotal to American history but also
significant in the world at large and especially influential on warfare and
military prisons and prisoners.[62] Accordingly, "the Civil War has been the
subject of more publications than any other episode in American history,"
perhaps as many as 60,000 volumes as long ago as 1969.[63] Nevins,
Robertson, and Wiley divide them into fifteen categories. "Prisons and
Prisoners of War," eleventh in size, contains over 200 representative titles,
mostly reminiscences of imprisonment. Many of the 200 are more or less
defective.[64] Byrne calls them bitter, disorganized, farfetched, exaggerated,
partisan, insignificant, vague, brief, confused, factually worthless, ram-
bling, lurid, superficial, pretentious, careless, rabidly hostile, often er-
roneous, and sarcastically polemical.[65] But he enters no defects against a
"memoir of a German who made the customary officers' circuit through
Libby, Danville, Macon, Savannah, Charleston and Columbia" (190),
Domschcke's *Zwanzig Monate in Kriegsgefangenschaft: Erinnerungen*. A
superior account of those important prisons, it deserves a distinguished
place in this flawed literature, an honor hitherto denied because it had not
been published in translation.

* * *

Bernhard Domschcke (1827–69), "an editor of exceptional ability," was
born in the German town of Freiburg near Dresden and educated at the

universities of Dresden and Leipzig.[66] He fought in the revolution of 1848 and, perhaps for being a revolutionary, allegedly served a two-year term in prison. In 1851 he arrived in the United States. An early backer of the new Republican party, he founded in 1854 in Milwaukee a weekly German-language newspaper of Republican orientation, to oppose the city's three German-language Democratic ones. For, though one of the German exiles called Forty-eighters after their failed revolution, he seldom acted like a German immigrant; except for language, he seemed more like an old-line Yankee of New England or New York. His *Corsar* ("Corsair") was "a very able paper" and he "really a very able writer."[67] It failed, however, because its intended German-speaking audience was overwhelmingly Democratic. In 1856 he founded a second weekly, the *Atlas,* which survived until the Civil War, and became a daily as the Republicans gained adherents among Germans, especially after the nomination for president of the appealing John Fremont in 1856.[68] By then, there were at least six German-language papers in Wisconsin, including Carl Schurz's in Watertown. In 1861 Domschcke became editor of the *Milwaukee Herold,* published by W. W. Coleman, who would also publish Domschcke's prison memoirs in 1865. In 1862 Domschcke took with him the *Herold*'s staff, and they enlisted to fight for the Union.[69] Thus he proved his hatred of slavery, his Republican sincerity, and his admiration for Lincoln. Those principles, together with his literary facility and journalistic skills, distinguish this "vivid and detailed account" of the Confederacy's prisons for Union officers.[70]

Promoted to captain in the Twenty-sixth Wisconsin after the Battle of Chancellorsville (May 1863), he was captured at Gettysburg (July 1863) and sent to the Libby in Richmond, where he took an active part in prison life, observing carefully the prison's people, customs, and events. His discussion of the Libby, the longest in his book, is one of the best we have: not only thorough and accurate, but also honest and as dispassionate as could be expected in such straits.[71] He was also a witness to the Sanderson controversy there, taking the position that Colonel James M. Sanderson was guilty of cheating fellow Union prisoners out of supplies from the North, and of collaborating with the enemy against prisoners. Domschcke's testimony must count against Sanderson in the tribunal of history.

Thus he created an eyewitness record superior to most in its comprehensiveness alone, and perhaps better than all in its literary and informational excellence. Indeed, of the many authors of Civil War prison memoirs, probably none could claim to be his equal in education and experience; none was therefore as well fitted to write such memoirs. How many of the memorists were educated at world-class universities, knowledgeable appreciators of the music of Wagner, and practiced newspapermen?

Exchanged at last about a month before the end of the war, he returned to Milwaukee and the *Herold,* and wrote *Twenty Months* and his editorials with "clarity and directness."[72] Captivity and its privation informed a good book, but they had ruined his health. He spent weeks as an invalid confined to his room, then died on 5 May 1869, his forty-second birthday half a year off. He left to posterity his study of Civil War prisons, a legacy as happily munificent as his death was sadly premature. Only now, in its first publication in English, can *Twenty Months in Captivity* reach the audience it deserves.

1

From Virginia to Pennsylvania—The Battle of Gettysburg—Taken Prisoner

On 12 June 1863, the Eleventh Corps [of the Army of the Potomac] broke camp and prepared to march. We had been ordered into camp [at Stafford Court House] after the wretched Battle of Chancellorsville [1–4 May 1863].[1] Here we stayed [from 5 May to 12 June. Drill and fatigue filled our days] in the desolate, steppelike region in Stafford County of northern Virginia, near Brooke's Station, between Aquia Creek and Falmouth. And now we marched because General Robert E. Lee was on the move. He and his Rebel hordes [were maneuvering before the invasion of Pennsylvania, which would end at Gettysburg]. We knew nothing else. Conjecture therefore abounded. Where would we confront him? Some thought our army would withdraw to defend Washington, to protect the capital from the enemy's thrust. Others imagined a third clash on Bull Run's charnel fields. Another group expected an engagement along the Shenandoah. In any case, we left camp in the bright heat of summer's noonday sun and in the evening reached Hartwood Church, a village of a few houses.

From there [the next morning] we went, via Weaverville, Manassas Junction, Centreville, and Gum Springs, to Goose Creek, a tributary of the Potomac. On 17 July [after a long and tiring march in heat and dust] we stopped a few miles from the creek's mouth about six miles from Leesburg, and stayed six days. It seemed unsure yet whether we would meet the enemy in Virginia or on the other side of the Potomac. An order soon erased doubt: *Cross the Potomac at Edwards' Ferry.*[2]

On the splendid morning of 24 June, after so many crusades and pilgrimages hither and yon in old decrepit Virginia, we gained the Maryland shore, God's country. Never shall we forget the impression of well-tended gardens, green meadows, and the buildings of Maryland farms—buildings that evidenced prosperity—after being long inured to nothing but dismally boring piny woods, exhausted and barren fields, and ancient, tumbledown houses. Everywhere in northern Virginia we met not progress but stagnation, not renovation but decay, and not freedom's blessing but slavery's curse. How antiquated and enervating everything seemed! A sad place [Virginia], a locus of damnation, of perdition, as still as the grave, everywhere. Only the plaintive monotone of the whippoorwill broke the nocturnal silence of a burial ground. The bodies of our comrades in arms lay moldering in the red soil of that stygian land: the thousands who had forsaken home, prosperity, and happiness to secure the Republic against its worst foe.

The route from Edwards' Ferry took us through a prosperous region [of Maryland] to Jefferson and then Middletown and Frederick, to Emmitsburg. There we paused to rest. We pitched camp beside a convent [Saint Joseph's Seminary]: an imposing edifice of many windows and numerous little doors on all sides; a handsome palace, with outbuildings, enclosed by splendid gardens. General [Carl] Schurz [commander of a division of the Eleventh Corps] set up headquarters here. The superior [a priest], most obliging, assured the general that if a battle occurred nearby, the wounded would have shelter; 1,000 could be accommodated. In the evening [29 June], Schurz ordered up the band of the Forty-fifth New York to play the songs, marches, and polkas they knew so well. The superior himself attended. A European in black robe, he looked like a man of the world and seemed invested with the irony often found in Catholic priests of high station.[3] When Schurz asked him, *Would the nuns enjoy the music?* the reverend father smiled ironically. "They will enjoy it, but they will not let on that they have heard it."

On 30 June the order: *March to Gettysburg tomorrow.* So we left on the morning of 1 July. Up and down miles of improved and unimproved roads, over fields and fences, across creeks and swamps filled by long rains the day before—then the command from Gettysburg: *Come here as fast as you can!* One of our hardest and most tiring treks began at once. Soon we reached the hilly region and scaled rocky heights on the run. Rain cascaded on soldiers scarcely able to proceed. Yet new orders demanded all possible speed; the Battle of Gettysburg had started [and Union forces clamored for help]. Exerting what remained of our strength, we finally reached the town and hurried through its streets at double-quick to an open field on the other side where the fatal battle lines of that historic struggle took shape forthwith.[4]

Fighting already engulfed the First Corps to our left. Soon we of Eleventh were also under fire. Our two corps, though totaling 12,000 to 13,000 men, proved too weak against the Rebels of [Richard S.] Ewell's command [First Corps, Army of Northern Virginia] opposite; they encircled us and drove us back to the town. During this retreat they took many prisoners, including me, together with another officer [Lieutenant Albert Wallber] and forty-six men of my regiment [the Twenty-sixth Wisconsin]. At that moment [at the instant of capture] a time of tribulation began, an ordeal of such pain that its victims will remember it with horror as long as they live.

The Rebel officer, my captor, let me, under guard, take one last look at the place where my regiment and the enemy had clashed a few minutes before. (The officer permitted it though I was his prisoner and already on my way to the Rebel camp.) I found many a dear friend dead or wounded. Compared to the wounded how fortunate the dead! The wounded usually suffer ghastly agony [on the battlefield], pitiful to behold. Here many cried out to me, but I could not help. Some called my name, but blood covered their faces and I could not tell who they were. If a man is to be shot, let the bullet smash his head or pierce his heart and dispatch him to eternal rest.

Short sad excursion done, I crossed with the young Rebel lieutenant to enemy ground. He had taken a certain dislike to a war that had inflicted him with a souvenir of itself: a piece of shrapnel in the leg. Enemy territory resembled ours, except that the dead outnumbered the wounded. Most of the dead had been shot through the head or in the chest, proof our men aimed well. The lieutenant, like several officers before him, pumped me for information: the strength of our forces, the direction of our approach, whether the entire Army of the Potomac had arrived, who had replaced the former commanding general, [Joseph] Hooker, and so forth. The curiosity of these worthy gentlemen went unsatisfied, of course. They also wanted to know the distance from Gettysburg to Baltimore, because most of them were sure their revered General Lee would lead them to Baltimore in triumph. Perhaps a few asked it out of fear, thinking that if distance intervened, many a battle must be fought before they could dictate the terms of peace from Baltimore.

Both sides of the battlefield confirmed for me that Rebel soldiers are notorious thieves. Wherever they could they looted bodies. A lieutenant of my regiment, killed beside me, fell victim in death to outrageous plunder. They even robbed their own dead. Indeed, theft in every form typifies Rebels. They had started [the Confederacy] in thievery [by seizing Fort Sumter]. The latest act of the Rebel Congress ordained an instance of theft best understood by the bankers of Richmond.[5]

I saw and spoke to a few more of our wounded near the Rebel-held part of the field. Then three Rebel soldiers escorted me to the prison camp in an open place next to a farmstead. There I joined several thousand fellow wretches. Next morning, officers and men were separated. A Rebel general told us [officers] that General Lee would parole us and send us to Carlisle, where we could cross to our own lines. But [on 3 July 1863] Major General [Henry W.] Halleck [the Union General in Chief] had issued an order [General Orders No. 207] forbidding such paroles and limiting places of exchange to City Point [Virginia] and Vicksburg [Mississippi].[6]

As for enlisted men, an officer must countersign a certificate of parole, but the order forbade such countersigning.[7] Therefore we [Union officers and men] could forget parole. We must that day face the sad prospect of being moved to Richmond—unless General Meade [commanding at Gettysburg] should be so lucky as to win, pursue the enemy, and free us.

The enemy took us a mile and a half behind their lines. The commander there, a Virginia colonel named French, a half-humane man, issued our first [Rebel] rations, homeopathic in quantity: raw meat with a handful of wheat flour and a few grains of salt [for each of us]. Malice accompanied this gift of rations, for we had almost nothing in which to cook or bake it. So, at first, this bestowal of largesse perplexed us [as to how to prepare it].

Rations in hand we must march a while again. I had wrapped in a small cloth my flour and that of my fellow prisoner Wallber. Marching, I lost my grip on the bundle. The flour spilled onto the wet grass. The two of us, famished, looked with pain at what we had lost. Wallber [fortunately] had a small tin kettle. In it, later, we cooked the meat: that day's sole nourishment.

Henceforth I handled flour with care. I even learned to bake, though we owned neither pot nor pan nor oven. I rolled dough on an oilcloth and shaped little loaves. Wallber meanwhile kindled a fire and hunted up small stones and ringed the fire with them. Stones hot, we put the loaves on them and with sticks tilted the stones to the fire and left them until one side of the loaves baked. We turned the loaves to repeat the process. Only with disgust could I nibble such bread now; but we wolfed it then and craved more.

The second day of battle drew to an end. We did not know if our side had won. Nor could we get reliable information from newly arrived prisoners. What aggravating ignorance! Having lost the first day, had our army been fortunate the second? We heard the rattle of musketry and the roar of cannon. Had the Federals succeeded or the Rebels advanced? Anxiety filled the suspense as we awaited a report. But we must be patient until evening, when the Rebel band struck up joyous tunes and the "gray jackets" chimed in with hurrahs. Victory—for our enemies! We comforted ourselves by wishing their joy premature, but that cold comfort chilled us to depression. Sleep temporarily interrupted our brooding, our foreboding.

On the morning of 3 July we enjoyed the dubious honor of being on view to the Rebel general [George Edward] Pickett. We had spent the night on the ground in front of his tent. The archetype of a Virginia slave baron strutted briskly, proud in bearing, head lifted in arrogance. On horseback he looked like the ruler of a continent. Obviously he took pains with appearance—riding boots aglitter, near-shoulder-length hair tonsorially styled—but the color of his nose and upper cheeks betrayed that he pandered the inner man. Pleasures of the bottle left indelible tracks.

Indeed, the coarse plebian features in no way matched the efforts at aristocratic airs.[8] He galloped proudly that morning, from his tent to the front. But when we saw him a few days later on the Potomac, a pall seemed to cloak the ruddy features. He had lost two-thirds of his division on 3 July.[9]

We heard only scattered shots during the morning. That eerie silence prevailed which usually precedes the battle's catastrophes. Sure enough, in the afternoon, hell broke loose. The thunder of cannon shook the earth. We surmised that this clash would decide the contest.[10] Our hearts throbbed at the thought: *Our side could lose.* We knew what importance attached to this battle, we appreciated the far-reaching consequences of a Union defeat [it could have meant the South would win the Civil War], and so our ignorance [of the outcome at Gettysburg] doubled our suffering. Meanwhile our men struggled in combat but we, in enemy hands, could not help.

Night fell. The cannonades and musketry died away—to what end? True, last evening's music did not recur, but could we pin firm hopes on such a doubtful sign? Heavy of heart, tired, hungry, we lay down on the ground to rest.

The sun of the Fourth of July awakened us. But to what kind of a Fourth? Normally on this day of joy for us, we would have participated in festivities memorializing the founding of the great Republic. But today we did not know if the malignant enemy had brought the Republic to its knees. Once free and at home with friends under the glorious Stars and Stripes, we now were prisoners, captives of the Rebels, who scorned the flag of the Union and trampled it!

Bright sunshine disappeared, dark clouds gathered, and the day matched our mood: sad.

We had been crammed into a field enclosed by a fence. Outside it, guards paced up and down, weather-beaten fellows in gray rags, who sneered at us. One of us thought to do at least *something* to signify recognition of this grand national holiday: he burst into patriotic song. We joined the refrain. The guards stopped short but permitted us to continue, which we interpreted as the best of signs. Had the Rebels won [yesterday's fighting], they would be reluctant to allow us even this small harmless pleasure. Notorious for malice toward us, why did they so indulge us now? Why "John Brown's Body" and "Rally 'Round the Flag, [Boys]" and "Down with the Traitors" unhindered? Such leniency [we cogitated] must have a reason. Perhaps the Rebels had *lost* on 3 July.

Soon there were peculiar movements. Detachments marched to-and-fro. Adjutants galloped madly about. The huge wagon train began to roll. One of us officer-prisoners, an American with an intelligent face and a long neck, went to a slight elevation, stretched himself to his full height, looked

around like a clever ostrich, and said at last: "Gentlemen, the meaning's clear, the Rebels are withdrawing."[11]

He was right. Lee had been beaten. Presently we got the order to join the column in retreat. Tempestuous clouds, having piled higher and higher, exploded about noon with storm and rain. We marched to a creek and stood near its stone bridge. Bolt upon fiery bolt of lightning. Thunderclap after stentorian thunderclap. The largest trees bent in the rampage. Rain fell in sheets.

Down the road a checkered medley galloped headlong: wagons of baggage and munitions, cannon, and all kinds of vehicles bearing the wounded. Those pitiful wretches groaned and whined. Our hearts rejoiced when we realized that the Rebels had lost and were fleeing. At the same time, however, we knew *our* fate. We would be carried along with the retreating army, away from the land of freedom, to the Hell of treason and barbarism—to Richmond, where the arch-Rebel Jefferson Davis reigned. Never had joy and grief so crowded at once into our souls: joy at the victory of our army, grief at our own lot.

But hope did not forsake us. Couldn't the [Union's] general [Meade] flank the retreating enemy and free us? And wasn't it possible that the magnitude of our victory guaranteed short life to the Confederacy and thereby ruled out a long imprisonment for us?

The unfortunate thus grasp at a straw. In this way they bear their misery of body and agony of spirit, sustained by a pleasant illusion of hope.

2

The Retreat into Virginia—The Shenandoah Valley—Richmond

Lee's army retreated [from Gettysburg] in two columns, infantry and artillery, crowding one another. Prisoners, escorted by infantry, formed an intermittent third. What with roads too narrow for such an agglomeration of men and cannon and wagons, we must often follow unimproved trails, marching across field and meadow, climbing fence and hedge, and wading creek and pond filled by [recent] downpours. On 5 July [1863] we reached Fairfield [Pennsylvania]. Women of all ages stood in doorways, saw our many blue uniforms, and wept, believing all to be lost. We shouted reassurance: "The Rebel army is retreating, we'll soon be back!" A beautiful young woman sobbed bitterly and begged God to protect us. [Later] the same day we entered the so-called South Mountain Ridge, a range of romantic elevations, some high, with deep valleys and ravines. Here we [prisoners], and the army with us, bunched often into a massive clump that lurched ahead with travail, unable to spread out as before on level fields. When the dark of night fell, safety demanded every precaution, lest we tumble beneath horses' hooves or slip under cannons' wheels. Some officer-prisoners took advantage of darkness and confusion, sneaked past guards, and hid in the forest-covered mountains until the Rebel hordes disappeared.

On the sixth we gained the spa of Monterey Springs. Here the Rebels opened new negotiations with us for our parole, having learned the hardship of moving such a clutch of prisoners.[1] They also probably feared another Union attack, in which we might escape. Moreover, they reasoned, we would in any event require a strong escort [of many guards] far better used otherwise in those circumstances. So the Rebels assembled us and presented approximately the same proposals as at Gettysburg. After long deliberation we decided, in view of Halleck's order, to decline them.[2] For, as of the moment, they would profit the Rebels alone. We declined, too, because we still hoped to be set free. We could see that the Rebels craved to be rid of prisoners once and for all. How could we agree to

something so desired by the enemy? We feared for our future, we pined for
freedom, but we could not do the Rebels a favor while disobeying an order
[Halleck's] that restricted exchange [and parole. Authorized commanders
alone could exchange or parole prisoners and only those] in "actual
possession."[3]

On the afternoon of the sixth, those negotiations over, we began a
torturous and exhausting march to Waynesboro [Pennsylvania] and
Hagerstown [Maryland]. What a horrid night! Our concourse moved at a
crawl, having to halt nearly every five minutes.[4] Given neither rest nor
enough to eat, and therefore tired and weak, we lay down at once on the
muddy road whenever we paused, so as to get the most of each moment of
every respite.

In the morning we entered Hagerstown, home to numerous secessionists, male and female. A female, face cheerful, stood on the sidewalk.
To the mounted Rebel heading the column she shouted triumphantly:
"Colonel, that is the way to bring them in."[5] Blatantly she thus asserted
membership in the nasty group of vixens so numerous in the South—
hellcats who goaded half-crazed men to greater ferocity and more treason.

South of Hagerstown we met a troop of captured [Union] cavalry who
had been sent on reconnaissance and forced to battle Rebels near the
town. In a field along the road, other cavalrymen lay dead, the bodies
plundered by Rebels, of course.

The Rebels had also arrested on some pretext several civilians whom
they put in with us and brought along. A cruel fate awaited them. Not
treated as prisoners of war, their kind frequently did not receive even the
trifles granted us by Rebel clemency.

A pause at Hagerstown, then they herded us farther, to Williamsport on
the Potomac. We camped in wet grass beside a wheat field on a hill.
Plucking heads of wheat, we sought in the incipient kernels a bit of ease
from hunger. The Rebels had posted strong pickets to the east, and we
heard an occasional mutter of cannon. But our hoped-for saviors did not
appear, and that sanguine glimmer faded. Ahead lay the Potomac, the
boundary between free states and the empire of the Rebels.

We had been optimistic for freedom—until now. A rose-colored whim?
Not after we knew the Rebel army's condition. Disappointed in their
expectations of marching victorious into Baltimore, demoralized by Gettysburg and its frightful casualties, they had fled along sometimes barely
passable roads toward the swollen Potomac. Our guards, remnants of
Pickett's division [devastated at Gettysburg], lamented to us that no other
battle demanded such sacrifices of them. Seeming palpably to expect
further assaults, the Rebels ran for cover beyond the Potomac. Now,
between Williamsport and the river and headed for its south shore, cannon
and wagons of food and munitions stalled, mired nearly to the axles, stuck

Barry University Library
Miami, Fla. 33161

in ground as soft as a bog and as sticky as glue. Only the cavalry had negotiated the Potomac's deluge, and the feat distressed them. Surely this situation must be known, however imperfectly, to [Meade] the [Union] commanding general? Surely it must compel him to a fresh attack that could destroy the enemy and free us?

Nothing of the sort. Instead, in the afternoon of 8 July, we began the travails that would get us over the Potomac. (We had crossed it in bliss at Edwards' Ferry two weeks before.) First we tried to wade, at a fordlike spot in relative shallows. The water proved too deep, the current too strong. So we resorted to an old flatboat pulled by one rope diagonally along another between poles driven one into each shore. This crude apparatus prevented the fragile craft's being swept downstream. In a few hours, we transported ourselves all to the other side.

Returned to Virginia, in the land of barbarism once more, we arrived not as victors but as prisoners. Gloomy prospects joined sad and poignant memories; recent days had been painful. When we looked back across the Potomac that separated us again from the land of the free, our eyes caressed longingly the Maryland mountains where our army must be. Reverie ended, we stopped woolgathering, at the savage command— *"March!"*

We went first to Martinsburg [West Virginia]. Spending the night in an orchard, many of us quieted hunger with tiny green apples. The next morning, near Winchester [Virginia], we got a day's rest and some flour and meat, in a shady place, under the massive limbs of a gigantic elm hundreds of years old, near the inexhaustible gush of a splended spring. Having to cook the food, we applied swiftly the primitive methods I have described.

On Sunday, 12 June, we passed Winchester, a town of tolerable aspect. Many old-fashioned houses, yes, but new and handsome ones, too. Elderly gentlemen and aristocratic ladies gathered on verandas to review us and gloat. They said nothing, but their faces radiated joy over so many Yankees in tow. Across town we saw the fortifications that figured in the recent defeat of [Union] General [Robert H.] Milroy [at the Battle of Winchester, 14 June 1863]. Officer-prisoners among us told many a story of experiences in bloody engagements hereabouts in days just past.

We reached the Shenandoah Valley in a few days, there to begin a march that exhausted us beyond description. Heavy rains came, remained nearly a week, fouled the roads, and swelled the creeks. Cavalry of [John D.] Imboden's command escorted us, forcing us [because horses set the pace for men] to cover fifteen to twenty miles each day without fail. Every night, after we built a small fire and struggled to nourish it with nearby brush and bits of scattered wood, and after we lay down drenched and tired on wet ground, a fresh cloudburst would startle us and douse the fire. We slept

anyhow, too tired to be concerned about rain. The next morning we would get up, soaked to the skin and chilled, to continue the march. Though rations remained as thin and skimpy as before, we could buy something here and there. Not yet alert to prices extorted in the South for anything edible, we bought food eagerly. Locals exchanged three Confederate dollars for one greenback and demanded royal ransom for what seemed the staple of the Valley: a sour blackberry pastry.[6] Edifying research later revealed to our shock that an item, at $3 there, could be purchased for perhaps ten cents in the North. Not even an army sutler would have overpriced it by more than one-third.

The valley, of fertile fields between mountain ridges and naturally beautiful, lacks the [human] asset absent everywhere in the South: the drive for progress. In the hands of free Northern farmers, the valley would become a paradise, a jewel of prosperity even more valuable than it has been.

After Winchester, at Newton, the Rebel captain in charge lost his way, and we had to wade a stream because water covered the bridge. The villages and small towns of Harrisonburg, Strasburg, Edinburg, Mount Jackson, New Market, and Middletown, though situated attractively enough, looked either old-fashioned or weather-beaten, like most such places of the South. The war, devastating to them (Harrisonburg perhaps excepted), had signed its bold signature here: many empty houses tending toward collapse; few commercial signs, stores and workshops locked beneath them; a male populace of only granddads, boys, and youthful cripples [except for cripples, men of military age had gone to war]; and women and girls mostly shabby and usually in black. In some towns we saw barracks where regiments had spent part of a fugitive existence, or where the wounded had been sheltered. In Harrisonburg the grand edifice of an academy had been converted to a hospital.

In Harrisonburg I met a German Jew, a real speculator of an Israelite, who talked about good business. Circumspectly mistrustful of Confederate dollars, he [secured their dubious value by] buying houses and farms with them, cheap. He gushed a kind of Pennsylvania Dutch replete with the expression [half-German, half-English]: "And just let me tell you *the reason why.*" He sold us blackberry pastries as sour as vinegar, and a loaf of bread, at an exorbitant price. To a mild remonstrance, he replied: "Just let me tell you *the reason why.* Everything is sky-high, especially the flour, and you ought to be happy to get anything at all, *sure!*"

Past Harrisonburg we crossed a fertile region, via Mount Crawford and Mount Sidney, to Staunton, last stop on our arduous, roughly two-hundred-mile trek. Railway cars waited at the station [of the Virginia Central]. In a few minutes [we were aboard and] the train ready to depart. But we must suffer one further disgrace. A lieutenant entered our car and demanded, by order of Imboden (general of cavalry and bushwacker), that we give up cloth blankets, rubber blankets, coats, and the like: meager things that had protected a scant few of us from inclement weather. As might makes right, we had to comply, though several cut blankets in two and threw the pieces out the window or onto the floor. The Rebel lieutenant expressed regret at having to rob us of these scarce possessions, but said in the same breath that the general had phrased the order in the sternest of language.

The evening of 18 July, nearly three weeks after capture, we arrived in Richmond. The train pierced to the city's heart and stopped in a busy thoroughfare. Hundreds of the curious, white and black, had gathered on both sides.[7] We formed a four-file column, guards took post, and the dismal procession moved out. We marched through several streets, including one that seemed exclusively of Jewish shops. It being Saturday, women sat quite richly dressed at the doors, faces unmistakably oriental of feature, inspecting us in silence. On the signs above, the familiar and often poetic names—Rosenzweige, Rosenhaine, Rosenbäume, etc.—had been curiously Englished. This was the street whose residents later provided copy to the *Richmond Examiner*. (Bear in mind [while I tell the story] that their presence disturbed the *Examiner*, which doubted their loyalty to the Confederacy.) That is, when a Northern paper spoke of a "crusade" against Richmond, the *Examiner* remarked that "northern vandals" could not be compared to the Crusaders. In one respect, however [the *Examiner* said], a similarity would exist: the Yankees would find many Jews here.[8]

A march of fifteen or twenty minutes brought us into Cary Street, beside the canal. Stopping at a big building of three stories, we asked: "What sort of place is this?"A small wooden sign [in English] on its western corner ended all doubt: "Libby & Son, Ship Chandlers & Grocers."[9]

3

The "Libby" Prison—Its Officials—Initial Arrangements

The prison [for officers at Richmond] was later called the Libby for short [after the old sign on the building: Libby & Son, Ship Chandlers & Grocers].[1] When we arrived, inmates appeared at the windows of the second and third floors: [Union] officer-prisoners who had preceded us by several weeks as captives of the Rebels. They had served under General [Robert H.] Milroy [of the Second Division, Eighth Corps] or under Colonel [Abel D.] Streight of the Fifty-first Indiana, the unit that raided into Georgia [out of Nashville in late April 1863. Streight himself was here in the Libby, with his men.][2] They threw down a note of warning as we stood in the street: *Hide your greenbacks.* (In a Confederate prison, Union currency doubled in value.) So of course we hastened to conceal them in our caps, in the linings of our coats, or in our boots.

The warning was timely and well-advised, very much so, as we quickly learned. For, on the building's ground floor the moment we entered, every last one of us was searched and robbed of what possessions remained after the bandit [General John D.] Imboden [the Confederate raider and cavalry leader] plundered us at Staunton [Virginia].[3] Had our money not been hidden, the predatory Rebels would have grabbed every cent.[4] This shakedown included our first meeting with Sergeant George and the infamous [inspector and commissary officer] Dick Turner, known now as a holy terror. Turner at once showed himself to be in his glory when he could with impudence strike an officer [of the Union army] who protested being searched. And George acted like nothing less than an uncouth beadle.

The shakedown over, we went to the second floor and met Streight's and Milroy's officers [now prisoners here]. They flung a thousand questions at us. A justifiable curiosity, what with the most exaggerated stories of Rebel victories filling the Richmond newspapers. And, seeing the arrival of so many prisoners, the questioners must have assumed our army had suffered misfortune. Naturally it delighted them to hear credible witnesses testify to Lee's [defeat at Gettysburg and] retreat [4–6 July 1863]. Having already had enough Rebel hospitality to depress them, the captives took heart at our report. The Rebels had been especially harsh and downright malicious to Colonel Streight and his officers [probably because he dared to raid and do so much damage so deep in the Confederacy].

The Libby was of three floors. The first consisted of the office together with the so-called supply room (here, a room without supplies) and a place for the sick.[5] The second and third had been storage areas for ships' goods, each about fifty feet wide and sixty deep. Both floors had three such areas. To distinguish among them we named them the Upper and Lower West Room, occupied by Milroy and Streight's officers; the Upper and Lower Middle Room, which would house officers captured at Chickamauga; and the Upper and Lower East Room, both to belong to us later. When we arrived, however, Lower East contained a hospital. Meanwhile we had enough space in the Middle Rooms, still free then, and in Upper East, the best of all.

Under the first floor something of a cellar served various purposes. There the terrible cells—tiny dark holes infested by rats and other vermin—horrified everybody so maligned as to be locked in them.[6] An olio of things rotted there, polluting the air. Even a short stay in those dungeons amounted, without a doubt, to an aeon of agony. One person, and one alone, took pleasure in them. With hellish delight—the ecstasy that devils are said to feel about the torment of their victims—Dick Turner committed helpless people to bread and water in the black and reeking pits.

The Middle Rooms, having lower ceilings, were darker than the Upper. Higher ceilings under the roof with skylights brightened the Upper. Windows occurred sufficiently in the Libby but were nothing but openings; panes and sashes had long since disappeared. Wooden stairs connected the floors, without landings, steep—typical for warehouses. Here and there the roof leaked. Wooden bedsteads, so-called bunks, filled Upper and Lower West. Every other room offered only empty walls. Except, in each, the wooden trough for washing. Water piped in from the nearby canal served drinking, cooking, and bathing—lukewarm in summer and (especially after a rain) laced with yellowish soil.

Initially we chose to billet in Upper Middle and Upper East. I've observed that they offered only their naked walls, but after our trek we delighted in a place that at least protected us from rain and gale. In times of sustained misfortune and continued torment, the smallest favors gratify a person, even tokens he might otherwise scorn. True, it spelled h-o-r-r-o-r to land in this Bastille and suffer stark emptiness. Yet who of us did not believe we would soon be exchanged? Had we been guaranteed we would never be exchanged, and being unprepared for the prisoner's lot, most would have retreated to the edge. People accustom themselves but slowly to misery, gradually with reluctance accommodating the fact of being

Fate's choice for torment. With humor one can endure even extended misfortune; the pain will not damage the mind. Some minds surrender, however, and remain scarred. Misery that can purify and ennoble may also consume and leave a person in ashes.

The next morning Dick Turner appeared. We would be brought something to eat, he said. This agreeable announcement piqued our curiosity— what would be set before us? Negroes appeared soon. They delivered some wheat bread, a measure of beef, and about a dozen containers of rice soup unsalted. The containers were of wood and had perhaps been used for several purposes before. This meal, we must confess, nearly exceeded our expectations—until we got it. Then we knew that the Rebels did not intend to fatten us. Portions were minute and, except for a second of bread at noon, our "hotel" served no other meals.[7] What a pleasure, this introduction to the bill of fare!

Innocent of the principle that variety brings joy, the next day's menu duplicated the last except that now there was too much salt in the soup. Portions in no way sufficed, and questions arose, of course. What was to become of us? How would this state of affairs end? Already in our dreams we saw ourselves as figures of pallor, walking skeletons. "I'm hungry," everyone said. Complaints were general, and in each complaint hunger echoed. We laid ourselves on the floor to sleep, and hunger lay down with us. We woke, and hunger glared at us. Hunger—the wretched acquaintance, the importunate companion, the hateful presence, the insufferable pest. It cannot be silenced, it will put you out of sorts, and it could not be evicted from a predicament like ours.

Who staffed this prison?

• The commandant, Captain (later Major) Thomas B. Turner. He smacked of noblesse but was a Rebel through and through, an accessory to all offenses to torment prisoners, and a hypocrite who masked with civility the temper that has little or nothing to do with humanitarianism. Though trained at West Point and active and vigilant as commandant, he had not, so far as we knew, been tested as a soldier in the field.[8]

• The other Turner, Richard, usually called Dick [a captain and the commissary], second in importance. He was about forty years old, thin and wiry, and of moderate height. His hair and beard were black, eyes dark and piercing, features hard and pronounced. The son of perdition itself, vicious, sinister, a born turnkey and a beadle by nature, he should have delighted Jefferson Davis.[9]

• The adjutant, Lieutenant [John] Latouche, a strong, stocky man of French extraction, outwardly friendly and ready to laugh, but treacherous and spiteful.

• The head [or adjutant's] clerk, a comical little fellow named [Erastus] Ross, whose father owned this building. Ross seemed to be a Rebel only because Virginians were Rebels. He delighted in new and diverse clothes, liked to chat, was pleasant to us, but never could cope with Yankees who teased and played jokes on him whenever they could. Roll call, his main responsibility, often caused him heartache and drove him to desperation after ten, twelve, and fifteen repetitions yielded the wrong count. One day, after failing again and again of an accurate total, he shouted in futility: "More are here than are here!" Again he complained, "I am too few for so many Yankees." Then he counted 143 more than were there. Discovering the absurd sum, he slammed his book shut and marched away double-quick.[10]

• Sergeant George [Stansil] has been mentioned. Nasty at the outset, he mellowed, probably as a result of bribes.[11]

Arrangements made after a few days—an eternity to us—bettered our situation, to be sure, but indicated that our incarceration would not be short. Turner ordered boxed off an area of Upper Middle and had cookstoves put there so that we could prepare our own meals. To oversee this task and superintend the keeping of order overall, Colonel [Charles William] Tilden of the Sixteenth Maine was appointed commanding officer. Lieutenant Colonel [James M.] Sanderson, head commissary for the First Corps [and former cook and hotel keeper] was named manager of the kitchen or, as he put it, "culinary director." The ladle was his scepter. Officer-prisoners were divided into so-called messes of twenty-five to thirty members each. A commissary [or mess sergeant] headed each mess and answered to a commissary in chief [or mess officer] who received rations from the Rebels and apportioned them among the commissaries. Daily, each commissary picked two members of his mess to cook and serve the food and wash the dishes. The culinary director set the hours for cooking and the order in which the messes would eat. The Rebels continued to deliver to us beef, rice or beans, and wheat bread.

Another arrangement concerned purchases. The Rebels, sly foxes, discovered we had something they lusted after: greenbacks. Trying to be clever in getting their hands on them, and hoping to turn a pretty penny by manipulation, Turner & Turner permitted us to buy food and other items. Here is how their scheme worked: One of us officers would give greenbacks to a Rebel sergeant, and he would return Confederate dollars. Though the exchange would seem to be by stealth, Turner & Turner would know all about it. At first such deals brought us for each greenback [dollar] $5 to $6 Confederate, and by 1864, up to $16 and $18.[12] Then, when we had Confederate dollars, any member of a mess who wanted to buy could place the order with his commissary. The commissary itemized all orders on a sheet of paper and handed it, together with the money, to the commissary in chief, who consolidated all the orders and presented the result, plus the grand total of money, to Inspector Turner. He directed purchasing and, the next day, would send the goods to the commissary in chief, who divided them among the commissaries. They were the retailers. From them the members of the messes each received his respective share, some more, some less.

To the Rebel officers this business was profitable threefold. (1) They went to brokers or private individuals and reexchanged the greenbacks for more Confederate money than they had given us. (2) They made 100 percent or more on the goods. (3) They could keep our rations as skimpy as possible, calculating that if we were hungry, we would gladly exercise the privilege of buying and not grumble about the meager table. So our money migrated into their pockets, without our being able to accuse them of outright theft. Moreover, they used these transactions occasionally as examples to us of how convinced we must be of their humanitarianism.

This buying and selling brought us advantages, but it had a dark side: it gave rise to suspicion that some of our comrades, involved as commissaries in the acceptance and distribution of goods, were interested less in honesty than in their own profit. Furthermore, those prisoners without money hungered while others more fortunate could at least get tolerable meals and eat their fill.

We were also granted the privilege of buying newspapers. Accordingly, early every morning, often about 4:00 or 5:00, a Negro came round. He had told us he had been sold [as a slave] seven times in his life. His was always the same cry on entering the room: *"Great news in the papers."* Frequently he quoted headlines, often in peculiar English. If he could not understand the headlines, he invented tidings from the Rappahannock, the Mississippi, the James, and any other river he might be able to name, in a colorful medley. At any rate, there was always "great news in the papers," an assurance delivered with sincerity and an air for all the world of the utmost importance.[13] Apparently lacking knowledge of the value of money, he would sell five copies of the day's issue for one Confederate dollar. Later, for reasons not divulged to us, he was forbidden to peddle papers. Colonel Tilden's adjutant [Sanderson] was given the task and, according to every calculation, earned a tidy sum.

As to sanitation, all that could be done was done. In the early days we officers had to scrub floors ourselves. Later a number of Negroes scrubbed them. Most of these menials had been Union army orderlies. Captured, they now suffered under Turner's thumb: scrubbing floors, cleaning stairways, carrying wood, delivering rations, etc. One of the Negroes, a funny old eccentric, every morning brought a pan of embers on which tar had been dripped. He, too, intoned a refrain: *"There is a good smoke."* Sometimes he also remarked, *"I save your lives, I will draw on you."*[14]

And so July ended. How long those two weeks seemed! The fact of having temporarily enough to eat could not blot from mind what we wanted most: exchange. Every day and each hour we expected [Dick] Turner with the announcement that a boat had docked at City Point [Virginia, the exchange point for the East] to take us out of the hated land of the Rebels. Turner did come often, to promulgate regulations in an imperious voice or, with a malicious air, to read orders from the other Turner. But not a word about exchange. Probably, we thought, imprisonment would last only until 1 August. Probably the details [of our exchange] were not yet worked out; it would take time, wouldn't it? Impossible that our government would forget us and let us languish.

The first of August found us still in the Libby. Oh, well, we would have to endure until the middle of August or, at most, 1 September. Deplorable indeed that we must sit in this infamous prison. But, surely, exchange was just around the corner.[15]

We'd be free on 1 September, wouldn't we? Of course we would!

4

Libby Society—Pastimes—An Intended Execution

The diverse inmates consisted of officers of all ranks; from most of the states; [educated,] half-educated, and illiterate; representing nearly every walk of life; not a select group, rather an accumulated rabble having in common only the tragedy of imprisonment. From the start it should have been clear that such a conglomeration would spawn and suffer nasty frictions and ugly misunderstandings.

Therefore some Americans' venom for Germans flourished. The American, despite his many excellences, finds it hard to free himself of nativistic prejudices. He likes above all to sink his teeth of scorn into the "Dutchman."[1] But the origin of this hatred should not be discussed here. Nor should what the Germans themselves contributed to its existence be considered now. Suffice it to say that in the beginning [here at the Libby], we [Germans] had to endure a hail of gibes, many of them about the notorious but false reports of German troops in the Battle of Chancellorsville.[2] Now, take the American who acquired at his mother's knee an unshakable antipathy for Germans. Give him those reports. Tell him that they originated at the headquarters of [the Union commandant at Chancellorsville, General Joseph] Hooker. The prejudiced American would then feel all the more justified in looking down on Germans, disparaging them, and sometimes expressing dislike in ways that hurt [us Germans]. It would never occur to him that the reports could be false. He would accept them as proof positive and use them to substantiate his disagreeable opinions.

Gradually, however, such harsh injustice [here at the Libby] mellowed in communication and the exchange of ideas. In addition, German prisoners' inimitable and almost impeccable behavior contributed to [creating] that [improved] state of affairs. Yes, obscenities and brutalities occurred time after time and again and again. But, Germans being in no way responsible [for those ugly acts and reprehensible practices], friendly relations formed inevitably between Germans and upright, well-intentioned Americans. In many instances this friendship prospered until the end of imprisonment, helping to squelch prejudice and encourage better opinions of German character. Today [after the war] I'm pleased to remember the special Americans [among my fellow prisoners] who distinguished themselves by virtue of clear minds, kind hearts, and uprightness among men. Unfortunately the tribulations of captivity killed many of them; they rest in foreign soil far from home.

To shorten the hours, American prisoners [here in the Libby] initiated all sorts of intellectual and educational pastimes. The impetus came from the Reverend Mr. [Louis N.] Bouldrye, chaplain of a New York cavalry regiment, a man of diversified education and rather liberal religious views. Bouldrye's idea, like all new fads here, burgeoned among the Americans. "Let's devote a few hours a day to things of the mind," he proposed. "Not only will we thereby educate ourselves; we'll end monotony as well." Presto! The Americans seized the idea, elaborated it with feverish haste, and [to implement it] organized every possible club. How they wanted to study and learn! An enthusiasm blazed, such that anyone unfamiliar with the American character would have thought the Libby verged on becoming a university.

The debating club [also called the Lyceum] took up bizarre topics. Queer notions and ridiculous opinions came to light. On one occasion a speaker tried to prove beyond doubt that intemperance [excessive drinking] caused the slaveholders' rebellion. Another gamecock of debate, ever ready for a fight, flaunted his virtuosity by reciting several minutes of references to Moses, Julius Caesar, [General] McClellan, Muhammad, General Grant, Jesus Christ, Shakespeare, Lincoln, and Queen Elizabeth—without a hint of the topic at hand. The club suffered the fate of all clubs [here]. Preparation for performance [in debate] demands ardor and diligence; club members fell short in both. Indeed, members lacked the education and the facility even to frame appropriate topics [let alone debate them]. The few worthwhile speakers wearied, and the club failed. No good had been done.[3]

I've already mentioned the Reverend Mr. Bouldrye [the architect of this inchoate university]. Bouldrye himself conducted two other classes organized at this time: stenography and French. Attendance prospered at first. Pupils doggedly enunciated those French nasals which Americans find renitent. Every pencil worked to crack the code of shorthand. French survived, after the officer-prisoner [E.] Charlier [157th New York Volunteers] replaced Bouldrye there. Spanish fared but little better though taught by a native Cuban, Lieutenant Colonel [Frederick Fernandez] Cavada. Well educated, he spoke Spanish, French, and English, besides being an excellent draftsman.[4] Spanish was Greek to the Americans, however, and only a few pupils stuck with it. Several prisoners even started to learn German.

Next, Bouldrye and some other preachers held daily religious meetings, often practically unbearable. The right to call such meetings, and to attend them, cannot be denied. Even we [skeptics and freethinkers] could stand an occasional sermon—one composed clearly, delivered effectively, and aimed at a useful end. But, again and again in the meetings, the windiest of windbags babbled and blustered. Worse, the manner, a sanctimonious chest thumping, would nauseate any honest, rational listener. We followed with interest the few homilies that Bouldrye preached. But other sermonizers—some were ministers, some not—reveled in histrionics of religiosity dishonest to the core. Bouldrye, for all the enthusiastic tone to his presentations, neither rolled his eyes nor contorted his limbs.[5] I took him, therefore, to be notably more devout than some of the others—I mean those who struck ostensibly pious poses for display, thereby profaning what (according to them) they considered most sacred. Respect for these guys deteriorated even more when they masterminded plots to work mischief or led in the laying of plans to do evil.

Other subjects addressed [and other projects launched] were mesmerism; a declamation of selections from Shakespeare's tragedies in the hair-raising style of the actor [Edwin] Forrest; and a handwritten newspaper, the *Libby Chronicle,* a sericomic weekly that appeared for the first month (it degenerated; the last number contained a lewd poem).[6]

Our [other] reading, limited at first to a few books and the [local] Rebel newspapers, included a volume on the life of Stonewall Jackson by a Rebel officer.[7] Southerners revered Jackson like a god, and his biographer portrayed him as one of the greatest men who ever lived. It cannot be denied: Jackson possessed elements of greatness. Indeed, when heroism joins religious fervor in one man, he must wield influence and exert magnetism upon others. But [in a book about such a man] blind reverence, [uncritical] devotion, the cult of personality, and the biased flourish of virtues [to the exclusion of vices] can never satisfy the levelheaded, impartial judge [of the book and the man]. Not the desired effect but the opposite can then be expected. In the book in question the pettiest of trifles often cast a halo around Jackson. The book's faults [in sum] practically wrecked its value as history.[8]

Jackson, stern and introverted, brusque and eccentric, taught at the military academy in Virginia [the Virginia Military Institute, in Lexington] where his peculiarities amused the cadets, and they called him "Old Jack."[9] At the outbreak of the Rebellion his pupils asked him for a speech. He replied: "Soldiers give short speeches. Draw the sword slowly at the threat of civil war. But when you've drawn it, throw away the scabbard." (Boundless applause.) Outside his academic circles, in the Confederate government for example, people said, "Jackson has learned a lot, but he can't put much to practical use." His appointment to colonel therefore demanded effort. Colonel Jackson took part in the First Battle of Bull Run and won the nickname "Stonewall." When our forces hurled back a Rebel division, he alone stood fast. The [Rebel] commanding general [Barnard Elliott] Bee, urging the retreating Rebels to renew the attack, shouted: "Look at Jackson. There he stands like a stone wall." At that moment, the rise of Jackson began: in rank, in the esteem of the troops, and in Southern public opinion. A religious mysticism dominated his character; the army knew his piety and devotion. His chief of staff, Ewell, once free with curses, supposedly said (referring to a time before he mended his ways) that he and Jackson got "along well. Jackson attends to the praying. I take care of the cursing." Earlier, Jackson tried writing religious lyrics and even composed music to them. In a conversation about campaigns and battles, he claimed something that illuminated his incantatory bent: "Mystery is the secret of success." In my eyes, [on balance] a character like his may interest psychologists; it may double his power to attract supporters; but he committed treason, partook of an inhuman enterprise intended to destroy freedom, and thus diminished his greatness.

Having little else to read, we studied Richmond's newspapers. Thin and scanty in general news as well as in journalistic versatility when compared to Northern, they nonetheless deserved admiration in one respect: [for energy and effectiveness if not ethics] in the way they defended the Rebellion and incited the public. Indeed, an incredible fanaticism animated the Rebel press. From every angle and with recklessness, Rebel papers splashed sophistry and distortion over their pages in a style like the impetuous vituperation of fanatical monks of centuries past. Southern papers accordingly represented the Rebellion as an event of global significance and a justifiable revolt of a great and glorious people against the tyranny of a malignant and brutal usurper. Furthermore, as if not rash enough in self-gratification, the press exceeded that madness with an insanity: it agitated the public's worst impulses with articles so rabid that they seemed written with daggers dipped in poison. Using every [inflammatory] device, playing every demagogic trick, the press tried both to convince the South that injustice had been worked on them, and to stir them to the sternest measures against it.

Every Rebel newspaper wrote that way, for the Southern press had (with rare exceptions) united in a unanimity largely responsible for the victories the Confederacy enjoyed from time to time. Meanwhile, in the divided press of the North, many newspapers did their best to hurt our government, demoralize our people, and help the Rebels. Yes, opposition to Jefferson Davis asserted itself [in Confederate papers], but those voices registered only personal antagonism. Backing the [Confederate] cause one and all, each [Southern paper] vied with the rest to calumniate the Yankees and glorify the Rebellion.

"The Southern people do not belong to the decadent Anglo-Saxon race.

Morally, socially, intellectually, and politically, the Southern people sur-
pass the Anglo-Saxons." Rebel papers and particularly the *Richmond
Enquirer* asserted that line most often when trying to agitate the Southern
populace and fortify Rebel confidence. The infamous Irishman John
Mitchel headed the *Enquirer* [and laid down that line in] the summer and
fall of 1863 [the time I spent in Richmond].[10] An informed and impartial
judge would deem the case absurd and ridiculous. An argument in its
behalf would seem impossible. Yet the *Enquirer* labored—falsifying history, twisting statistics, drawing bogus conclusions—to prove to Southerners that they were, simply and clearly, God's chosen people. They
"must [therefore] unsheathe their flaming sword in defense of a new order;
and of course they shall conquer the stunted people of the North, those
dwarfs, scorned by the world, who don't respect even themselves."

Thus the *Enquirer* blustered, day in, day out. The *Examiner* joined it,
thundering against arrogant Yankee fools. "They fancy that Lincoln the
barbarian, the son of an orangutan, can lead them to victory over the high-
minded Southern nation, which will fight to the last man!" Though the
editor, Edward A. Pollard, seemed to have learned a thing or two, he
retained his obnoxious style, disgorged an olla podrida of references, and
mounted historical analogies that usually went lame. He wrote a few
political pamphlets, too. Like his newspaper, they reflect bias, being more
the ravings of a polemicist than reasoned analyses by a calm, clear-eyed
observer of current events.[11]

The *Dispatch,* the *Sentinel,* and the *Whig* joined [the *Enquirer* and the
Examiner] in [Richmond's] mad quintet. The *Whig* differed [from the
others in one respect]: it opposed Jefferson Davis.[12] Never missing a
chance to assert anti-Davis rancor, it often lashed out at the Lord of All
the Rebels. Item: his proposal of a day of prayer and repentance in the fall
of 1863. Item: the time he issued a proclamation to Southern women,
urging their fullest cooperation in the Rebellion.

Now and then it amused us to read those fanatical sheets. But the same
fare, every day without variation, must at last provoke disgust.

As I've said, we read newspapers, attended classes, heard sermons and
speeches, and prepared meals. Empty time still remained.[13] We tried to fill
it by sleeping, by pacing back and forth, and by conversing. Many also
indulged in shenanigans and monkeyshines, rightfully to be expected only
from schoolboys.

I refer especially to what would happen in the evenings. Guards would
call at 9:00 from posts on the streets on every side: "Lights out!" We
would lie down in our places, but not to sleep. Every evening at that
moment, hell broke loose. Sleep? Out of the question—for hours. The
disorderly among us, those insolent high spirits as yet untamed, screeched
and howled like Indians. They shrieked hilarious songs in shrill, cacoph-

onous voices; they pounded the floors with everything they could lay hands on; they raged like lunatics. From top to bottom, the building reverberated. In short, if you did not help produce the infernal uproar, it would drive you nuts. One evening's hullaballoo erupted in such clamor that Turner, the commandant, sent a lieutenant up with the order to *stop this tumult at once or every man jack will march to the street and stand there a few hours.* Success—that time. The following evening a rumpus burst forth again.

Indeed, once such devilry starts, no doubt the American appetite for foolishness and love of mischief will create bedlam. I blame excess energy, too, or the adolescent departure from self-restraint, not intended to offend but potentially offensive. Yet the equally strong American tendencies—to gravity and moroseness, stern and surly—contradict unbridled merriment. An astonishing contrast. Consider the man given to unbounded mirth. He would engineer outrageous pranks; yet how often we saw him on other occasions—sullen, black browed, dejected—as if he suffered the world's woes.

An incident, early in our Libby days, caused [another sort of] uproar. I refer to the threat to hang two captains [here] because General [Ambrose E.] Burnside had made short work of two spies [at Knoxville, Tennessee], by stringing them up. As soon as Rebel officials heard of it they decreed: *From among Streight's and Milroy's officers, choose two captains by lot. Hang them.* Lots were drawn and two wretches clapped into the underground cells: Captain [Henry W.] Sawyer of [the First] New Jersey Cavalry Regiment, and Captain [John] Flynn from one of the New England states [actually, of the Fifty-first Indiana Volunteer Infantry].[14] Every day, gleefully, Turner told them to prepare to die. In suspense they hovered quite a while [confused and anxious] between life and death.

A happy accident redeemed the captains from a nasty plight. Late in June 1863, our forces had captured Brigadier General [William H. F. ("Rooney")] Lee, son of the [Rebel] commander in chief, together with Captain [William S.] Winder, son of General [John H.] Winder, commander of all [Rebel] military prisons. Now [July 1863] the Confederate government received notice: *Let harm come to Sawyer and Flynn, and Lee and Winder will hang.* The stratagem worked. Sawyer and Flynn's morbid anguish ended. But look at Flynn—pale, features blurred, a young man with hair grown gray—only thirty years of age, yet how a moment of tormented uncertainty harrowed him! In battle he had gazed fearlessly into the eyes of Death. But to be murdered [here in the Libby] in a manner so foul? The thought cut him to the quick, shook his innermost soul.

5

Exchange of Prisoners—The "Royal Family"— Shipments from the North—Rebels as Thieves— Belle Island—General Neal Dow

Steal an individual's freedom and you take his natural joy, you plunder a legitimate buoyancy of spirit, and you pile upon him a load to twist him emotionally and cripple him physically, if not to crush him. Deprived of personal liberty, the victim at once directs each thought and all feelings to his miserable condition. Should he parry the stab of pain, silence the gnaw of care [and bring a moment of light into his darkness], worry and sorrow soon cast once more their grim shadows. Of course his thoughts concentrate on the wish to be [free and] rid of oppression, to be his own man again. [Accordingly] each of us strove every which way to shorten the summer days, which seemed endless. Yet we could neither stifle boredom nor banish the thought of exchange. Our every conversation concerned exchange.

Through August and September we awaited fulfillment of our wish. In vain. Then we explained away its postponement: Our government did not want to exchange before the autumn campaign ended. For, to return to the enemy a large number of well-cared-for prisoners would strengthen him with troops fit for service [against ours]. We thus rested assured that, come winter, we'd get out of this trap.

Still, even so early [in our captivity], something grieved us: the so-called special exchange. That is, if our exchange bureau wanted somebody freed, it gave notice, and with the next boat (or the one after it) the man went north.[1] If the Confederates wanted to bring one of theirs out of Union hands, or free a Union man because he somehow made himself worthy of freedom, a mere message would do the trick. Simple, this procedure. Harmony thus seemed to prevail between exchange agents [General Samuel A.] Meredith [of the Union] and [Robert C. S.] Ould [civilian judge advocate of the Confederate armies], though each occasionally wrote a discordant letter to the other. Meredith especially expressed himself with a certain coarseness. Ould tried to be more diplomatic. Correspondence between them grew more waspish until their negotiations broke off at last. Yet special exchanges of privileged prisoners continued uninterrupted (in fact, they increased) even under the later [Union] agent, General [Benjamin F.] Butler [appointed 17 December 1863].

When we enlisted, we knew that the army would be no picnic. We had resolved to have to chafe and ache and even die for our cause. If our government could not honorably agree to Rebel proposals for exchange, if political necessity must keep us in prison, then in either event we possessed the capacity for self-sacrifice and the patriotic will to suffer and agonize in our government's interest. Still, were we to brook a long incarceration for our cause, no exceptions must be made, no distinctions drawn with respect to person; we expected justice whenever and wherever circumstances demanded [and permitted] it. Any deviation would cause the severest pain and be the worst of injustices. Small comfort, true, but some consolation to bear misfortune equally with others. Special exchanges denied this justice. Moreover, if you favor one man and slight another, you intensify the suffering of the one slighted and bring upon yourself the rebuke that such unfair treatment [rightly] provokes. And if injustices done by a person deserve rebuke, those of a government deserve it more, for a government represents a nation. Individual thoughtlessness can be easier forgotten. From a government we expect [proper behavior after] mature reflection.

Brigadier General [Charles K.] Graham won dubious honor as the first special exchange. He spent a few weeks in the Libby's hospital after a scratch at Gettysburg and an ambulance ride to Richmond. We heard that he got every favor, and then exchange itself, without pain of imprisonment. Special exchange sent others after him. It became routine to see a fellow selected from our midst for the privilege of exchange. Injustice aside, the practice demoralized in more ways than one. Not a few of us, to win exchange, bowed and scraped to Rebel officers. Others, again, using as levers influential relatives and friends in the North, moved heaven and earth to influence our government to get them exchanged. [In short] many [of us] forgot decency and dignity when the practice [of execrable special exchange] began. How disgusting to see [Union] officers fawn upon Rebels and humiliate themselves. Nor did the debasing obsequiousness stop there. Officer-prisoners subsequently gave money or watches to curry Rebel favor. Even religion took part in this rotten affair. Richmond's Catholic bishop visited the Libby several times, to preach and to share the evening meal. Catholic prisoners flocked to him, of course. Word was, others did likewise who regularly disregarded Catholicism. Behold the miracle! Soon, with few exceptions, Catholics and all who claimed to be Catholics were exchanged. One prisoner, piqued, nailed up a caustic placard of classification by belief. His category number seven (those who could least expect to be exchanged) consisted of Jews, Mormons, and atheists. And then, [worst of all,] suspicion had it that, to gain favor and win a place on the list of those recommended [for exchange], some [of us] did obscene favors for Rebels.

Among those who toadied for favor, a small but salient clique got the name "Royal Family" for their snobbery and their daily [and extensive] association with Rebel functionaries. The family conducted with aristocratic dignity all necessary mediation between prisoners and officials, occasionally favoring us with a glimpse of their scorn for us. Sundry miscreant inmates attended the family as cooks, lackeys, and stooges. Obviously they delighted in being permitted at the family's usually abundant table and took joy in being able to catch a word of praise or an approving smile for their sycophantic subservience.

Lieutenant Colonel Sanderson, the "culinary director," headed the clique. Early in our captivity he besmirched his name [with us] when officials asked him to sign a statement and he signed. (I've already mentioned Colonel Tilden, who also signed at the Rebels' request. A member, too, of the family, he enjoyed privileges granted for their comfort, as well as access to officials.) "The Rebels treat us with laudable humanity," the statement said. Of this humanity, we had seen nothing. Director Sanderson however, guided by personal designs, scarcely cared if he distorted the truth. He had owned a New York hotel popular among Southerners before the war. Several of his remarks [in the Libby] revealed sympathies more or less with the Rebels. He visited Richmond at will, having been granted permission to do so. One day the *Examiner* included a little panegyric to him. Nothing to ingratiate him [with us], it conformed our every suspicion against him. He sank [in our eyes] daily and at last had to resign as director. By true and faithful service [to the Rebels], he continued to enjoy Rebel benevolence until exchanged in March 1864. His bitterest enemy was the honest, upright, worthy Colonel Streight.[2]

Meanwhile, little by little, rations diminished and worsened. Bread changed from wheat to corn. Meat appeared less and less, replaced by sweet potatoes and cabbage—cabbage often rotten. I recall days in the fall of 1863 when we got nothing but a chip of corn bread and half a potato, medium sized. The notorious rice/bean ration had begun. Each of us received three and never more than four tablespoons of rice, or two to three of small beans, frequently worm-eaten. Prisoners with money could improve their situation somewhat, but for many cash began to disappear. Meanwhile, the nearer the winter, the dearer the prices, until they stopped at exorbitance. In these circumstances, we wished for nothing more fervently than permission to request packages from friends and relatives in the North. Turner issued a directive permitting requests for clothing and food. The list of forbidden items included alcohol.

Jubilation greeted the canal boat with the first packages from City Point, though a minimum of us received anything. Transferred from boat to warehouse [across the street from the Libby], then opened and inspected, the packages arrived at the main entrance on the Libby's north side, after a few days, and each went to a recipient after he signed for it. He must sign in good faith, no matter that some of the contents might be missing. The packages usually contained (besides clothing and footwear) hams, dried fruit and vegetables, and the like. And reading matter.

Having long seen nothing in print from the North, we welcomed [non-Confederate] reading material. Local Rebel papers did carry extracts from the Northern press, but mostly out of the *New York World* and *Chicago Times,* deservedly dubious in credibility and despicable to us. Papers from the North circulated from man to man. Every article, each advertisement, was read. [In packages from the North] some inmates got stories of hunting, robbers, and ghosts: tales that pullulate in Philadelphia or New York. They deserve a place beside their German counterparts in dime novels and other pulp trash. Many of us would never think of seeking entertainment in this stuff but, at time of deprivation, even tales of horror and the likes of Munchhausen and Eulenspiegel refresh the parched spirit.[3] So we amused ourselves with the bear hunters of "old Kentucky," with bloodthirsty pirates on the Mississippi and crafty horse thieves in Arkansas, and with the gruesome slaughter of Indians. Let a pair of clumsily described lovers struggle against rascality and intrigue; let everybody, including the villain but not the lovers, die in various ways in the end; let the wedding take place beside the corpses: even [such a preposterous yarn] would please us.

Although delivered promptly and conscientiously at first, packages caused us vexation later. The Rebels, ever itching to steal, stole as never before. They plundered our packages in the warehouse across the street from the Libby, helping themselves frequently to more than half the contents. And after rifling packages, the Rebels would delude us with any ruse to delay delivery.

When a great load arrived on the boat one day, we each wanted to know, "Is there a package for me?" (By this time, with many of us, the answer to Will I be hungry? depended upon getting a package.)[4] None appeared at the Libby's door. Our query went unanswered. Days and weeks passed; our property remained out. At last the announcement: "Be ready to take your packages." They came—but with contents in a state! By "contents" I mean the dregs; for most packages had been nearly emptied by theft. What survived Rebel rapacity had rotted to putrefaction, and the swelling stench so fouled the warehouse that the Rebels decided to deliver at last. To what depths of infamy could the Turners sink after they gave us our property when it had rotted beyond use?

Of course, with rapacity the soul of the Rebellion, and Rebels the most ruthless of thieves, it follows that they robbed prisoners. Our government meanwhile fed and clothed prisoners as well as possible: the Rebels ought to have honored the responsibility to do likewise. Instead they added to the insult of neglect the criminal injury of stealing what the prisoners' government or families and friends sent to reduce suffering.[5]

In the late autumn of 1863 [the Rebels robbed us again, for example, when] our government dispatched a big shipment of uniforms for us and the prisoners at Belle Island.[6] Cold had set in—every one of us suffered the lack of clothing—and we (those at the island in particular) needed this shipment above all. But much had been stolen, especially coats. Even Rebel newspapers had to take note of that theft, which indicates its monstrousness. Many men in blue coats popped into view, the newspapers said, "coats probably swiped from the canalboat." The Confederate government ordered an investigation, the papers continued, "whereupon the costs vanished." (They had been taken to the dyers and dyed black.) There the matter rests, inquiry out of the question now.

Little [other] news reached us from the island until a few of us got permission to go there with things to distribute. Word of bad conditions had come to us accidentally in the Rebel newspapers. [We read that] General Winder, commander in chief of Rebel prisons, asked the Richmond city council to relinquish the poorhouse; he wanted to lodge prisoners and the wounded there. (I've mentioned Winder before.) During the discussion in council, a member said that the request must be denied. "Belle Island is the unhealthiest and the most wretched place in town."[7] The newspapers published the council's proceedings, which convinced us of the misery of our soldiers [at Belle Island].[8]

[Their troubles began when] enlisted men captured with us at Gettysburg had been forced to walk the approximately 130 miles from Staunton to Richmond, arriving at the island in August. (We meanwhile had traveled the distance by train.) Their rations, though small, came regularly at first. But at about the time [that ours were cut and] we at the Libby got little more [than they at the island], theirs shank to the minimum. Hunger prevailed there; our men killed and devoured dogs, mice, and rats. Human beings, however cruel and callous, would relent at such misery; but the Rebels did not swerve from a policy of persecution. They even scoffed at the wretches. Witness this article from the *Examiner:*

Notice to Dogs.—A citizen writes that Belle Island, Richmond's prison for Yankees, poses hazards for dogs, especially those in good flesh. The Yankees eat them. Our correspondent bases this conclusion on facts that have come to his attention. Several men recently lost their best friends on the lonely, barren island. Furthermore, our correspondent assures us, the guards know that the Yankees have caught, roasted, and eaten dogs. Moreover the guards understand that Yankee prisoners have begged people to leave their dogs for the Yankees to eat. If we doubt our correspondent, he advises we take a dog there: "You shall return alone and convinced of what I say." We have nothing to add to this dog story, except that we never respected Yankee taste. If Yankees prefer a piece of dog to the beef, bread, potatoes, and soup dispensed in the commissary—that is to *their* taste, not ours. Some carnivores adore the flesh of their own kind. Here we have a case of "dog eat dog."

This article suffices to show that the "Southern nobility" verges on barbarism. Later, Edward N. Pollard, editor of the *Examiner,* got regular rations when a Union prisoner and, soon paroled, had the run of Brooklyn until he returned to the South. Thus our government treated heartless people who mocked our soldiers because, racked by hunger, they ate dogs.

The head of the Royal Family [Sanderson] had gone to Belle Island first. Of course he saw nothing of the misery there. He told us that the officials did what they could for prisoners. General Neal Dow visited the island next; from him we heard the shocking truth. Hunger tormented the inmates; they needed clothing; they lacked shelter; the guards maltreated them: Dow withheld nothing. Turner, the day he learned that Dow spilled the beans, forbade him to visit the island again. Sanderson continued to visit as before.

A few months after we entered the Libby, Dow joined us—himself a prisoner then.[9] Indeed, he had been one in Alabama for a while. A reputed fanatic, he met a cool reception here. But he surprised us pleasantly and we warmed when we came to know him. An inveterate apostle of temperance, yes, and he seemed possessed by the idea of it; yet he must be respected as modest, well intentioned, and patriotic. He entered the Libby quietly, and his bearing and his way of life contradicted [everything about] the Royal Family. How well I remember him [and how he behaved unlike expectations for a general], standing with his small tin kettle at the stove, preparing his portion of beggarly grub. By and large, he lived like the most wretched of us; he did not assume authority but scorned it.

He could not forsake his temperance mania, of course. We had nothing to drink but canal water at the Libby (no place to urge abstinence in any event), yet the old gentlemen delivered two temperance lectures nonetheless. They served no practical purpose? He replied that they "*can* be of use. Somebody might now learn something that will benefit him later." Neal Dow, fixed on one idea, puts his faith in it and does not swerve from it.

6

A Winter in the Libby—"Fresh Fish"—Music and Theater—The Kitchen—The Sanitary Commission—Hunger

Autumn had nearly ended, but we knew nothing for sure about exchange. Feverishly we read the Ould-Butler correspondence. But the closest study and the keenest inferences produced no comfort: nothing to justify new hopes.[1] The two bigwigs quarreled about numbers, like schoolboys over a problem in arithmetic. Each, to the other, added or subtracted wrong. Each reproached the other rudely or with malice. We believed at first that nothing blocked exchange but differences over numbers of prisoners and parolees. We concluded at last that the cartel, agreed upon in 1862, had suffered an irreparable breach; the responsible parties [henceforth] neither wanted harmony nor intended to allow it.[2]

Then Northern newspapers quoted Lincoln: "The time is not ripe for a general exchange."[3] Several such quotations strengthened our revised opinion, which proved unfortunately to be correct. Now we said for the first time, "We'll be in prison until the end of the war." Of course, we followed military developments all the more intently meanwhile, for we understood victory in other than a general sense. To us, victory meant something personal: the sooner the end of the Rebellion, the nearer our day of freedom. But [military] events sadly promised little and seldom brought hope. General Meade advanced the Army of the Potomac briefly, then turned back when scarcely across the Rappahannock.[4] With winter crowding in, a new campaign could not be expected. So we comforted ourselves that we would pass winter safely in prison. Perhaps spring would bring us freedom in 1864.

In October, so many officers captured at Chickamauga [19-22 September] joined us that "Fresh Fish!" seemed endless.[5] This cry when greeting entrants, now customary, startled and puzzled recent arrivals. They did not know what it meant. The first inmate to spot a new face at the main entrance or on the ground floor would shout "Fresh Fish!" and be echoed at once in every room. Surrounded the instant he hit the top of the stairs, the arrival would be bombarded: "What regiment? What corps? Where captured? What's your name?" Sometimes we learned interesting things. Many arrivals, however, overwhelmed by this peculiar reception, could scarcely answer myriad questions asked in anxious inquisitiveness. Learning nothing, we sniffed, "Fresh fish are ignorant."

Chickamauga, as I've said, brought a shoal, packing every room. Even the space at ground level near the cellar had to be used to billet prisoners, for others had already arrived, individually or in small groups, from various places. The officers of the gunboats *Satellite* and *Reliance* had been captured in disgrace at the mouth of the Rappahannock [23 August 1863].[6] We prepared food on the ground floor.

When Chickamauga prisoners moved into Lower Middle and the one opposite, in late fall [1863], they displaced civilians caught at Gettysburg and elsewhere. The civilians, miserable victims of Rebel cruelty, suffered the most brutal treatment. We communicated with them through a hole in the floor (carefully concealed from Turner the bloodhound). They lacked water, they suffered vermin, and they got almost nothing to eat. Their frequent ration, only a little soup of rice or beans, teemed with worms. Every possession confiscated [including money], they could have bought nothing had anything been available. They begged and beseeched us for help. We passed food through the hole whenever possible, usually bread. It had to be cut to bits; the hole was small. Later they were transported I know not where; perhaps the poor devils entered another house of torture—Castle Thunder near the Libby, said to be the site of the most vicious scenes.[7] A motley assembly [largely political prisoners] populated it: Northern civilians, Southern Unionists, deserters, confidence men, soldiers who violated parole, and the like. (Even women.) A Captain Alexander commanded the castle.

In November the cold had already become painful. Trying above all to protect ourselves against frosty blasts roaring through windows that lacked both glass and shutters, we covered the windows as tightly as we could with bedding and rags. At night we wrapped ourselves, usually fully clothed, in blankets issued by the Rebels. Enough of us died of cold anyway; few received blankets from the North. The cold at the end of 1863 and in January 1864 exceeded what we had expected, with some days as bitter as in Minnesota or Wisconsin. The heating system? The stove in each room could not have produced enough heat had we been given fuel. Here Dick Turner proved mean with a vengeance. We had stoves but often no wood to warm them. We got rations but no wood to cook them. We had to defer the meat of a cold Christmas until the day after, we had not a stick of wood to cook it. (Dick Turner's Christmas largesse!) At first we could alleviate the lack by ripping out boards and gathering old lumber not nailed fast, but these reserves dwindled to nothing.

Meanwhile we made our quarters as comfortable as possible. With the lumber of crates from the North we fashioned tables, benches, and chairs. Having requested and received lamps [which came in the crates], we could sit and read or otherwise shorten the aeons of evening. The few of us with good voices entertained the rest. Many with awful voices sang, too. The small repertory mattered not at all; we attended to one and the same tune a hundred times. A schoolmaster from Pennsylvania directed our quartet [or glee club] with gravity and did second bass in the usual hymns and spirituals while the first tenor's face turned syrup-sweet with song. After the quartet warbled to the end of its pious enthusiasm, somebody would strike up an Irish ditty or a Negro ballad. The company would join the refrain and usually emit a roar.

We lifted our voices so wondrously in the Libby—I believe Satan himself enjoys no concerts more beautiful in Hell. A talented composer among us could have studied the effects, applied them [to his work] later, and thrown into the shade the Flying Dutchman's peculiar cadences and dissonances. Even an orchestra formed. To its main instruments—banjo, guitar, flute, violin, and drum—a craftsman added a triangle, improvised of old iron rods. It approximated the form but produced none of the sound of the true triangle. But such minor defects could not stop the music. Strumming, piping, drumming, the orchestra belted out the words of favorite composers. On musicians' Olympus, Lanner and Bellini must have been overjoyed.[8]

A minstrel society [the Libby Prison Minstrels] also appeared.[9] Its performances, at brief intervals, delighted the Americans among us. The performers (in blackface, of course) presented songs, instrumental pieces, and what they did best: buffoonery and droll skits, called farces. Modeled on the comic acts of professionals, and featuring abundant broad humor and myriad dirty jokes, the farces would have been inappropriate for an audience of women. The Americans loved them nonetheless. They rejoiced in the funny situations and lewed jests—and even in the Negro-like but overdone mugging and dancing. The minstrels stopped [performing] chiefly because the repertoire grew monotonous, and no new acts could be created to vary it.

We honored the muse of the dance, too, often three or four times a week, usually in the evenings. Frequently, right after devotionals, a dancing party began. Or men danced in one room while others prayed next-door.[10]

A world unto itself, the Libby, then. In this corner, three or four men at whist [or other games of cards, checkers, or chess]; in that corner, one studying a religious book.[11] Here a group would discuss their common fate or the question of exchange, earnestly and with zeal; while others, there, amused themselves over silly anecdotes (in good supply among the Americans). In this room, in a so-called raid, a number of younger prisoners (those given to boisterous tumult), joined hands in single file in what they termed a "snake" and, on signal, blustered around the room at full gallop, not only along passages among the rest of us reclining or sitting, but also slap-bang over chairs, tables, and boxes, upsetting everything in the way, in storm and riot, like the age-old chase, and final hunt. Meanwhile in yet another room, preachers preached morals and Christian behavior. Seriousness and frivolity, cheek by jowl. Peaks of joy amid depths of depression.

The [musical and minstrel] performances, which I've discussed, took place on the ground floor, in the spacious kitchen. We also exercised there. On cold days [to warm up] when we had no wood, we formed a four-file column and moved at a healthy double-quick, often led by old General Neal Dow.

The kitchen [thus] throbbed from morning until night. Cooking began at the crack of dawn and, except for a few hours, men remained at the stoves, preparing their often plain and frugal fare. The old arrangement, of messes cooking together in prescribed order [described earlier], had been given up because the Rebels no longer delivered rations as at first. Each prisoner now cooked for himself, or a few would join a private mess.[12]

Early in the morning we prepared only coffee. Many of us received the real article from the North.[13] Others brewed an ersatz of rye, common in the South then, available at $2 or $3 a pound. The rest, destitute of packages and money, made do with roasted cornmeal. Rations worsened daily; now and then we got meat that nobody would set before a dog. In January 1864, many of us called it mule meat, probably its right name. Others, however, said that it came from animals dead other than by slaughter. That conjecture, too, may have been correct. (We read at the time in the papers that a herd of cattle perished of cold and hunger on a train from Danville to Richmond. As likely as not, their carcasses went to prisoners.) Occasionally we received salted meat, of as little use as the problematical flesh just mentioned—hard, tough, tasting salty beyond belief—inedible whether boiled or roasted. No alternative remained to our poorest men but to cook in water the tiny ration of rice or beans, without so much as a drop of fat. This miserable soup, with a slice of cornbread and nothing else, had to suffice unless somebody with more to eat contributed a scrap now and then.

At this time a few individuals, the Royal Family in particular, lived like sybarites. They enjoyed practically everything available at the Richmond market and feasted to satisfaction while others went to hard beds of hunger. On Christmas Eve the family ate a sumptuous meal, laid in the kitchen, as if to deride the rest of us.

I've mentioned hustle and bustle at the stoves, producing plenty of comic scenes. A man can't ignite his wood, which is wet as usual; so he whittles shavings, lights them, and blows for dear life, trying to transfer flame to chunks piled in the stove. Repeated efforts produce nothing but smoke. Another man, clumsy enough, knocks over his kettle or somebody else's. A long face, or volcanic cursing, shall follow. A third man suffers a different misfortune. Meal in hand, he mounts the stairs toward the top floor, slips, drops the kettle down the steps—*crash!* Men who see the accident laugh, notably unsympathetic to a ruined meal. Pity the hungry one who lost his dinner, especially since he has nothing else. Devastated, he looks down, with touching sadness, at the food on the floor, lost, neither to be recovered nor replaced. He has been cut to the quick. The man beside him chuckles, titters, and guffaws.

Smoke frequently filled the kitchen, making cooking a hardship. Several times we had to spend hours in smoke while officials tried to take an exact count of us. We had to leave our rooms then and report to the kitchen. When satisfied nobody remained behind, the officials read the roll aloud. Each prisoner, name shouted, returned to his room. Smoke intensified the ennui of a roll call.

The kitchen served two other purposes. (1) A place to practice fencing, which a number of prisoners did with swords they contrived of wood. (2) Distribution point for rations. A door [handy for this purpose] gave onto the street, open but a few hours a day, however, and of course guarded then.

Many of us would not have hungered had the food the Sanitary Commission sent been properly dispensed. (The Commission did much good [throughout the war] and everywhere helped relieve the suffering of our wounded, sick, and captured soldiers.) To us [at the Libby], from the commission, came clothing and food—in heaps. To the Royal Family the Rebels assigned distribution. If ever injustices were done, they were done then and there. Some prisoners, the family's pets, received to excess; others, without a friend in the family, nothing. We deemed it a fact that Rebel officials got part of the shipments and that the family helped themselves to a glut, especially of food. The family's agent [in this atrocity], one Captain [Edward A.] Fobes [131st New York Infantry], complied with instructions from Sanderson & Company—to the letter. Fobes treated with arrogance anyone not enjoying protection or favor from a member of the family (I speak from experience; I was there). And the family? They acted as if rations originated with *them*.

What sorrow for us, thus to have the commission's humane purpose blunted. I have already observed elsewhere the unfair distribution of "sanitary goods." The Libby flaunts one more example. Corrupt, underhanded scoundrels penetrate nearly every charitable enterprise. They worm into the administration, to indulge congenital dishonesty in yet another place, or wield fraudulent authority on one more occasion.

The populace of Richmond suffered the same regime as ours: scarcity, need, and hunger. Children and adults assembled outside our walls nearly every day, seeking a bit of cornbread. The poverty-stricken begged from the impoverished! The notion pervaded the city that at the least we had enough food. (Mendacious newspapers never missed the chance to spin for the public the yarn that the commissary supplied us prodigally, in addition to loads sent us by friends in the North.) "Though a prison," the *Examiner* said one day with the greatest of ease, "the Libby measures up to a good hotel in the way it feeds its occupants. Prisoners enjoy not only a surfeit of staples but also plenty of the choicest delicacies." Again, "what a shameful injustice to treat humanely and feed well the captured 'barbarians' who trespass upon the South's sacred soil—plundering and burning and endangering Southern ladies' innocence—while Confederate soldiers, ill-clad and suffering in camps in Tennessee and on the Rappahannock, defend Southern freedom and the security of hearth and home." These statements, repeated by Richmond papers over and over, must have led readers to believe the Libby a huge larder, where we lived off the fat of the land.

When a few of us spoke on the sly with guards through kitchen windows, we learned in detail of privation and want in Richmond. The guards said that they by and large got barely enough to sustain life, while famine stalked their families. Gratefully the guards accepted bread from us. A few thirsty prisoners traded corn bread for bad apple brandy, and in due course ached accordingly.

Although [Rebel] newspapers disliked speaking of misfortune [on their side], even they could not avoid mention of deprivation and financial ills, widespread here and now, in addition to [physical] damage and [human] losses inflicted by the war. The papers viewed as calamitous the fact that so many Negroes "upped and left" with their "hypocritical friends."[14] The labor force thereby reduced, the white man must work if he wanted to eat. An entry about Suffolk [Virginia] in the *Examiner* of 7 December 1863, stressed that the "white ladies and gentlemen must do the work their servants had done." Unless necessity pinched [let me add], the "ladies and gentlemen" would not have worked. Absolutely not! To the Southerner, work is a disgrace, especially work done once by Negroes. In the proverb, necessity is the mother of invention. In the South, necessity compels work.

Attempts to Escape—The Grand Tunnel— Hullabaloo in Richmond—Return of Escapees—The Cells—Colonel Streight

No doubt about it now: mountains blocked exchange. Inevitably our thoughts turned therefore to escape. An example inspired us. The first to try to take leave of the Libby's hospitality, Major Houstain and Cavalry Lieutenant Volziehn, reached the North after a cunning and masterly flight. Nearly everyone [consequently] dealt [optimistically] with *the* question, How can *I* get out of this rotten hole?

Considering each possibility, weighing every contingency, we inspected and studied all windows, each door, every wall. Officers of engineers among us drew maps of Richmond and environs. We tried to contact people in the city, to communicate with Negroes who worked in the Libby, and to get the lowdown on their white overseers. In short, we did everything possible to inform ourselves fully and to prepare for escape.

We even discussed forcing our way out. Colonel [Philip de] Cesnola [Fourth New York Cavalry] labored over the plan. We officers, organized with enlisted prisoners in big buildings nearby [Castle Thunder], would break out at night, surprise the guards, seize weapons, and in serried ranks penetrate Rebel pickets and march to the Union lines. This plan, which could have worked, came to grief the morning the rebels removed enlisted prisoners.[1] "The 'Yankees' were preparing a grand escape," the papers said, "but officials learned of it in time." Most [papers] connected one man with the foiling of the plan: Lieutenant Colonel Sanderson, mentioned several times [in this book].

Americans [among us] put to it their native shrewdness and brooded and mulled and beat their brains over ways and means of escape. A few individuals succeeded with plots long-cherished and carefully elaborated. An escapee left by the door from the kitchen to the street. Several others disappeared via the hospital. [Then a cheeky fellow] obtained a Rebel uniform, donned it, and descended the steps of the west wing to the ground floor. (And with such brass and so much grit!) Easily passing the guard there, he strode unchecked into the office and asked the way to the desk of a [certain] captain [outside the Libby]. Could he have been answered in a friendlier manner? The adjutant accompanied him to the sidewalk to show him where to go. The guards, having seen them together, took nothing amiss. So the bird flew the coop.

Some attempts failed. Major [H. A., or Harry] White, of Pennsylvania [and a member of its senate], tried to slip out with physicians being at last exchanged after long months in prison. At City Point, the place of exchange, Rebels detected him and sent him back. [Though his senatorial status was urged] every effort to have him exchanged failed as miserably as all his foiled escapes.

Colonel Streight, trying to get away, bargained with a guard and gave him a gold watch. Perfidious, the guard seized him on the verge of flight. The guard's rascality delighted the Turners. (All Confederates nursed a special hatred for Streight.) Clapped into irons, he endured three weeks in an underground cell, fed nothing but bread and water. So the Rebels exacted revenge on the man they feared [because of his raids, deep into their strongholds, before capture]. He looked pale and wretched when he rejoined us after three weeks; but his spirits remained high. One of the most honorable among us, unlike the Royal Family, he neither dealt with nor toadied to the Rebels. "I could have gotten some favors and little privileges from them," he said once, "had I been willing to enter into certain arrangements. I rejected such things out of hand. I wanted no truck with Rebels. I mean *none*."

On 7 February 1864, alarm swept the Confederate capital [Richmond]. According to the newspapers, bells pealed in such fury that one of them cracked. Cannon sped at a gallop through the streets. Troop units, large and small, hustled east to the fortifications there. Trepidations gripped the populace. The cause? Part of Butler's forces had gained Bottoms Bridge. They stopped there.[2] The Rebels calmed a little then, only to be riled again.

That is, on the evening of 9 February, in the Libby, the hour of "lights out" had passed, but the inmates had not thought of sleep. A scurrying here, a whispering there, a bustling somewhere—continuous agitation means an unusual game afoot, no doubt about it. How true!

Colonel Streight, with several prisoners he trusted, planned a tunnel and started at once.[3] For over two months [since early winter], tireless moles labored at night—subsequently during the day as well—until they reached their goal. Enumerate the leviathan obstacles to this caper and be compelled to marvel at the energy and the endurance the little band devoted to it. (1) The distance between entrance and exit. (2) The lack of proper tools. (3) The utmost caution obligatory lest guards and officials get wind of

conceal the plan from the many fellow inmates who,
with the Rebels.

th utmost caution, yet several times brushed within a
. One day [for example] in a cellar room, a mole
sacks of cornmeal stored there. The door opened. In
walked an o.... astonished, of course, to find somebody in the locked
room, he asked, "What are you doing here?"

The mole answered with presence of mind: "I wanted cornmeal. I'm
hungry. What I get to eat doesn't satisfy me."

He added that he had clambered down here on an unused staircase—
unused and therefore boarded up. The official swallowed this "explana-
tion": neither he nor his colleagues had the faintest notion of current
events underground. Nobody suspected an entrance to the cellar from the
kitchen, covered in the daytime by a cookstove.

The tunnel itself, [which had to go] from the cellar to the yard of a
warehouse across the street, exacted the harshest travail. (The warehouse
held our packages [from the North] before distribution.) Granite hid the
tunnel's entrance; a big block had to be broken out of the building's
foundation [before digging could start]. From that point, the tunnel dipped
beneath the street and rose to open in the yard.

On the predetermined night, 9 February [1864], lights went out, guards
as usual announced in loud voices their posts and numbers, and the
typical peace settled on the street. Inside, agitation prevailed. Especially in
the kitchen. The stoves had already been shoved aside and the hole
exposed. Word [among inmates] flashed like lightning: "A tunnel's been
dug! There's a big break!" Hundreds swarmed to the kitchen. The clamor
aroused fear that the guards would be tipped off. Arriving in the dark
kitchen, the mob shoved for the hole. The rush upset a stove. The crash
produced flight back up the steps, a chaotic retreat to the rooms because
everyone thought the accident had exposed the plot [and that the jig was
up]. Indeed, a sergeant opened the door from the street to the kitchen and
glanced in. But he shut the door without suspicion. Nocturnal tumult did
not impress guards used to uproar. Inmates, convinced that the coast was
clear, filled the kitchen again, after a while.[4]

Escape continued until 3:00 or 4:00 A. M. From the upper floor of the
east wing, you could see fugitives pop out of the tunnel, cross the yard,
clear the gateway to the street, turn left, and disappear into the dark. A
gaslight burned on the corner a few steps from the gateway—and across
the narrow street the guards paced back and fourth—could they have seen
nothing? Conjecture has it—and I believe—they took the escapees for
fellow Rebels leaving the warehouse after another instance of the notori-
ously frequent crime of looting our packages.

On 10 February, a day of amused excitement among us, we began as, at the crack of dawn; "How many got away?" The number, we learned exceeded a hundred. Intending tricks to confound the clerks during roll call, we looked forward to the customary [assembly and] count at 8:00. [Ours was a worried anticipation, however, for] though we had become skillful at this mischief, we could not be sure our humbug would work. As luck would have it, Dick Turner wanted Colonel Streight before roll call. Steight not to be found, Turner suspected escape. The count commenced at once. The tally stunned Turner and little Ross.

Ross, the imp, asked; "Where *are* they all?"

We answered; "They fell out the window."

A hundred prisoners missing—how did they get away? An investigation began. How in the world could a hundred men escape and not be heard and the guards know nothing of it? Every last official stood [on the carpet in the office] dumbfounded and helpless. Thinking the guards bribed, [Major Thomas] Turner [the commandant] arrested them on the spot and ordered them taken to Castle Thunder. Duck Turner, for his part, had his horse saddled, then galloped off in search of spoor. He wanted especially to nab the despised Colonel Streight. Later, Major Turner and Adjutant Latouche appeared in the rooms. Nothing to be discovered there, they went into the street, ramrods in hand. They poked into each handful of loose earth, delving for the crack by which the birds had flown. Watching from the windows, how we rejoiced at those futile probes! Turner glared one way and another, wildly, and thrust and stabbed at the ground. The fat adjutant peeped into the cellar's every opening and ran his hands over the walls; he wanted the honor of solving the riddle. So they circled the building, hunting high and low, stamping their feet in search of possible burrows—in short, seeking in desperation the key to this incredible, audicious "Yankee escapade." Meanwhile a wag [among us] cut strips from a blanket and fashioned a makeshift rope and lowered it from the uppermost window in one of the wooden additions to the [Libby's] south side. The end of the rope hung about five or six yards from the ground.[5] Suddenly the adjutant spotted it and shouted in a paroxysm; "Here's where they got away!" Turner, cleverer, disagreed. The search continued. At last they happened into the yard of the warehouse and saw the pile of soil and the hole. Returning to the cellar, they found the block of granite and the tunnel's entrance. They called for a young Negro and ordered him to crawl through. The puzzle had been solved. Only where were the [missing] Yankees?

The escape caused an uproar in Richmond beyond description; the break from the Libby became the talk of the town. Continually the next day, people came [like tourists] to the yard to view the mouth of the tunnel. Two days later the newspapers devoted long articles to it. The *Whig* spoke of a fetid rat and its disappearance via a gigantic burrow. This adventure of Streight's, the *Whig* added, doubtless overshadowed the flight of the Rebel John H. Morgan from Columbus, Ohio.[6] "Yankees, the damned moles— we must be on guard against such people."

Meanwhile the Rebels exerted every effort to fetch back the escapees. Ecstatic over our comrades' success, we had rejoiced at the Rebels' dismay—but then, learning of measures [for recapture], we grew anxious. We knew too well the Rebel character; we must expect rage to be vented upon recaptured escapees. We agonized especially over Colonel Streight. Fate decreed ill for him, should he be retaken.

Suddenly, on the third day after the break, a cry: "Yanks! Yanks!" We dashed to the windows and saw the return of the first to be recaptured, brought back under heavy guard. In the days to come, others followed: fifty or sixty in all. They had to state their names in the office, then, with few exceptions, repair to the black cells below and endure several days (nearly two weeks in a few cases) under lock and key there, with bread and water but without enough clothes or sufficient blankets.

They [the recaptured inmates who went below] discovered a man prostrate in a cell. They entered. "Bread," he begged. "Give me bread." During the night he so hallucinated that they decided he must be gravely sick. The next day they mentioned him to the sergeant who brought bread and water: "Can't he be removed?" The sergeant reported to Turner. "Don't be concerned about what does not concern you," Turner said. The following day the newcomers to the cells called for the Rebel physician as if *they* needed him. When he came, they said: "We found this man in the cell. Obviously he's sick. He's not had a bite to eat." The physician, accepting responsibility, ordered the man removed to the hospital. Thus the invalid and his illness came to light together. He must have had to endure many days in the cell's blackness without food and sick. Smallpox. He would have died had not the new prisoners happened into his cell. They spent a day and two nights with him. Later they learned from the sergeant that Turner had banished the man, a Union soldier, to the cell, for reasons of (alleged) theft.

Each [survivor of the cells] described the ordeal: "Appalling." What prevailed in those holes—cold, isolation, foul air—exacted toll on the health of many a man. All emerged pale and emaciated. They agreed, "It's barbarous to put and hold people in those rats' nests." Dick Turner's face glowed in those days, radiating hellish delight. He knew how many had been forced to suffer.

Returned escapees had been telling us of the dangers they faced and the hardships they endured [in trying to flee to Union lines]. Some individually, some in small groups, they mostly headed east afoot, having to wade swamps and swim rivers, chilled and without food for days on end, hiding in the bush, often losing their way at night, feet gashed, exerting supreme effort to avoid pickets and patrols, until they reached our lines or were recaptured. Many ailed for months. A few weeks later the news delighted us: fifty-five escapees had reached Butler's army [about forty-five miles east of Richmond, around New Kent Court House].[7]

Colonel Streight had been among the fortunate. The Rebels sought him above all [but he made good his escape].

[He left such fear behind that] shortly after he got out [of the Libby], commotion erupted in the streets of Richmond. [It began one day when] police chased several of the hazard players abundant then in Richmond. One player fled to the roofs to escape. People below saw him and took him for Streight fleeing arrest. The resulting uproar no doubt struck terror into the player, with stones hurled at the roofs and shots fired. Knowledge ended the misunderstanding. The incident dramatized the eagerness to nab Streight.

8

Stern Measures [against More Escapes]—General Butler—The Richmond Press—Exchange—Hope and Sudden Disappointment

The getaway by Streight and his party flabbergasted the Libby's officials. Though flawed, it succeeded well enough to horrify them. On the qui vive, they lay down rules to foil others. Our Rebel keepers henceforth supervised us with suspicion and mistrust, and daily looked for new deceptions and took every pain to put the quietus on fresh schemes. The Turners must have been vexed that they, reputed to be super jailers, had been too dumb to discover Yankee burrowing. [Moreover, according to a report] Libby officials had let Streight's "execrable Yankees" dupe them; lightheartedly and without concern, [the moles] dug the tunnel that became the talk of the town for weeks. The report had probably been ill received in high places, [indeed] by General Winder and Jefferson Davis [himself].

The order to sentries to fire at any prisoner seen at the windows showed how jittery the Turners had become. Would a prisoner jump from the height of an upper floor? Would he let himself down by a rope in view of sentries pacing back and forth below? The Turners accepted nothing as impossible. Committed to making life disagreeable for us anyway, they gave all the more willingly their order [to shoot on sight]. Sentries obeyed punctiliously and fired at prisoners too near windows.

Sentries one day let go into the south-side addition. Death brushed cavalry lieutenant Imboden. The bullet that pierced his hat would have finished him had it penetrated but a few more millimeters. Another prisoner missed death because the iron of the window's bars deflected the bullet. A short while earlier, Adjutant Forsyth of the 100th Ohio had not been so fortunate. He sat at his table reading, at least ten feet from the window. A shot rang out. He fell dead, a bullet in the chest. Of course, "the shot had not been deliberate," the Rebels said. "The gun discharged of itself during the loading of a percussion cap." We believed with justification that a vicious Rebel had fired into the building to murder a detested Yankee for no reason but pleasure. As honor among Indians accrues to the warrior who slays as many as possible of a hostile tribe, so does a Rebel gain heroism for killing Yankees, even one unarmed.

Patrols prowled rooms at night, too, against escape. During the day, while we answered roll call in the kitchen, our belongings [in the rooms] often got ransacked. Now, many of us passed the time carving bones [into chessmen and various notions and trinkets], mostly with knives and files bought during times of milder supervision. The Turners knew we used the files but, haunted by [the memory of] Streight and his tunnel, they took the files for dangerously suspicious items and, one day in a general search, confiscated a number of them. Who could be sure; with them might not the crafty Yankees pierce the walls and dig a new tunnel?

Of captured Union enlisted men we heard little, none of it good. Most had been taken to Danville, where sickness struck and smallpox especially ravaged them. As early as 18 January 1864, the *Examiner* observed that, come spring, at their present rate of mortality, all Danville prisoners would be dead. Hearing of the smallpox epidemic, General Butler sent 6,000 doses of vaccine and a letter to [Rebel] exchange agent Ould. Newspapers added theirs to Ould's amiable response, praising Butler's humanitarian kindness.

[Until now] the Rebel newspapers had lambasted Butler, the man the Rebels hated most. The *Dispatch* once called him "the paragon of wickedness" and likened him to [Jean Marie] Collot d'Herbois [who drew a blood bath at Lyons in the French Revolution]. "The South long recognized [Butler] for what he was, and scorned him, and therefore he revenged himself through the meanest and most savage treatment" of Confederate prisoners. This denunciation alluded to the execution, at Butler's order, of the scoundrel [William B.] Mumford in New Orleans [for tearing down and destroying the American flag over the mint, 26 April 1862, during the Federal capture of New Orleans, led by Butler]. The Rebels revered Mumford thereafter and wanted to raise a monument to him. Butler they called nothing less than "The Beast." To besmirch his name as much as possible, their press sank to the depths of filth. Without occasion or reason, papers lied and calumniated brazenly, and printed the most daring and shocking tales, to agitate their harebrained and irresponsible public. When he began his campaign [up the James toward Richmond] in the spring [early May] of 1864, Richmond papers said that he had no sooner left [his old] headquarters than he assaulted a Negro woman—"shamefully." [In general] the Confederate press, a slough of baseness and cruelty, fed such stuff to a Southern populace gone wild and pandered to the tastes of the Rebel mob. What an event, such a contrast, then, the newspapers' tribute to Butler's humanitarianism at Danville!

Still, that press hurled invective daily at the Yankees. Regularly it boasted of Rebel courage and blustered about the certainty of the eventual

Confederate triumph. Besides those topics, newspapers in the winter months [1863–64] reported chiefly on the Congress [of the Confederate States] convened in Richmond and the important measures it considered. In other words, monetary policy, taxation, and military law gained the attention of congressional wisdom and set journalistic pens in motion.

Day by day, the worth of Confederate money declined. The Congress, foreseeing the result to be a bankruptcy of sorts, decreed that, up to a certain date, money in circulation could be exchanged for new [and dollar for dollar]. Thereafter, old money could be redeemed only at two-thirds of face value.[1] Libby officials took according advantage. They received Confederate money sent from the North to inmates [and exchanged it] as legal tender and at full value but distributed it later [following devaluation] after deducting a third. When $150 Confederate came for me from a friend, I waited a long while before I got $100 in old notes; in other words, $66.33 ⅓ at current values. I repeatedly applied for the rest but received not a cent. Many men suffered likewise. (The Rebels excelled at fraud and theft, especially against prisoners.)

Taxes in the Confederacy could far easier be imposed than collected, especially in areas lost to Union forces or expecting imminent occupation by them. Yet taxation occasioned debate as hot and as protracted [as that on money].[2] But the so-called impressment law aroused the most opposition, by empowering government agents to seize for the army a part of basic commodities.[3]

The "military law" (chief sponsor [Louis T.] Wigfall of Texas), next in resistance incited, obligated all men eighteen [i.e., seventeen] to fifty years old. The law also vested in President [Jefferson Davis] the unheard-of power to grant so-called exemptions. Confederate citizens [i.e., most males] thus being under his thumb, Davis could at his pleasure excuse anyone from service or dispatch an unpopular man to the front regardless of his justifiable claim to exemption. The law, illustrating the Confederacy's tendency to monarchy, imposed an incredible despotism.[4]

After enacting those measures, intended to cure the Confederacy's chronic consumptive diseases, the Congress adjourned on 18 February with a eulogy to the Rebel general [Robert S.] Garnett, killed in action [13 July 1861, near Corrick's Ford, West Virginia].

Richmond newspapers meanwhile described a South radiant with well-being. The South, they declared, would win the war. Amid such messages intended to maintain popular morale, plenty of fears nonetheless emerged [as well as reports of unfavorable conditions]. The *Whig,* the most realistic, viewed things less often through rose-colored glasses and expressed much sadness. For example, were the Confederacy to entertain [legitimate] prospects of [military] victory and [political] success, public trust must reside in the president's office. Jefferson Davis enjoyed far too little public trust. Imperious, vindictive, openly intent on gathering unto himself as much power as possible, he alienated many otherwise-passionate Rebels. Furthermore, in a miserable monetary situation, people in the streets of Richmond paid $18 to $20 Confederate for $1 in Union greenbacks. Food plummeted in quantity and quality while its cost skyrocketed. Many items commanded ten times what they cost six months before. Prices of cloth for apparel, and of leather, shot up to the fabulous. Animals for slaughter diminished persistently while the famished Rebel army on the Rappahannock devoured the few still to be found. Only the rich could secure a paucity of comforts; the poorer classes must accept unpleasant guests: poverty and hunger. Fewer and fewer horses would not suffice to restore the cavalry's heavy and daily-worsening losses. To that tale of woe, add the news of the mass mobilization in the North. Though scorned by the [Richmond] press, such news helped worsen the Confederate situation, which became wretched. Still, whenever Northerners spoke of fresh levies of troops, new ships to be built, and other martial measures, [Richmond] newspapers sneered. Accordingly, when Senator [Timothy O.] Howe of Wisconsin broached in Congress his admittedly bizarre proposal to draft a million men to be used to free Union prisoners in the South, the *Dispatch* remarked; "Let them come, our vultures want to eat." And Richmond newspapers were calling the [Southern] people heroic, portraying theirs as the richest and most productive of countries, labeling Northerners as pygmies and cowards, and predicting the unavoidable financial collapse of the North. Some papers, writing this way to maintain the morale of the army and the people, stated such assertions and prophecies as acts of faith rather than matters of fact. Other papers, blindly fanatical, took for granted the Confederacy's ultimate victory.

Rebel big shots visited us several times that winter. The mayor of Richmond, Joseph Mayo, so honored us. [Mississippi] Congressman [Henry S.] Foote, too. Jefferson Davis's inveterate opponent, he provoked scenes in [the Confederate] Congress. The notorious [John C.] Breckenridge also paid a call [he the presidential candidate in 1860, now a Confederate general, and to be Davis's secretary of war]. As well as [George P.] Kane, former United States marshal [and the chief of police] of Baltimore. And the cavalry general and raider John H. Morgan. (In Richmond [by the way] the people adulated Morgan after he escaped from prison [on 27 November 1863]. Rebels flooded the Ballard House, where he lived at public expense, to see the "brave chieftain" lately incarcerated by repugnant Yankees in the [Ohio state] penitentiary at Columbus.)

"We regret that you must endure such limited and unsatisfactory issue," these Libby visitors said when we showed them our miserable and scanty rations. "The Southern people do not want you oppressed this way." A few, Breckenridge for one, promised to speak with authorities about our treatment. Nothing improved, of course. Either the visitors mouthed empty phrases so we'd think their interest genuine, or if they in fact attempted what they freely promised, their influence proved too weak. Besides, Davis and his secretary of war [James A.] Seddon did not intend to treat us as human beings—even though, in one of his messages, Davis (the hypocrite) spoke of the humanity and compassion that the Confederate government would show prisoners of war.

At the end of March the newspapers astounded us: the commissioners had agreed, and the first exchanges [under the Dix-Hill cartel] would leave on the next boat. Too often misled before, we believed not a word now. We took it for a ruse to stall us and prevent new attempts to escape. This time, however, facts belied skepticism. Inspector Turner appeared and read aloud a list of forty or fifty to be conveyed the next day to City Point for exchange. Words cannot describe how happy we were. "At last the ice is broken," we thought. "At last the commissioners' quarrels have ended. At last we can return [home] and be free again."

Several times in the following weeks, groups of prisoners were sent away, and we presumed exchange to be proceeding smoothly and on schedule. Each of us calculated the approximate time when it would be *his* turn. We lacked an intecessor, we did not belong to the Royal Family, [and so we must rely on our own devices]. We delighted in [imagining] the glorious moment when Turner would appear and call *our* names. We anticipated the journey on the James. We fancied our arrival in the North. Some of us even cogitated on our first meal there. Would it be the fresh fish that Pastor Bouldrye wanted? Or another tasty morsel. And noble Bacchus—how we wanted to embrace him! As for our old coats—worn out and home to tiny creatures infamous for widespread unrest and discriminating palates—how we wanted to buy new ones *fast*. Reveling [thus] in thoughts of freedom, we dreamed of meeting and greeting friends and relatives, we forgot [the Libby's miserable surroundings, and we entertained again the highest hopes [for exchange]. After a long night we enjoyed the first ray of sunshine; after a long pain, the first pleasure; and after a long winter, the first breath of spring. (Weren't we fools to cherish hope again? Hadn't we learned to stick to reality and leave hope to softies, dreamers, and romantics?)

One day at the end of April the call came for another group. Like those who preceded, they left amid shouts of *good-bye* from us who remained. Soon they arrived at City Point and saw the Union steamboat they expected to carry them home to the land of freedom. Then: "Exchange has ended." The message jolted like a thunderclap and flabbergasted the poor devils at freedom's gate, about to enter, but flung back into the misery of incarceration. The next day, bearers of bad news, they rejoined us. [Their report] knocked us out of seventh heaven and into a chasm of disappointment and anguish.

Exchange had ended! Therefore we stayed in the Libby, where one more amenity had just been added. We sat on a volcano now. Turner, the man of humanitarian intent, had ordered an enormity of powder installed in the cellar. He intended to blast us to smithereens if our government staged another raid to free us. Colonel [Ulric] Dahlgren had undertaken one [with General Judson Kilpatrick] and had even reached the outskirts of Richmond. Rebels repulsed his troops and killed him [from ambush]. Libby officials did not feel safe for a moment thereafter, fearing another raid or a [new] attempt to escape. (Reason existed [unknown to them] to fear escape: preparations to dig a second tunnel had begun.) Turner had decided not to let us get away so easily another time.

The Negroes first brought word that something, they knew not what, had been buried below. Soon we learned the facts and asked Turner why he mined the cellar.

"I'm going to blow you all to bits if you try to escape again."

Hence our pleasure to spend every hour for several weeks, awake and asleep, on top of a malignant explosive.

On 6 May, Turner appeared in the evening and read us an order. "Be ready to be moved elsewhere tomorrow early."

Whither? To our own lines perhaps? Or deeper into the Confederacy? No answer from Turner.

9

Departure from the Libby—From Richmond to Danville—The Prison in Danville

[Dick] Turner read us the order to depart. Hustle and bustle erupted in every room at once. We began to assemble our belongings as the cry rang out again and again—countless times—*"Pack up! Pack up!"*

Not knowing whether we would go on foot or by train, we had to limit baggage to essentials. During the course of [the] time [of our confinement here], packages from the North and things we had purchased had multiplied our possessions. Choices were therefore necessary—and difficult. Some of us had collected chattels enough for a household; a load impossible to bring along. All of us had grown accustomed to a lot of things and wanted to keep them, even those of little value.

We believed our destination and mode of transportation had been omitted from the order, deliberately, so we would leave the maximum behind. Were the Rebel officials already delighted that they would get what had been ours? We would not oblige—not in the least! If we were unable or unwilling to take something, it was left unfit for use, if not demolished.

Those nighttime scenes should have been made into pictures. In the dull glow of tallow candles, everybody was busily at work. A general inspection of everyone's effects came first, followed by the review and study of everything that was to be abandoned. Condemned items were put aside and then destroyed. Here a man drove a nail through a plate; nobody would eat bean or rice soup from it anymore. There a man smashed under a boot heel a tin kettle in which many a gruel had been cooked. Here a man was demolishing a chair he had so painstakingly devised from the boards of a crate. In this corner a man ripped to shreds an old shirt on whose threadbare surface he had so often given chase [to lice or fleas].[1] In that corner a man cut to bits a pair of crippled boots. Fragments of tableware and cooking pots, of clothing and cabinets, were flung about amid facetious comments or wild shrieks; the rooms became a bedlam of mad destruction. Pieces of wood and old clothes were piled in a middle room and, shortly before our departure, ignited. Rebel officials discovered the fire in the nick of time. We would not have minded abandoning Richmond by the light of this bastille in flames.

About 2:00 A.M. the order came: Leave the rooms and report to the kitchen. After we mustered there, the rooms were searched for anybody who might have remained in hiding. Dick Turner sat by the kitchen door that opened onto the street, calling names from A to Z. One by one we exited by that door and assembled in the street, cordoned off by Rebel soldiers. The recitation of names was so slow that our column formed only in time to be greeted by the first rays of dawn. Before we marched, several of the Libby's slaves with wheelbarrows rolled up a batch of corn bread. Each of us got a slice: the ration for twenty-four hours and the last memento of the luxurious Libby: bread baked of unsifted cornmeal and burned.

Captain [W. Kent] Tabb, commanding the escort and responsible for moving us, finally dressed the column after several headcounts. We trooped down Cary Street, past Castle Thunder [a big, brick tobacco warehouse converted to a prison, with barred windows and a wooden fence] and across the bridge over the James, to Manchester [later South Richmond, part of the city proper]. What an odd feeling to walk on solid ground again, having been so long off it. The earth seemed to sway in the manner of the illusion experienced after a long sea voyage.

In Manchester the buildings nearest the bridge are factories. Our column approached them. Workers, mostly of the African race, gathered at doors and windows and reviewed us. Their curiosity was profound—with good reason. Not only were we some of the captured Yankees who piqued interest everywhere in the South, but we also looked downright comical. True, what we were wearing was decent enough, but we carried such grotesque loads: clothing and other things of every sort. Here and there on somebody's shoulder rode a ham, already half devoured. A frying pan swung in somebody else's right hand. This marcher lugged a chair; that marcher toted a washboard. And there were the instruments of the Libby's band.

A beautiful morning: sun bright and clear; sky cloudless; trees gleaming in spring's shiny new green. Outdoors for the first time in ten months, we were almost blinded. Our eyes, used to the Libby's half-light, had been hurt by it and the kitchen's eternal smoke. Some of us, nearly dazed by the coruscation, could scarcely distinguish colors. How our hearts would have sung if, on that unforgettable morning of fresh air and splendid Nature, we had been told we were free! But that news was not forthcoming. Though pleased with pretty views, we could not be truly happy while we brooded on a captivity that seemed endless.

Opposite Manchester, Richmond rises on a line of hills sloping gently to the river. The capitol, about in the city's center, towers over the other buildings. Large and attractive homes and elegant villas grace the city's upper part, the beauty enhanced by avenues and gardens. Below along the river lie the quarters with the large businesses and big warehouses. There, too, is the Libby, and we took a final look at it. Farewell, old gray fortress of dark rooms, barred windows, cells, and a smoky kitchen. Farewell, bastion of misery, where, for months, we craved freedom and bled in our struggle against a species of insect [soldiers and officials of the Confederacy]. Farewell, hall of sadness, where we ate tainted meat and black beans gnawed by worms. You will not go up in flames but stand forever, a monument of the Rebels' inhumanity.

Directly we reached the station [of the Danville & Richmond Railroad] in Manchester, drew up along the tracks, and were all present except a few officers of Negro regiments and some others left behind as hostages.[2] Among the latter was a German, Captain [Emile] Frey, of the Eighty-second Indiana [or the Eighty-second Illinois]. A pause. Then a locomotive brought up a string of cars. We were packed in, fifty to sixty per car, which still carried the residue of earlier loads.[3] Side doors remained open. There and on the roofs, Rebel soldiers took post. Captain Tabb and Adjutant Latouche counted us. We saw Latouche's malignant leer for the last time, the locomotive whistled, and slowly the train rolled forward. Farewell, Richmond. May you soon have the pleasure of meeting General Grant.[4]

Most of us realized that we would be moved deeper into the Confederacy because our army was threatening Richmond. But a few of us still entertained a slender hope for imminent exchange, believing that we would ride this Danville [Virginia] train only as far as the junction with the Petersburg [Virginia] train [of the South Side Railroad], then go to City Point [Virginia], the place of exchange. A few hours shattered this dream.

The route is mostly through forests. Occasionally we glimpsed short stretches that had been made arable. Negroes worked there. We also observed houses of the old style, and small, squat cabins for Negroes. The train, very slow, did not arrive in Danville until the next day at 2:00 A.M.

The town is on the Dan River's south bank, near Virginia's border with North Carolina, some 140 miles from Richmond. When the war began, Danville had about 2,000 people; this number later doubled, as many families moved from the battlefield to temporary homes here.[5] At the town the river was swift and quite wide, and crossed by a long covered bridge. Earthworks had been dug along the heights on the north bank, and cannon placed in town near the hospital. Danville looked desolate.[6] Only a few people were present when we arrived. Not far from the station stood six brick buildings, about the same size and structure, of three or four stories, so-called tobacco warehouses [numbered One, Two, Three, etc.], where tobacco had been prepared and stored. We were put there. I and about 200 others went to Building One.

Ground level remained vacant. (Later we learned the reason.) Stairways, worn and steep, led to the second and third levels. The cramp between the third and the roof had to be used, too, because the second and third would not suffice. In weather already hot, we suffered almost unbearably under the low ceilings of these rooms, especially during midday. We glutted the floors, each man having barely enough space to lie down. We avoided the windows because the guards were to shoot anyone seen there. Long was the wait to satisfy our first desire: water. Rebel officers let only a few of us, perhaps twelve, go at a time to a nearby river and return with buckets. When one group came back, another could leave, but often only after having thirsted two hours for this most essential substance. So not enough buckets could be delivered to keep us adequately supplied. As to men compelled to visit the little place on the side of the building, even they frequently marked time unwillingly for an hour.

The food was a little better than the Libby's. In a small addition to the north side, prisoners of enlisted rank cooked for us, making every effort to prepare meat and soup as best they could in three or four cauldrons embedded above the fireplace. Other such prisoners had already been transported to Georgia; these few remained. Daily we got an adequate ration of salt pork, bean or rice soup, or gruel, and a slice of corn bread baked of sifted meal, its redeeming feature. We ate the bread in the morning. At noon we took food in buckets used also for water: meat first, then soup or gruel. No food was served in the evening.

The cooks were allowed to visit us, an unexpected privilege. They told how they had spent the past winter here. The prison's commandant, one Major [Mason] Morfit, a merciless beadle like Dick Turner, had terrorized the poor prisoners in every conceivable way, giving orders that increased suffering daily. Prisoners initially received meat and a little wheat bread. The meat dwindled to nothing. Then that bread disappeared; a small portion of rough corn bread replaced it.[7] The severity of that winter has been noted elsewhere, yet little wood was provided here, and neither ax to split it nor stoves to burn it. Fires on sheets of scrap iron produced unavoidably a room full of smoke. Many men fell victim to chronic diarrhea and other illness. Then smallpox broke out. The sick had to languish in the rooms until a hospital could be set up—to the disgust and terror of healthy men nearby.[8] The Federal government had sent clothing for the Danville prisoners, but Rebels stole much of it, along with the contents of packages from [people in] the North. Some prisoners were shot near windows while many starved. So, driven to desperation by cold, pain, and want, Danville's inmates finally decided to escape.[9] After a few succeeded individually, the rest chose flight en masse and planned to break out. Successful tunnels took a number of fortunates to freedom. Other tunnels were discovered [by guards] or betrayed by squealers. At last the [remaining] prisoners were taken to Georgia's horrific prison, Andersonville. There, with huge success, Captain Wirz continued Major Morfit's fiendish handiwork.[10] Listening to our soldiers' stories convinced us that the Rebel government intended to decimate us by hunger, want and disease.

Lack of space especially troubled us. With anxious expectation we pondered the future. Summer was at hand. Were we to spend the hot months in these cramped and sultry rooms? If so, at least half of us would contract fatal illnesses. Within two or three days after our arrival, talk began on escape and forcible breakout. We reconnoitered as much as we could. A tunnel posed problems: the Rebels had kept us off the ground floor to prevent tunnels.

Time dragged.[11]

Our moods alternated between good and bad.

One of the men near me had been an old settler in East Tennessee. Although of German extraction, he retained little of the language. Firmly pro-Union, he had raised a company in his region and commanded them until captured by guerrillas. He told me of much destruction and many atrocities by Rebels in east Tennessee. But he was ignorant of places and events outside his region. I told him about Wisconsin. Yes, he had heard the name; but he gaped, astonished, when I informed him that Wisconsin has nearly a million people and at least a third are Germans. He did not expect that [sort of population] in the "Land of Bears, Wolves, and Badgers."

On 12 May 1864 came the order that the next day we were to say good-bye to Danville's tobacco houses. The stay had been short. We did not want it lengthened.

From Danville via Columbia and Augusta to Macon—The Prison in Macon—Our Stay There from 17 May to 29 July 1864

When we arrived at the station [of the Richmond & Danville Railroad], a long string of freight cars rolled past, drawn by an old locomotive.[1] We thought they were for us. Wrong. They were for cattle and grain. We Yankees went on open ones, the so-called platform cars, all the more uncomfortable when it started to rain. We took seats on the dirty wet planks, the guards were posted, and the train left—slowly.

After about twenty-five miles we had to dismount at the end of service-able track and walk about seven miles. Heavily loaded, no longer ac-customed to marching, we labored on this excursion. Many panted like beasts of burden under their onus of baggage, cursed the Rebels, reviled the world, and damned their own existence. Here and there along the unfinished roadbed we met groups of Negroes improving the embankment or digging ditches. Ours was a terrible path, if a crude roadbed—lined with tree trunks, stones, holes, puddles, and morasses—can be called a path. We could not walk on the embankment, we had to struggle beside it, through puddles and morasses, over stones and tree trunks. We even had to negotiate an incomplete bridge of considerable height, on narrow boards laid tie to tie. Some of us, finding repugnant the crossing of a chasm on such skimpy footing, were forced to turn back and then wade to the opposite shore. After some hours we reached the place where ser-viceable track resumed. Then we bivouacked until after midnight.

About 2:00 A.M. we left [by train of the North Carolina Railroad] and via Greensboro [North Carolina] gained Charlotte, North Carolina, late in the afternoon. We camped in a nearby forest and drew our first rations in two days: crackers and boiled pork. Toward evening it began to rain hard. Soaked, we boarded cars whose roofs provided insufficient protection against the downpour. Each car carried sixty to seventy men, including the guards; doors were not opened because of the rain; and the atmosphere was stifling. In wet clothes, so packed together that no one could move freely, we lay or stood in the miserable cars while an old locomotive rolled us slowly along until noon the next day. The weather cleared in the meantime. When the train stopped, we were permitted to dismount and dry our clothes and blankets. Then the train proceeded, at last reaching Augusta [Georgia] on 16 May, after passing Columbia and Branchville [South Carolina]. A circuitous route [on the South Carolina and the Charlotte & South Carolina railroads], as a glance at a map will show.

Georgia's second [oldest] city, Augusta, on the west bank on the Savannah River, is pleasant with wide streets, many fine homes, and various public buildings. The authorities had been notified, and a company of militia was posted to guard our arrival and escort us to the station of the train to Millen [Georgia]. Allowed to leave the cars, we soon struck up conversations with the militia, many of whom were Germans. I chatted with one of them. He said it saddened them to see us in captivity; they were fed up with the Confederate government. I asked, Were there many supporters of the Union [here]? Yes, he replied, many Americans and a notably large number of Germans had always been, and to this day remained, true to the Union.[2] But, he continued, Confederate terrorism, in severity and amount, beggared description; and Union sympathizers had no choice but to suffer the government. Recently their numbers had increased when many aristocratic families relocated here from Charleston.

Captain Tabb galloped up, tall in the saddle, interrupting our conversation. With grand pomposity, as if it was a matter of forming an army for the assault, he ordered the sentries to keep a sharp eye on us. (Unfortunately we would later have far too much to do with him.) Beyond the sentry line, a crowd had gathered to look at us. The captain could think of nothing better than to prance up and down [in front of this audience], flourish his saber, and show off like a general. He had tricked himself out in a red sash, probably stolen from a Union officer, and was brazenly trying to persuade the citizens of Augusta that he was a great war hero. At departure time he ordered us into four ranks. When said ranks did not immediately appear as he wanted, he roared, "I'll cut your heads off, you damned Yankees!" One of the damned shouted back, "Go ahead and try!" The big hero in the red sash turned his Rocinante to the right and rode toward our left flank.[3]

We got two crackers and a small piece of salt pork, again our first ration in forty-eight hours. Once more we were locked in freight cars, this time for the bumpy ride to Millen [Georgia, on the Augusta & Savannah Railroad], and then to Macon [Georgia, on the Georgia Central Railroad], arriving the morning of 17 May. We marched through several streets of the attractively situated town and stopped at a fenced area that resembled a park [about a quarter-mile east of Macon]. The inscription above the barred gate said "Camp Oglethorpe."

A space of about three acres adjoined the camp; a board fence separated the two enclosures.[4] We were ordered into the second, formerly known in Macon as the Old Fair Ground, now a prison pen created for us. A twelve-foot board fence surrounded it. Sentries stood or paced back and forth, at intervals of some ten yards, on the catwalk attached to the outside of the fence. Inside, eighteen to twenty feet from the fence, ran the deadline. Elsewhere it might be marked by stakes or a ditch and thus be made more dangerous than it would be without them. Here in Macon another fence, three-and-a-half feet high, signaled the line. Sentries have strict orders: Fire on anyone who enters the area between them and the line. The prisoner who crosses it puts his life in hock.

On the south side of the enclosure a creek flowed hard by the line, and nearby was a spring, but available water was inadequate to so many people's needs. Three wells were added later. Two buildings stood near the entrance. The long one, a single story of wood, served in part as a hospital. A partition of the front half created a room for generals and [other] field-grade officers. A second, larger building bulked to the east of the first. On the northern and southern sides of the enclosure a few trees offered a measure of shade. The western side was flat and without shade. The southern sloped downward toward the creek.

The gate was large and of two wings. We entered. An old acquaintance (but not therefore a dear friend) met us. We had known when still in the Libby that Major [Thomas P.] Turner was going south to seek "suitable quarters" for prisoners. But we did not expect the sight of this personage to surprise us so soon. Yet there he was at the gate, in his gray uniform with gold braid, counting us.

En route, every opportunity to "dart sideways into the bushes" had been taken. If some would-be escapees were captured, others had fled to freedom. Our numbers had diminished significantly, therefore, and Turner's count did not agree with the inventory delivered by the belligerent Tabb. Turner looked displeased. Tabb seemed to feel that his genius had been put to its first test, with poor results. Something like this could be read on his face: "Poor me! It's not my fault that the Yankees outsmarted me." But the face soon darkened. He glared at us, eyes glittering with rage, as if to say: "O you dirty vagabonds from the North, I'd like to massacre you!"

When all of us were inside the gate, we formed a single rank. Turner was so kind as to give us a speech. This place belonged to us now, he said, and we were to make life as pleasant as possible for ourselves. Avoid the deadline, he continued: whoever climbed the fatal fence, or even touched it, would meet a Rebel bullet. In other respects we had complete "freedom" to do as we pleased, except when limited by special order of the commandant. For the time being, we could take up quarters in the buildings or under the trees or elsewhere until his requisitioned lumber arrived. Then we would build barracks for ourselves, so-called sheds. Axes and saws would be issued, as well as tin kettles, iron skillets, washtubs, and something to eat. (This [we thought] was true benevolence.) Moreover— yes, he said it—the authorities would do all they could for our comfort.

Hearing that pledge, we stared at one another, amazed. Was this the voice of mendacity? And what a curious speech, such a unique scramble of heterogeneous terms: "freedom" vs. "special order," "deadline" vs. "comfort."

When the Speech of Great Promise ended, we were divided into squads, each of 100 men. Each squad's senior member became its leader. A chief commissary, appointed to receive rations from the Rebel quartermaster, was to apportion them among squad commissaries; they, in turn, among "messes." Twenty men composed a mess; hence five messes to a squad. The ranking general of prisoners was our commander in chief: General [Henry Walton] Wessels. He had been forced to surrender himself and all his men to the Rebels at Plymouth, North Carolina.[5]

We heard that he had been a brave officer. But he met much more blame than praise in his role as senior prisoner at Macon. On one occasion he issued an order: "In my room an officer must take off his hat, whoever he is, whatever his reason for being there." A silly order, smacking of the notorious arrogance of European martinets.

Of the officers captured at Plymouth, only he had joined us in the Libby; the rest we did not see until the day we entered Macon. Our other general, who had spent several months with us in the Libby, was Brigadier [General Eliakim Parker] Scammon, captured in West Virginia.[6] Three more generals appeared later. Neal Dow had already been exchanged.[7]

We took an exact reconnaissance of the enclosure, then hunted up billets. The two buildings could not accommodate everyone, so a large number had to camp outside. Some burrowed under the first building. Others improvised little tents of blankets, scanty defense against rain and the broiling sun. At last we got lumber, busied ourselves at construction, and quickly put up barracks for several squads. But there was not enough lumber to create shelter for every prisoner. True, small amounts were delivered from time to time; but prisoners increased almost day by day, to total about 1,600.[8] Therefore, several hundred always lacked adequate refuge. The tiny makeshift tents offered neither protection from days and weeks in succession of unbearable heat nor cover against rain in typical Southern torrents: a situation at once miserable and unhealthy.

Inside the barracks we fashioned lumber into beds, which stood a few feet off the floor. Scrap lumber, left after major construction, became benches, tables, and chairs. An open space between barracks was for cooking and baking. A similar space in front of the first [permanent]

building served exercise, assembly, ball playing, etc. Every morning the
occupants had to tidy the area in front of the barracks. Two-wheeled carts,
pulled by horses or mules driven by Negroes, came around and removed
trash. Every morning a certain number of men from each squad, under
escort, went outside, where firewood lay, and brought back their allotted
amount. A guard carried in the axes and spades in the morning, and they
had to be returned to the gate before dark. (These tools, by the way, were
of very poor quality.) Should one be missing, all were withheld until it
reappeared.

We drew rations every fifth day, in these grand amounts: about seven
pints of rough cornmeal; a fifth or a fourth of a pound of pork, ostensibly
salted but actually preserved with ashes; a half-pint of syrup, usually
called sorghum; two tablespoons of rice or bad beans; two tablespoons of
salt; and, out of marvelous concern for our hygiene, a tablespoon of soft
soap. That much and no more was one man's ration for five days. Divide it
by five and you'll scarcely believe that the daily ration could be so
minimized and still sustain life. Yet prisoners in some places got even less.
The cornmeal went mostly into bread, baked in the skillets. Recipe:

• Combine water, meal, and a few grains of salt (two tablespoons of this
valuable stuff must last five days!).

• Mix this dough thoroughly.

• Grease the three-legged skillet or, lacking fat for cooking, dust with
meal to keep the bread from sticking.

• Pour in the dough.

• Set the skillet on a fire and build another fire on the skillet's cover, so
that the bread bakes on both sides. The fire on top must be hotter than the
one beneath.

• After about a half-hour, the bread is done. Americans call it *pone*.

Others made gruel of the meal, rather than bread; the so-called *mush*.
Here, for the edification and delectation of gourmands, is the recipe for
that delicacy:

• Fill a kettle or a pot with water and set it on a hot fire, the hotter the
better, until the water boils.

• Strike a graceful pose in front of the kettle.

• With the left hand, slowly sprinkle meal into the boiling water.

• Meanwhile, with a stick in the right hand, which does not know what
the left is doing,[9] stir the mess until it is as thick as bookbinders' glue.

• Add salt to this dish, too, if you have it.

• When the mush is cooked, pour sorghum over it, dig in, and flatter
yourself that you are better off than the residents of Olympus, who had
nothing but ambrosia.

We poured sorghum on the pone, too, but that petrified corn was and
remained a tough, indigestible lump. Today I think back on it with horror.

A serious inconvenience was the shortage of knives, forks, and spoons, and the lack of containers to store rations. We who came from the Libby did have eating utensils; but newcomers brought none, and the Rebels supplied them nothing of the sort. (The Rebels probably thought of Yankees as savages who could use their teeth as knives, fingers as forks, and cupped hands as spoons.) Consequently, an extensive lend-and-borrow system developed.

"Would you lend me your spoon?"

"Of course. But A is using it right now, and then I've promised it to B. Talk to him about it."

The prospective borrower would have to wait until B devoured his mush. The same situation prevailed with plates, kettles, and skillets.[10]

When rations were distributed, the mess commissary assembled his twenty men. First, the cornmeal. A man stepped forward holding a leg cut from an old pair of pants and fastened together at one end. In this ingenious and disgusting sack he took his cornmeal. For the same purpose another man used an old stocking, its mate long since missing. Rice and beans went into our caps, salt into a piece of clothing snipped from the faded lining of a tattered coat, and sorghum into any old can or a tin cup. Meat was clutched in the bare hand and soap put on a chip of wood. Carrying this load, each man headed for his billet. When the last man was some distance from the commissary, the can and the chip could be expected to fall, and syrup and soap mingle into a potion fit for allopathy.

We received the Macon newspapers [the *Confederate* and the *Telegraph*] almost every day, but their information was as thin as our soup. The lead articles, written in the spirit of the Richmond press, were nothing but calumny or bluster. According to this systematic slanting of the news, the reader was to believe that the Confederacy had reached its objective and that the Union lay permanently in ruins. Glorious Rebel victories and the sad situation of the North—nothing else was reported here. The papers proclaimed: Grant shall never take Richmond, nor Sherman reach Atlanta.[11] At Richmond "our great Lee" was digging a mass grave for Grant's forces. "Our celebrated General [Joseph Eggleston] Johnston" was withdrawing—the better to prepare Sherman's destruction. At any rate, "Come what may, we shall fight to the last man." Such were the phrases printed on inferior, grayish yellow sheets. These mendacious stories fooled Southern people who deluded themselves with sweet dreams of absolute security. We were skeptics who, of course, did not believe in the [tales of] Rebels triumphs.

Meanwhile, Grant and Sherman surged forward. Our first reliable reports, concerning both the eastern and western theaters, came with the many "fresh fish" [newly captured prisoners] brought in at the end of May. Some had been exchanged in April and then captured a second time. One,

Lieutenant Colonel Gustav von Helmerich, an ex-Prussian officer and later of the Fourth Missouri Cavalry, had been taken in June 1863, in Tennessee, imprisoned in the Libby for nine months, and exchanged in April 1864. He returned to his regiment, joined General [Samuel Davis] Sturgis's deplorably led expedition, and unluckily fell into enemy hands.[12] He was a friend of mine. Unfortunately, two weeks after he and I were exchanged in Baltimore, he died—of an illness originating no doubt in his long imprisonment.[13]

Ecstatically we heard from the newcomers that, despite the strongest of Rebel resistance, Grant had penetrated to the James River while Sherman, confident of victory, bore down upon Atlanta.[14] Having thus learned of the valiant efforts of our armies, we read with all the more amusement the braggadocio of the Macon papers. The fresh fish told us of prisoner exchanges, but we had lost all hope that we would be exchanged. Worse, it was now utterly unlikely that, with our armies fully engaged [and winning], our government would reinforce the enemy with an exchange of several thousand able-bodied men. Still we were yet weak enough to lend an agreeable ear to rumors of exchange. Soon, however, we scorned anybody who thought of starting another such rumor or of believing one.

Indeed, many of us became increasingly bitter and as sardonic as a misanthrope, deaf to pleasant conversation. This acerbity of mind grew more and more understandable as we sank lower and lower into indigence and could find no oasis in a desert of misery and want. Already many went barefoot; clothes turned daily into rags; veterans of captivity had spent their money long ago and even sold their coats and watches. To those miseries add meager rations, a wretched and inconsolable monotony of life, and the advance of disease—a list to sour even the sweetest disposition.

Oh, those long midsummer days, how they dragged! We had daylight from 3:00 or 4:00 in the morning until 8:00 in the evening; but what to do to quicken the sluggish hours, each weighing like lead on our souls? Time had once shot past with the speed of light—but now it crawled. Orientals dream away the time, the long days, meditating in noiseless tranquillity, but excessive sorrow kept us from peaceful contemplation. Bored yet restful, feverishly agitated yet convinced that hope was useless, members of a large group yet wishing to be alone at the ends of the earth: thus we passed a sad existence. Rob a man of freedom; take away the pleasure of company freely chosen; drive him into the direst poverty, so that his appearance repels him and he curses his eyes because they show him how he and his fellows look in a beggar's world; put time in chains to protract his day into a week and his week into a year; let his body hunger and his spirit thirst—and you commit him to a hell worse than any theologian could imagine.

How sad, then, to have to watch yourself pass from good to bad and not be able to prevent such misfortune. Every shred of cloth that falls from your coat seems to carry away part of your very self; you shudder to think of the moment when destitution will be total. Unfortunately, some of us lost character along with clothes. Or, the more holes the sun found in one's coat, the more one's true nature came to light. Many a fellow [here] was a fine gentleman when he wore the beautiful blue uniform with gorgeous epaulets. But, given the looks of a *Lumpaci vagabundus* [tattered vagabond], the fine gentleman disappeared, transformed [as if] by witchcraft into a specimen best viewed at the distance of a mile.

The day we arrived, Major Turner left Macon and returned to Richmond. Captain Tabb, who had wanted to cut off our heads in Augusta, became commandant—Tabb: half barbarian, half fool. One day a captain of a New York regiment [Frank Irich, of the Forty-fifth New York Volunteers, a prisoner here] handed him a watch and chain, asking that he sell it, but not for less than $400 Confederate. A long time passed without word from Tabb. At last the owner went to him and asked what had happened with the watch.

Tabb said that he had sold it for $200.

"How is it, then, that you are wearing the chain that went with the watch?"

Tabb replied that the buyer had given it to him.

"I want the watch and chain back, or $400, or I'll make the whole affair public."

This justifiable demand enraged Tabb. He bombarded the owner with the foulest invective, had him stretched in the rack for several hours, and then returned the watch.[15] General indignation erupted at that worthless Rebel's outrageous behavior. But *he* had the power, and *we* were prisoners without rights.

Some prisoners often held religious services evenings in the open area in front of the first [permanent] building. One evening, as a service was about to begin, Tabb rushed up and addressed Chaplain White, "I can no longer allow prayers for the president of the United States in these services." Chaplain Dixon stepped forward at once and in a loud voice prayed for the president, his cabinet, the Congress, and generals Grant and Sherman. Tabb heard the prayer to the end, thunderstruck.

"Well, your prayer won't do much good."[16]

He said nothing else and left us fast as he had arrived.

On another occasion he discovered in one of the barracks a tunnel that opened under a major's bed. Dirt from the tunnel had been hidden under other beds.

"Take this spade, Major, and shovel that dirt back into the tunnel and fill it up."

The major refused.

Tabb repeated the order.

Again the major refused.

Tabb hit him and he bled from the nose and mouth.

Yet, on occasion, Tabb would beguile. Sometimes he seemed to suffer remorse at his brutality. Our General Shaler had for a while commanded a Union prison.[17] One day Tabb asked him whether that assignment had caused him regrets.

"No. I always obeyed the laws of humanity and justice."

Tabb said nothing.

After about a month he was posted elsewhere. Captain (later Colonel) George C. Gibbs replaced him.[18] Though more civil, calmer, and more reflective than Tabb, Gibbs was nonetheless spiteful and malicious. Some prisoners once sought his permission to gather bark from white oaks nearly: medicine for our chronic diarrhea. He knew we had no medicine; he knew there was no danger in letting a few prisoners out (they had requested to go under escort); yet he refused.

Another incident shed equal light on his character. One evening, soon after dark, Lieutenant Otto Gerson, a German of the Forty-fifth New York, went to the creek on the south side of the enclosure. Standing under a tree, two steps from the creek, he remained well inside the deadline, which was across the creek from him. Shots rang out, fired suddenly by a sentry on the platform opposite. Gerson fell, mortally wounded, and died in a few hours. A vile murder by gunshot, committed without provocation. Gerson had stood quietly under the tree, having neither said anything nor touched the deadline, which was at least six feet off. Obviously the sentry had wanted to make a joke of killing a Yankee.

The senior prisoner carried to Gibbs the next day a written request for an investigation of the outrageous incident. Gibbs returned the request with a notation: "An investigation such as I deem appropriate, shall be conducted into this matter. The conclusion of said investigation shall coincide with that into the murder of Confederate officers by Negro troops at Fort McHenry and elsewhere."[19]

Gibb's answer contained a bald lie. We heard, straight from some of our guards, that Gerson's murderer was promoted to sergeant and granted a thirty-day leave. (So much for Gibb's promised investigation.) Such a reward was likely to inspire similar acts of heroism.[20]

On 4 July [1864], immediately after roll call, a celebration took place in the first [permanent] building: speeches, hymns, and patriotic songs. One speaker was the senior officer of prisoners, Lieutenant Colonel Thorp, of the First New York Cavalry [Dragoons].[21] The celebration displeased Commandant Gibbs. At noon he issued this order: "Lieutenant Colonel Thorp, having violated regulations, is relieved as senior officer of prisoners, and Lieutenant Colonel [David Berkley] McCreary appointed in his place. Peace and quiet are to be maintained today as every other day. Whoever disobeys this order will suffer unpleasant consequences."[22]

The celebration being over, the order meant little to us. But Gibbs's behavior to Thorp was malicious and a revenge of sorts. Nobody had bothered us when we observed the prior Independence Day in a similar manner and near the Rebel army. Yet our innocent manifestation of patriotic spirit had irritated Gibbs. He threatened to clap Thorp in irons and lock him up, but he backed down after Thorp said to him; "When it comes to the free expression of my principles, I'm not afraid of torture, and I'm not afraid of death."

During our last weeks in Macon, command shifted to Lieutenant Davis, a young fellow who acted like a buffoon. Some thought he must have been a circus clown.

Soon after we arrived in Macon, illnesses broke out, especially the chronic diarrhea, or dysentery, and eventually scurvy. To fall ill was vile, to stay well a miracle in these circumstances: intense heat, insufficient and unhealthy food, lack of exercise, the impossibility of keeping oneself as clean as one should like, no shelter for many of us, and, on top of those evils, melancholia—enough to induce illness and shatter even a strong constitution. Yet some of us did not fall ill. Still, conditions were enervating; and we had nothing to refresh and invigorate us. Many of us lay in bed ailing for weeks on end—others hobbled about with effort on canes—none could have obtained the slightest help. True, there was a hospital, but its treatment amounted to nothing. Why? First, because the blockade had cut off most of the South's medicines.[23] When some were available, Confederates thought of their Union prisoners last. Furthermore, the little that might have been done was not done; and our own physicians were to blame. Yes, a Rebel physician supervised our hospital; but he left the details to captured [Union] regimental physicians. Contrary to what should have been expected—so the sick themselves told me—these physicians did not treat our sick [their comrades] compassionately in Macon.[24]

In one place or another, the Rebels provided somewhat better rations so sorely needed by the sick. But in most of those instances, what was delivered for the sick did not reach them. As to nurses and orderlies, the physicians had chosen young prisoners from among us. But the sick complained about them, too. Physicians, nurses, and orderlies led a nice life while the sick often got scarcely the essentials. Nurses and orderlies were not paid, so it could easily be presumed that they seized any small advantage. Nobody believed that they took their disagreeable jobs for humanitarian reasons.

Since the hospital was almost always overcrowded, many of the sick had to remain in the billets with the rest of us. Some died there. Feet tied together and arms crossed on the chest, a corpse was wrapped in a blanket and removed on a stretcher. The grievously sick were taken to the hospital the same way, including one of my dear friends, Captain J. Riley Stone of the 157th New York, captured with me at Gettysburg. Robust by nature, he had kept his health at the Libby; at Macon, however, diarrhea and fever so weakened him that he could hardly rise from his rigid bed of boards. When he was carried out, I walked beside the stretcher, to speak to him one more time. He was too weak to hear me. Death soon ended his suffering, and I never saw him again. In the Libby he had whittled small crosses of bone: souvenirs to be given his children after his ardently desired return home. But he was not to see his loved ones anymore.

Attempts to escape never stopped while we were in that tiresome Macon. Most failed. One evening, however, several prisoners sneaked out the south side. Unseen by sentries (the evening was very dark), they crept with the greatest stealth into the creek, crossed the deadline, and slipped through the main fence by the hole that admitted the creek. A daring exploit: sentries were near. The last man out made a little noise by accident. A sentry fired in that direction, fortunately hitting no one. Alarm, immediately, among the Rebel troops in Camp Oglethorpe. Drums sounded the long roll. In less than ten minutes the hunt was on. Around our enclosure we saw lights of torches and heard shouts of command, blasts of horns, and the baying of hounds. After about a half-hour the uproar subsided. We assumed that the fugitives were caught; pursuit had begun too soon after flight. Presently the officer of the day appeared and ordered us to our billets. "Stay there until daybreak. Sentries have been instructed to fire on anyone who disobeys." Our humane OD ignored the objection that prisoners with diarrhea could not remain inside all night.

Shortly after daybreak the hunt resumed. The same shouts, the same horns, the same baying—and the same results. Sly Yankees had outwitted the Rebels.

We answered roll call about 8:00 A.M. Rebel soldiers drew a line straight across the enclosure, dividing it exactly in half. Prisoners had to leave one half, enter the other, and (one by one) pass an officer standing at the line, counting. If the count miscarried [in following days], the procedure was repeated, often three or four times.

On the day in question, when half of the enclosure had been evacuated, a rigorous search of the barracks met some success: three tunnels were discovered. Long in the digging, they were nearly done. The tireless energy of Yankee moles astonished the Rebels. The moles were distressed that their hard, protracted work was in vain. (To appreciate the difficulties of tunneling, consider the fact that the guards watched us like hawks day and night and reported to the commandant any trifle that seemed amiss.) Still, one failure did not demoralize the Yanks; they soon started other digs. In my barracks, for example, a tunnel that began on the building's north side, hard by the deadline, would pierce the relatively short distance under the line and the wall, as far as the hospital. But this "rat hole," too, was found. Guards thereafter kept a double-sharp eye on our barracks.

Partly to intimidate us, and partly to be doubly prepared against fresh attempts to escape, the Rebels erected platforms about twelve feet high, at three places outside the wall, and on them mounted cannon that could sweep the enclosure. From time to time, their crews conducted drills to show us the deadly intent; if need be, they would riddle us with grapeshot. Fires blazed nightly between the deadline and the stockade. Several times a week the barracks and the hollows under the first [permanent] building were searched. Our captors trusted us as little as you trust a scoundrel. They believed we directed our every effort and pointed all our thoughts toward escape, a fairly accurate estimate. Our captors' apprehensive concern amused us. Lieutenant Davis and his many probes with a ramrod were especially entertaining. One day, just after finishing some energetic sniffing, he remarked: "Yes, you Yanks have the right to try to escape, if you can. But, by George, you aren't going to get away from *me*."

One prisoner hatched an ingenious plot to have himself shipped out. Now, almost every day, the sutler, a Rebel, delivered a quantity of food, in boxes, to be distributed to our commissaries. One day the gate opened as usual. In rolled his two-wheeled cart, loaded with a rather large box. One of the commissaries took it down and emptied it. As was typical, a large group gathered around the cart and the sutler's booth. Meanwhile the sutler busied himself with accounts, and several prisoners talked with his carter (a Negro) and with the Rebel soldier who had escorted the cart through the gate. A prisoner seized the moment and slipped into the box. Several of his friends, acting as if it was empty and light as a feather, lifted it high and put it on the cart. The sutler finished his accounts, the Negro mounted the cart and whipped up the horse, the soldier followed calmly, rifle on shoulder, and they quietly transported "Yank" outside.

But in a few days he was back. He had been caught several miles from town.

Another [would-be escapee], [H.] Bader, a German officer from Missouri [Twenty-ninth Missouri Volunteers], was among the most persistent of the bolters. One day, when the Rebel detachment that supervised roll call was leaving, he brazenly joined them—he had made himself a jacket and trousers of a gray woolen blanket and thus looked like a Rebel—and they all marched out. But he, too, was recaptured. I believe he attempted escape at least a half-dozen times.

Meanwhile, fifty prisoners had been transferred out of here in June: all the generals, colonels and lieutenant colonels, and half the majors.[25] At last, in the final days of June, the directive arrived to send the rest of us elsewhere. Transfer did not surprise us. For we had learned that Sherman was driving relentlessly ahead; and we knew that the Rebels, fearing he might order a cavalry raid on Macon, fretted about our safekeeping. The faster he closed in upon Atlanta, the more Macon [about seventy-five miles from Atlanta] was threatened; the Rebels deemed this the most sensible decision: Order prisoners away from a place where danger increased with every passing day.

To us, what the order lacked in surprise, it made up in joy. True, we could not hope for anything so pleasant as improved conditions elsewhere; but we still longed to move. At least a change would vary the uniformity and momentarily break the vicious monotony of our lives. When I think back on a long captivity, and compare the various prisons and their situations, Macon springs to mind as the saddest place to be dumped by the cataclysms of war. In other prisons we suffered even more indignities and at least as much misery and want. But an accidental concatenation of disparate circumstances rendered Macon the gloomiest of all:

• A hopeless situation in which exchange was unthinkable and the end of captivity unforeseeable.

• Less money and more raggedness—rising poverty—daily.

• The meagerness of rations.

• Widespread illness and many deaths.

• An almost total blackout of information from the North.

• Utter boredom.

Of course, taken together, those horrors so depressed us that we cursed our lot with all our might. When the order came—"Prepare to leave"—we saw it as nothing but a message of happiness. We packed joyfully, wanting to put Macon behind us as soon as possible.

11

Savannah

They divided us into three units.[1] Lieutenant Davis told the first to be ready to leave on the evening of 27 July [1864]. About 5:00 P.M. [of the twenty-seventh] the unit was counted. It left the next morning by railroad.

On the twenty-eighth the second unit (mine) got its orders. About a hundred officers from Grant and Sherman's armies had just arrived [as prisoners]; and the latest news of the war heartened us. All day we prepared to depart. Though the chief task was to bake bread, knives and files were sharpened zealously, and files turned knives into saws: tools to cut holes if possible in the floor of the car; holes to freedom. Escape was paramount with most of us; and during the railway journey, every attempt was made to escape. It was no easy task, then, for the assigned Rebel officers and men to guard us [in transit] and to deliver *all* of us to our destination.

In the afternoon [of the twenty-eighth], Lieutenant Davis and the adjutant called our names. One by one we assembled in the space between the deadline and the stockade, and stayed until all were counted. About midnight we marched to the street in front of Camp Oglethorpe. There we had to wait, almost until dawn, before going to the train station.

The third unit remained. Some of them intended to hide in the enclosure, wait for the rest to go, then escape.

In the afternoon of 29 July we arrived [on the Georgia Central Railroad] in Savannah. Several of us saw a good omen at the end of the line: Liberty Street. First, sentries were posted along the bright, pretty thoroughfare lined with trees on the outer edges of the sidewalks. Next came the signal to dismount. A crowd had gathered. We formed our usual column, four abreast. The crowd accompanied us on the hike to the United States Marine Hospital.[2] They looked at us meanwhile, but said nothing. Nor could we detect gloat or scorn in their faces. They eyed us with curiosity, rather, and seemed to pity us.

The Confederates used the United States Marine Hospital as one of their own. It was an edifice of stone with about an acre and a half of garden attached. Between the hospital and the garden a board fence about twelve feet high had just been erected. An eight-foot brick wall enclosed the garden's other three sides, and boards had been added to raise it another four feet. Around the outside [of the wall], as at Macon, there were a catwalk and boxes for sentries. The various trees in the garden included several water oaks [or possum oaks or punk oaks] whose thick canopy cast pleasant shade. Gray moss hung in long tresses from the limbs of tall, slim pines, imparting a peculiar look, almost of a weeping willow.

The Savannah authorities seemed to have been notified about us only a few days before we arrived. Wooden huts were barely done and only a few tents pitched inside the enclosure. So as at least not to have to lie on damp ground, we put to use the lumber scattered all around [arranging it into platforms as places to sleep]. This sensible precaution did no good the first night. Mountainous thunderheads gathered in early evening, and volcanic roars and flashes accompanied a downpour of several hours. Storms in the North do not rage nor rains gush like the ones we saw in Savannah. Tents and [makeshift] barracks are inadequate against such cloudbursts.

About 3:00 that morning the storm dispersed. At sunrise we sought to dry our clothes and the sacks containing our belongings (including bread). Of course everything was soaked, and the bread was nearly reverted to dough. We ate it anyhow; nothing else was served for breakfast. We tried to build small fires of the chips and scrap lumber lying about, but great effort brought scant flame to that watersoaked fuel. Yet, despite this disheartening start of our prison life in Savannah, the future turned out better than we had expected.[3]

Tents were delivered the same morning. They would be pitched in orderly rows. Each tent was intended for sixteen occupants, and there were 600 of us [so the tents did not suffice]. I was among the few, about twenty, who, after some days without shelter, contrived a kind of barracks [a lean-to] against the small, frame building erected for the chief commissary and the sutler. Three trees shaded the site, delightful on hot days but also the cause of an ugly situation: many prisoners fled from tents in full sun to sit in our cool bower; and sometimes they annoyed us.

Our circumscribed existence thus imitated the world at large. Friends and close associates either congregated or visited one another readily, and such visits were always welcome. Meanwhile a circle treated as strangers the men outside it, feeling for them in general no sense of comradeship. The reason for this factionalism lay largely in our heterogeneity, which caused much animosity and many quarrels, leading sometimes even to fistfights. Furthermore, our prison life increased egotism—to the extreme. Liberality comes easier to the comfortable, and sociability thrives better in the sunshine of happiness than in the frosty, winterly chill of poverty and want. Most of us moved each in his own narrow orbit of grouchy self-centeredness and, over time, had unlearned all concern and every sympathy for anybody else. If, like many of us, a man by nature inclines to this egotistic exclusiveness, then our kind of prison life, more than anything else, will worsen it.

Besides tents, each squad (one hundred men) received a big iron kettle, eight small tin kettles, eleven skillets, sixteen tin pans, four wooden buckets, two axes, and two hatchets. Axes and hatchets were drawn every morning and returned every evening. We also [each] received a pound of fresh beef a day, five days a week, and two-and-a-half pounds of salt pork the other two; as well as [every day] a quart of cornmeal, a pint of rice, a tablespoon of salt and another of vinegar, and a piece of hard soap. These rations were our best ever; we could congratulate ourselves on moving from Macon to Savannah.[4] A better diet undoubtedly helped many recover the health they had been losing and to forestall additional illnesses.

The beef arrived punctually every morning at 6:00 for distribution among squad and mess commissaries. It was freshly slaughtered and always good. After our long privation we feasted in delight on soup and steak, which we prepared with finesse. Here the pork came in handy; we used it to fry steak and bake bread better in the skillet. We got more rice than we could eat—cornmeal, too—so when we departed we had a bit in stock and, of course, took it along. The salt was sufficient. We welcomed the vinegar, the most effective agent against scurvy. The soap sufficed to keep us clean and to launder what was left of our clothes.

Indeed, many prisoners now owned only one shirt or one pair of pants. Therefore on wash day they wore almost little enough for the Garden of Eden. Usually they wrapped themselves in woolen blankets and cooked their laundry in the big kettle or scrubbed it on a washboard they had made themselves. A few times, Rebel officers on duty were showing some women around when many prisoners appeared in their underwear, looking like Adam or at least Jefferson Davis on the day of his capture.[5] If the women were secessionists, the spectacle probably filled them with loathing for "the barbarians of the North." If the women were Unionists, they must have pitied us. We deserved it. For, to be seen undressed among 600 people is disagreeable; to have to suffer the unaccustomed labor of the laundry, outrageous.

Our water system consisted of a pump [and a well], later augmented by a pipe from the river. Many disliked water from our well: a foul tincture of sulfur. Some therefore thought that the well contained something rotten, so boards were removed and the well inspected. It was clean. Guards told us afterwards that water from wells in town smelled and tasted like ours. I don't remember whether the water [from our well] made anybody sick. At any rate, it was much preferable to the turbid, tepid stuff out of the pipe. We usually used the latter for washing and cooking, however, because the sulfur water, perhaps good enough to drink, did not qualify for soup.

Our guards were the First Georgia Regulars, headed by Colonel Wayne.[6] Though sometimes strict and harsh, all in all he gave us no reason to gripe. He was more humane than Major Turner and captains Tabb and Gibbs. Under Wayne's command the [bad] scenes of Macon and the Libby did not occur. His orders were stern and his supervision exact, but his sentries never fired on us and always gave warning to anyone getting too near the deadline. During the day we were allowed to hang clothing and blankets on its fence.[7]

The following facts further characterize the colonel, his officers, and their staff:

● One day he decreed that beds in tents be raised several feet. Purpose: to discourage tunnels and facilitate inspection. By happenstance, the command did not get around. Still, had communication been perfect, the result would have been the same because we lacked material to raise the beds. When the colonel came to inspect, he saw that his command had not been obeyed. Without listening to excuses by the prisoners under scrutiny, he ordered the tents struck and removed. He returned them only after remonstrances by the physician.

● At a roll call (they occurred twice daily: morning and afternoon) he gave an order, and a prisoner objected. His face darkened. "Sir [the colonel said], I'm here to give orders, and all of you must obey them."

● Were axes and hatchets not turned in promptly in the evening, we could wait a long time for them the next day. One very hot morning we needed hatchets to cut meat, but the colonel did not send them until 10:00. By then the meat was half spoiled.

● He did not let us take Savannah newspapers, but he did allow that whenever they said anything about exchange, the articles be posted on the sutler's booth.

● He saw to it that we received good-quality rations promptly delivered. One day the commissary brought a big cask, or tierce, of bad rice: moldy. When this defect was called to the colonel's attention, he ordered that good rice be sent us.

● The other officers were friendly to us, especially Major Hill, a refined and an educated man, wounded at Morris Island and not yet fully recovered.[8] What most deserved praise from us in these officers of the First Regulars was their truthfulness. When questions on the war were asked, they politely refused to answer. When the initial rumors of the entry [by Sherman] into Atlanta reached us, Major Hill was begged for details. "I know nothing for sure. Battles have been fought. It seems that the outcome was not what we expected." Unlike the mendacious officers at

Richmond and Macon, those here did not lie about exchange. When we asked about it, they would respond in one of two ways. (1) A frank statement: "Sorry, we're not in a position to report anything positive. We've received no official news and don't want to repeat rumors as authentic information." (2) As already mentioned, they provided clippings and let us make up our own minds about what they said. Once a lieutenant took the liberty of conveying the falsehood that the [Union and Confederate] commissaries had agreed on an exchange. We never saw him in our vicinity again.

• Some officers conversed with us often, saying that they understood the tragedy of our circumstances and sincerely desired our prompt release.[9] Were such statements perhaps only [empty] phrases? Consider [the evidence to] the contrary: courteous behavior and a friendly tone—in pleasant contrast to the savage, beadlelike manner of other Rebel officers with whom we unfortunately had to deal.

• Common soldiers also treated us well. Some showed several prisoners various kindnesses: selling small articles of value or bringing newspapers.

Although Colonel Wayne ordered close inspection of billets, we dug a few tunnels anyway—with dubious results. He was too circumspect for us. One tunnel was so near completion that it needed only to be opened at the other end. On a black night a digger went into it for that purpose. He stuck out his head and heard, "Go back, Yankee, or I'll shoot you." The mole ducked back in a flash and quickly crept into the tent with sad tidings: the tunnel was discovered.[10]

The sentry, who had shouted at that apparition rising suddenly from the ground like a ghost, was part of a cordon on the perimeter, posted by the colonel, unbeknown to us. The next day he sent two occupants of our tent to the city jail, to spend a few days in a darkened cell. One of those unfortunate diggers was Captain [Albert] Grant of the Nineteenth Wisconsin. Always trying to escape, he incessantly laid plans to get to Fort Pulaski, only seventeen miles away and held by our troops.[11]

When the [Savannah] *Republican* heard of the tunnel, it published a nasty article advising prisoners to behave; hundreds of well-trained dogs from Savannah would be set on Yankees trying to escape.[12] Except for local variations, the southern press was of a piece, and the *Republican,* edited (like the Macon newspapers) in the spirit of the *Richmond Enquirer* and *Examiner,* teemed with vulgarity, secessionist lies, political folly, and vainglory about [Rebel] victories. The following incident characterizes the *Republican.* When a Union officer died in a hospital, a [Southern] lady, who looked after the sick with compassion, had him buried in the municipal cemetery at her expense. The *Republican* was prompted to call this interment of a Yankee "a desecration of the cemetery and a disgrace to others [Southerners] at rest there. The municipal authorities are obligated to undo such a shameful act of mischief."

Around mid-August, prisoners put significantly more faith in exchange. The cry of a hundred voices sounded repeatedly: "All aboard! Pack up!" Our government, according to reports, had concluded an agreement with the Confederate usurpers: prisoners would be traded man for man, and the places of exchange were to be Savannah and Charleston. A letter from Rebel exchange agent Ould to General Butler, clipped out of a newspaper, was posted about this time.[13] From it we learned that negotiations on exchange did take place.[14] An official notice to chaplains and surgeons lent credibility to such news. Be ready to travel to Charleston, it said, and there you will be exchanged. On this information, the sanguine pinned hopes that once the start had been made, we would all soon follow and be set free. In fact, chaplains and surgeons were exchanged but we were not.

For us the happiest event was the Rebel retreat from Atlanta and Sherman's defeat of Hood. We rejoiced: our army had won a glorious victory, and the enemy's prophecies had been mocked. We delighted to think of the fall of the supposedly impregnable Atlanta: it must have appalled the arrogant Southern people and demoralized their armies. And our old hopes were stirred. Such a decisive win brought nearer the coveted triumph (the destruction of the Confederacy) as well as the day we would be freed.

Meanwhile, health [among us] left much to be desired. True, shelter and rations sufficed; but significant numbers suffered fever, diarrhea, and dysentery. While treatment of the sick was better here than in Richmond and Macon, and Union physicians here exerted themselves to the limit, often they could do no good because they lacked essential medicine. Yes, the more seriously ill were brought to the Marine Hospital [next door] and treated with the same compassion as shown the Rebels there. Yes, a number of [Southern] women volunteered for the difficult service as nurses and cared for our officers as carefully as any other patient. Nevertheless, many died.

One was Lieutenant [Jakob] Leydecker of the Forty-fifth New York, young and strong and never seriously ill in the Libby. But when we had been locked in the Charlotte-to-Columbia cars for almost twenty hours in wet clothes, he had caught his death. A cure would have been easy in Macon—if the administration of the hospital and its treatment of patients had not been so wretched. He grew weaker and weaker. In the first days of September [here in Savannah], he disappeared into the hospital [and expired]. When word came that one of us had died, many of the living probably thought, When will it be *my* turn? Indeed, the Angel of Death was as apt to visit you in these prisons as on the battlefield.

Let me ponder another event that casts a lurid light on conditions in the

South before and during the war. The great and enduring heat had turned the *sink* (as it was called) into a pestilential hole that exuded miasma. The colonel therefore ordered it filled—it was on one side of the enclosure—and another dug on the other side. For this purpose he sent several male and several female slaves who set to work at once with spades and shovels. Most disagreeable to us, to watch women thus used. In addition, one of the slaves, a young fellow, was almost white. So we saw with our own eyes a living example of the slaveholding aristocracy's barbarous practice of keeping their own children in bondage or selling them as slaves to others. This aristocracy, while always claiming with boundless arrogance that they were of better stuff than "despicable workers and shopkeepers of the North," nevertheless flaunted the impudence to traffic in people, including their own offspring—a crime never committed by the worst tramp or the most evil brute in the North. The slaveholding aristocracy, the cultivated "first and best families," dealt in their own children as one of their noble passions and a pet and profitable economic sideline. This aristocracy, formerly the dominant [American] party, once dictated to the Republic disgraceful laws against freedom, in a time that, fortunately, lies behind us now. [15]

12

In Charleston—In the Shadow of the Gallows— "Under Fire"—Roper Hospital

We left Savannah [for Charleston, South Carolina] on 13 September 1864]—grudgingly, because we could hardly expect to be treated in the arch-Rebel state as we had been treated in Savannah. Looking with misgivings to the coming days, we put little faith in Colonel Wayne's cheerful assurance that we were being taken to Charleston for exchange. Yes, Rebel officers, in numbers corresponding to ours, had been brought to Morris Island, which lent a measure of credence to talk of exchange.[1] But none of us expected to be exchanged.

Our cars were not excessively crowded, so the journey [on the Charleston & Savannah Railroad] was relatively comfortable. We crossed lowlands and went mostly through miles-long marshes incised by slow-moving streams. Grass and reeds covered the marshes and sheltered alligators and snakes. The alligators seemed accustomed to the sound of trains. At any rate, one of the long-snouted beasts paused quietly on the bank when ours passed.[2] Here and there we intersected forests where many tresses of moss hang from gnarled oaks and the tarantula nests in scrubby pines. At some stations—Pocotaligo, for example—we saw reserve troops doing outpost duty on lines extending in a southerly direction toward the coast. After a trip not overly long, we reached the long wooden bridge over the wide estuary at Charleston. Soon we were in the city itself.

We dismounted on the other side of the bridge and followed sandy Coming Street to the prison. Many colored people accompanied us.[3] We kicked up so much dust that clouds swirled around us and we could scarcely see the houses. Walking swiftly in oppressive heat, and as usual carrying all our belongings, we sweated amply and were happy to reach our destination.

The prison is tall (four stories of stone), and to it an octagonal building is attached, surmounted by a tower of about forty feet. The workhouse, also of stone, occupies the adjoining lot.[4] The octagon faces a yard of less than an acre enclosed by a high wall. A massive, ironbound gate opened. We entered the yard. That small area, in which 600 were to camp, was empty except for a row of little tents, occupied in part by Union prisoners, enlisted men, recent inmates of Andersonville, later to be sent to Florence [South Carolina]. A patch of grass and a tiny tree prospered in a corner of the otherwise sand-covered space. In the middle stood a pump, nearby a deep cistern, in the corner toward the Marine Hospital a little old house over the sink, and near the sink a gallows reaching above the wall. The main building held Negro soldiers as well as vagrants, thieves, swindlers, deserters, and prostitutes.

The balcony of the Marine Hospital overlooked the yard. Part of our first unit, having left Macon the day before us, were in the hospital now. They shouted and threw us letters tied to small stones. Sentries posted on that side of the yard soon hampered and almost stopped that communication. Though instructed to cut off all messages, they were not able entirely to block our unique postal system. We corresponded similarly with members of the third unit, confined to the workhouse. There, previous prisoners had atoned for crimes with hard labor, and even slaves had suffered the lash at the order of their humane masters.

We took possession of the tents. Though each gave four men a cramped and wretched shelter, many still had to make do in the open, exposed to rain and the blazing sun.

During our long imprisonment we had endured myriad indignities and insults. We had felt the Rebels' malice and fury a hundred times. We were used to being herded like cattle rather than treated like men. But the worst had been reserved until now. Here at Charleston we were locked in a pen under a gallows and with society's dregs. This abuse, in the state whose ruling class commended itself on the finest civilization, showed the true character of the Rebels of South Carolina.

We had not abandoned in Savannah our stores of cornmeal and rice; we had disobeyed orders and brought kettles and pans, and now we could be happy at our prescience. For, here, under the gallows, the Rebels issued us nothing the first two days: neither rations, nor wood, nor cooking equipment. Except his twice-daily roll call, the captain in command, [S.H.] Sheldon by name, did not concern himself with us. He died some days later, of yellow fever.

On our third day he was at last friendly enough to send some stringy beef, about a quarter-pound per man, and cornmeal, rice, sorghum, and a little salt. Lest these splendid gifts swell our heads, he withheld firewood. So we collected every splinter in the yard and even tore up the planks from the sink—fuel to whet the appetite when put under a pot of soup. Without doubt, we would have cut down the gallows, had a Rebel soldier not been guarding them.

The load of wood that arrived the next day was so small that we had to be miserly with it. We got scarcely enough to bake bread and cook soup; on more than one occasion we had to feed ourselves bread not fully baked and soup half cooked. Longingly we remembered Savannah, where rations and wood had been sufficient. And here, cooking utensils were not forthcoming. If at last a man acquired meat or rice or cornmeal, and even a miserable stick of wood, he still lacked kettle and pan, and would often have to wait hours to borrow them. One prisoner chanced upon (in a corner) a few old cast-iron spittoons. At once they were cleaned and used for baking. We could buy wheat bread from the guards, but few of us had money. Besides, the price was exorbitant: $2 Confederate for a small loaf.[5]

Vermin overran the place. Not only the species we met in the Libby, but also a small beetle with many legs that carried it swiftly across the floor. With astonishing vigor, it gnawed through clothes and blankets left there. A piece of cloth, belonging to one of the men in my tent, was perforated to shreds in two days. For our added comfort, mosquitoes attacked; constantly we fought those damage-minded and bloodthirsty hordes. Mephitic vapors did no less to make our stay pleasant, discharged incessantly by the abominable sink. And out of the pump, another horror: water that tasted of salt and caused many a man to vomit.

Every day, as evening fell, bedlam erupted. The criminals [the nonmilitary inmates] shouted like hungry beasts in a zoo, pounded with sticks on the floor or on the bars of the windows, and rattled the bolts and bars of the doors—violently. One malefactor in particular shrieked and wailed—inarticulately—in a hideous voice for a half-hour at a stretch, as if possessed. What made him screech like an animal; was it a guilty conscience or an insane despair at having lost his freedom? Had we not known who inhabited the octagonal building and its tower, the demonic screams and rages could have led us to believe that we were in the courtyard of a madhouse.

When we encountered prisoners from Andersonville, they told us much about their pain in that torture chamber, that hell. We heard then for the first time of Captain Wirz, who has since paid with death for his countless crimes. Andersonville's unhealthy location, lack of shelter, hunger madness that gripped hundreds, scandals of ravaging diseases, barbaric harshness in the treatment of prisoners, executions of thieves and murderers, and many other things let us comprehend the agony our brave soldiers had to suffer in that prison.

Had those we met here in Charleston not told of horrors inflicted by Wirz and [John Henry] Winder,[6] a pitiful appearance itself would have convinced us that a cruel fate had knocked them into a pit where brutality ruled and the agenda decreed anguish and torment. All were pale, indeed ashen; emaciated to skeletons; unsteady and faltering of gait; and without luster in their eyes. Prisoners from Andersonville had not seen soap for five or six months, and he who owned a shirt was rich. A man in my tent, Captain [C.A.] Hobbie of the Seventeenth Connecticut, recognized one of his sergeants and, together with Lieutenant [D. S.] Bartron of the same regiment, gave him a shirt and a piece of soap. The sergeant, in indescribable joy at this small kindness, said thank you repeatedly and declared that he would never forget it as long as he lived. Later we heard he, a young man about twenty years of age, died soon after this incident.

Negro soldiers, imprisoned in the main building, were allowed in the yard during the day: intelligent fellows, devoted to the Union's cause, and seemly of behavior. Many had lost an arm or a leg in skirmishes and battles on the islands.[7] In the evenings they sometimes belted out songs whose texts they had composed themselves and set to existing music.[8]

In the notorious yard we not only endured in the shadow of the gallows but also prevailed "under fire." The Rebels had prudently arranged that we be in reach of General [Quincy A.] Gilmore's cannon, which blasted from the islands at the city, day in and day out.[9] Not a continuous bombardment but red-hot greetings roared in from the general usually morning and evening, now in long intervals, now in short. Occasionally the guns were silent the whole day, in contrast to another day's rapid shot after shot. In the beginning [of our time here] the projectiles aroused our curiosity, rushing at us in an arc from a distance of three miles and often exploding at the acme, like thunder. But after the first few days, we grew so accustomed to the shelling that we rarely took interest in giant missiles whose appearance at night is so brilliant when a flaming streak follows them like the tail of a comet. Shrapnel of an explosion overhead alarmed us but once: four rather large, sharp-edged fragments fell in the yard, but fortunately hit no one. Indeed, during July, August, and September, only one of us prisoners exposed to fire was actually hit, and the wound was not serious.[10]

One day General Gilmore seemed intent on something special:
- A rapid cannonade.
- Soon, thick smoke near the workhouse.
- Then the fire bells.
- And a cannonade more violent than the first.

"Twenty houses were burned," a Rebel soldier told us in the evening. "A shot even smashed one of the fire engines."

Prisoners in the Marine and Roper hospitals were not sent there as soon as they arrived from Macon. They, too, camped a while in the yard and got their subsequent billets [in the hospitals] only after signing a parole. In time the rest of us were offered the parole, and we put our signatures to it:

We the undersigned prisoners of war, in the city of Charleston in the Confederate States of America, herewith pledge, individually, as soldiers and men of honor, that we shall not attempt to cross the lines that have been drawn, and that are under guard, around our prison; and that, except by permission, we shall not communicate with persons outside the line or with visitors, either in writing or by word of mouth or by signs. We affirm that we make this pledge of our own free will and in return for privileges granted; and they are that we will be less closely guarded and may go freely indoors and out, during the day in specified areas, thereby getting fresh air and exercise that aid our comfort and contribute to our health. At the same time we attest that this pledge is binding on us in letter and in spirit, that we shall not interpret it otherwise, and that violation of it will constitute an act of permanent disgrace.[11]

(Obviously the Rebels were admitting, in this parole that they wrote themselves, that we had hitherto been disagreeably confined.)

On 26 September, after almost two weeks in an atmosphere of stench and suffocation, we abandoned the gallows yard for Roper Hospital. There we greeted old friends from Macon. (Those not here had escaped between Savannah and Charleston.) The first unit to leave Macon (28 July) had plotted to overpower the guards and seize the train when it neared Pocotaligo, when our [Union] lines could be quickly reached, and flee en masse toward Beaufort.[12] But this well-laid plan, which perhaps could have worked, failed out of hesitation when the time came to act.

Roper Hospital is of brick, grand and beautiful, four stories in the center and three in both wings. Two square towers rise from the center, and one, of about twenty feet, from the end of each wing. A broad, pillared veranda graces every story at the front of the wings. The whole contains six or eight spacious wards and many smaller rooms, lit at night by gas. In front a nicely arranged garden had flowers and shrubs. A wrought iron fence enclosed the garden along the street. Behind the hospital a yard, muddy and full of nooks and crannies, extended to a wooden structure once used as a prison, a cell block [to be exact]. (Some of our men had to billet in it because the hospital lacked space.) This yard boasted a cistern and the sink: as repugnant and nauseating as those of prisons past. West of the hospital a narrow passage led to a tall and roomy building: the medical school before the war, now closed. In a corner in front of this abandoned spot, several stunted fig trees surrounded the half-decomposed skeleton of a whale. Assorted skulls of Negroes, and broken medicine bottles and jars, lay nearby in a small pit. The entire campus, where students may have taken siestas, now appeared deserted and sinister.

The hospital is named for Thomas Roper, who gave the Medical Society of South Carolina land worth $30,000 for a large hospital. The city of Charleston, the State, and individuals contributed the additional money needed. Between 1850 and 1852, under the society's supervision, the hospital was built.

Prisoners here since August had organized the hospital as agreeably as possible. Most possessed a bed—perhaps issued, perhaps purchased—and tables and chairs bought in town at prisoners' requests. A chair cost $5 to $6, and table $10 to $15. Many of these prisoners, having received packages from the North, dressed better than we did. They and us—what a contrast! They appeared healthy and well groomed; we, more or less like vagabonds.

I entered the portal of the beautiful edifice and looked at bright, spacious wards with candelabra and immaculate floors. I even saw a carpet in the vast central ward on the first floor, where the senior officer of prisoners, Colonel Pennock Huey of Pennsylvania, was quartered. Had I been transported to another world? A clean floor—what luxury! Gaslight and carpet—such sybaritic splendor! And a roof, a tight cover overhead, protection against the tropical sun and the rain! Should I, in my once blue, now colorless clothes—should I, in shoes with uppers defiantly separating from rotten soles long without heels—should I thus enter this marvelous palace? Though almost overwhelmed by good fortune, I had not yet seen all. My friends, Lieutenant Colonel Helmerich and Lieutenant Newbrandt, met me with a cup of, not the thin and despicable brew of roasted cornmeal, but pure, unadulterated *coffee*. Beside it lay a cigar. At that moment I felt more blessed than all of Lady Luck's favorite children. How merrily the little blue clouds billowed from the burning cigar! We sat in quiet satisfaction on a veranda enclosed in green vines. Below in the garden, flowers shone forth in magnificent pomp amid luxuriant shrubs and cacti.

Rations were delivered every ten days—cornmeal, wheat flour, beef or sorghum, rice, beans, and salt—but in smaller amounts and of lower quality than in Savannah. Prisoners with money could buy all sorts of goods, however, because female greengrocers, as well as other peddlers and vendors, male and female, mostly colored, were permitted to offer wares on the sidewalk in front of the garden. He who wanted something went to the fence, handed money to a guard, who paid, then delivered the item to the buyer, through or over the fence. Chiefly for sale: sweet potatoes, cabbage, tomatoes, squash, apples, bread, and milk. Prices were enormous: a pound of flour, $3; one squash, $5; a small loaf of bread, $2; one quart of milk, $1.50. In the hospital the sutler marketed tobacco, cigars, soap, knives, spoons, forks, etc. Daily a hawker brought writing paper, pens, pencils, envelopes, and the like.

How did we come by money? Certain persons in Charleston were in the business of providing it for prisoners. Those brokers knew that prisoners, in order to buy necessities in a desperate situation, would take any terms, and so the terms would have been intolerable in other circumstances. Brokers made contact through influential Rebel officers. Two Confederate dollars would be advanced for [a pledge of] one greenback, and, in a promissory note countersigned by the senior officer [of prisoners], the customer would obligate himself to a person or a firm in the eastern states.[13] The broker in turn would dispense the desired Confederate dollars in exchange for the note; send it, probably with blockade runners, to the North; and have his agents redeem it there [with the person or firm named in the note]. Since family and friends of prisoners almost always honored such notes, brokers obviously netted a tidy profit.[14]

Day to day we occupied ourselves with the usual culinary tasks or laundered clothes if the cistern held enough water. Supplying ourselves with drinking water was often a problem. One day, when our pump would produce none, we had to buy it from outside sources for $1 a kettle. At other such times we were permitted to go out in groups under guard and draw it from a nearby well. Entertainment consisted of walking in the garden and reading newspapers and magazines from the North. (Charleston newspapers—like those of Richmond, Savannah, and Macon—were worthless.)

Charleston lies [between the Ashley and Cooper rivers] on a delta they have formed. The conflagration of 1861 burned to the ground, from river to river, a stretch of houses and churches, which had not been rebuilt. From our veranda we could overlook a large part of Charleston, especially the section destroyed by the fire [the Burnt District]. On nights of bright moon the view of the devastation was almost ghostly: a broad belt of rubble and ruins where tall grass throve and bushes flourished. Elegant homes, where rich aristocracy used to live in the most exquisite luxury, had collapsed into piles of wreckage. The churches had once been meeting places for the elite; now only walls remained. Grass and debris choked the streets where slaveholding nobility had promenaded. In the burned-out zone, a living thing was seldom to be seen.

A rich and proud city had been badly damaged. Moreover, now daily the cannon of the Republic smashed houses and mansions where [in the bombardment of Fort Sumter in 1861] the first shots rang out against the New World's great nation of freedom. In this seat of luxury and aristocratic arrogance, treason had been born and raised. And to what end, now that this resting place of the bones of the man who concocted the cursed idea of dismembering the Union, this center of treason, was exposed to fire and the sword?[15] The annihilating flames, which often mercilessly lay waste the huts of the peaceful and the innocent, had there begun the good work our artillery was continuing with praiseworthy zeal.[16]

Always the thought of exchange haunted us; we bore it like Jews the idea of the Messiah. Even here it vexed us, after a hundred disappointments, when reason told us we were fools to follow again the ignis fatuus of [a false] hope. But a number of prisoners from Sherman's army had been exchanged after an agreement with the Rebel Hood,[17] and the captured naval officers had been told they would be exchanged.[18] Therefore not a few [of us] believed that negotiations had resumed between the two parties at loggerheads over people's bodies and souls, and that the matter in which we must serve as scapegoats had been settled to mutual satisfaction.

By the end of September, numbers [of us] had yellow fever, perhaps giving reason to move us from Charleston. The Rebels were not worried about our health—not at all! They wanted purely and simply to keep alive as many as possible, to use in some eventual exchange. In other words, not altruism but opportunism and self-interest saved us from the threat of the fever. On 4 October we were told we would leave the home of the fever and be reinterned in "healthy" regions around Columbia.

The next morning we marched to the train in the usual manner, down several streets, past houses evidencing Gilmore's bombardment, and during a fierce cannonade. A crowd, mostly Germans, Irish, and Negroes, had gathered in the streets to see the prisoners. Loaded like beasts of burden, the prisoners struggled ahead under the scorching sun.

For, this time, made wise by bad experience, we brought along everything that could be of any use. Like emigrating Europeans, who gladly include on the long trek all household effects, we insured that we left behind in the hospital nothing but bare walls. We carried away even the iron plates off the kitchen stoves, regardless how onerous they might be, on this hot day, to those who lugged them.

In King Street, Charleston's former main street, several prisoners took advantage of the crowd, slipped between guards, and escaped. An old acquaintance of mine from the Libby, Captain Eugen Hepp of the Eighty-second Illinois, had gotten civilian clothes in the Marine Hospital, and on this march to the station, he disappeared easily into the crowd. After hiding a long while among friends made by accident, he fled the city and reached our ships.[19] Escape proved hard in King Street [on the other hand] for those who wore blue uniforms marking them as Yankees. When the train left, assembled Negroes and Negresses, waving hats and hands, shouted a hearty Good-bye and wished us farewell to Columbia.

13

Columbia—Camp Sorghum—Camp Asylum

After a twelve-hour ride [on the South Carolina Railroad] through a desolate, sparsely settled region, we arrived at night in Columbia [South Carolina]. We dismounted in the morning and, for the time being, camped in the station itself. In the afternoon we moved across the station and settled down again. [It was early October 1864].

Rations were not issued until evening. Meanwhile, women and boys, mostly colored, soon appeared at the fence between us and the street, and offered bread at fifty cents a loaf. But the cadets of Columbia, who guarded us, would have nothing of such transactions. One of us tried to buy bread to still his hunger despite the restriction, but a cadet bayoneted and wounded him, fortunately not seriously. Several of us discovered in the cellar a vat full of sides of bacon. We fished some out with a long pole and a bent nail [as a hook] at its end. At last Captain Semple presented himself—he commanded [prisoners] here in Columbia—and told us he had sent for a sutler who would sell us bread. The sutler duly emerged but demanded seventy-five cents for [a loaf of] bread. The hungry, indignant, declared that if he insisted on this exorbitant price with this crowd of famished prisoners, his load [of bread] would be seized forthwith. The threat produced the desired result. Later, two barrels of crackers were delivered, and each of us got a couple of the hard biscuits, our first rations in forty-eight hours.[1]

Toward evening, Jupiter Pluvius assigned a cloudburst to baptize us poor homeless devils—thoroughly and free of charge.[2] Water rushed like Niagara out the gates of heaven and flooded our place. Fires doused, we stood in pitch darkness in the water, unable at all to protect ourselves. Next morning, Captain Semple, thinking last night's storm had brought us to heel, suggested a comfortable and beautifully situated camp—ours if we would sign the parole. With the glibness of Reynard the Fox,[3] he painted word pictures of a paradise; but we did not lend an ear to this siren song, we knew too well the Rebels' mendacity and deceit. We surmised that Semple wanted only to spare sentries, and the future proved us correct.

Our senior officer stated plainly to the Rebels that we were perhaps inclined to the parole, but only after we had visited the camp and witnessed the alleged comforts so eloquently described by the captain. Seeing we were too experienced for him, he rode away without having fooled us.

In a few hours the order came to depart. Several wagons were ready to take our baggage. With many guards on either side, we went southwest on the road to Augusta and crossed the Saluda River on the long, covered bridge. About two miles from Columbia, we turned left off the road and stopped at last. The site was on an elevation, half a field and half a pine forest. Through the forest a long, narrow lane had been cut and pickets set out.

"This is your place," Captain Semple said. "Make the most of it."

It was the same one he praised to us earlier, but, even with our best effort, we could not detect the beautiful features he had described. We were to have signed the parole in order to become temporary occupants of this barren field! As to the promised comforts, we got neither lumber nor tents, neither axes nor spades. We were driven like a herd of cattle into the field, and sentries served as fences. Yes, Captain Semple spoke of tents in his possession in Columbia, and of the telegram he sent to Charleston requesting more. Soon (he said) all of us would have shelter. He could have saved his breath; we believed not a word. We began as soon as possible, therefore, to build huts as well as we could of branches—protection against the sun but not the rain.

The huts sufficed during the day in the bright, clear weather of the first week. Nights were cool, however, and dense fog often formed before sunrise. Soon the weather changed: prolonged rain. Badly clothed and without [adequate] shelter; soaked to the skin, unable to maintain fires, and chilled to the bone—so we suffered a sad situation. There was one way to warm up: pace rapidly back and forth in pouring rain.

Finally seeming to take a little pity on us, the Rebels sent eight axes and ten shovels, so that we could build better housing. Since the trees in our area had been used for firewood, we were allowed to fell others beyond the limits, and to drag the trunks to our side. Trouble was, those few axes could not serve 1,200 men. Thus, November arrived, and many, not having wooden huts, still had to live in our original "bowers" or in burrows "deep in the ground."[4] A few who had money bought axes from the Rebels: $45 each.

Despite the shortage of tools, the forest around the camp thinned as blows of new settlers' axes resounded among the trees and they fell from early morning until late at night. Logs, brought in each by six to eight men, were hewn and fitted one atop the other. Cracks were chinked with clay and then the roof was added. Hustle and bustle, therefore, everywhere.

With many man-hours and much effort in construction, a little town of "wooden houses" with shingled roofs soon took shape.

Who can better colonize, who in the world can better pioneer, in wilderness and virgin forest, than the American? Gifted and sensitive, he makes much of every small advantage. Clever and practical, he organizes for results. And with restless energy he conquers the greatest difficulties. He sets his goal and concentrates on it until it is reached. If diverted by bad luck, and even if everything goes wrong, he never thinks of giving up. Rather, he resumes with new strength and continues until the task is done.

Several hundred huts, each accommodating small groups of two to eight men, were completed by the middle of November. In this, our finished town, every feature was American but one: disorder. The two principal streets ran haphazardly across confusion, because each group had built where they pleased. What trouble making your way, especially at night! And, except on the two thoroughfares, another obstacle especially impaired your getting about: deep holes around houses. Builders needing clay had dug close at hand.

A creek on the southwestern slope supplied enough potable water. Bringing it home was hard at first, because only a few men at a time were allowed out. Later, an adjusted boundary put the creek at least twenty feet inside the limits. Initially the same problem arose with firewood. You had to often wait your turn for hours before being able to gather the next day's supply. Later, larger groups went out under guard. For a while, those who wanted to gather wood had to sign the parole.

Rations consisted of cornmeal, a little rice, salt, flour (sometimes replaced by grits), and sorghum. There was no meat. Sorghum being the chief article, the place was named Camp Sorghum.

Daily our clothing worsened. In the end many of us had to go barefoot, footwear was so bad. Among those thus blessed, I trudged shoeless many long weeks on cold, damp ground, until Captain Hobbie at last made me a pair. He used an old piece of cloth, and they were quite serviceable in dry weather.

How miserable to be brought that low! Today, therefore, I need only see somebody in cracked shoes in winter and I pity him.

In October the Sanitary Commission sent some boxes of underwear, just what we could use.[5] Though distributed as equitably as possible this time, it was not enough for so many men. Still we were grateful for every gift, even a handkerchief. Our greatest needs: coats, trousers, and shoes. We had already decided (in Savannah) to ask our government for uniforms, but I doubt that such a letter was ever dispatched [by the Rebels].

Wretched circumstances engulfed most of us now. Cold and hunger, our chief enemies, were always on the offensive. Many suffered effects of severe chill. Every morning, when an assistant to the Rebel physician visited the camp carrying a medicine chest, a pitiful sight would unfold: pale, emaciated creatures standing in the cold, shivering before that Aesculapius. And all to receive a powder probably thought of as a panacea! About 200 feet from camp, across Augusta Road, a hospital tent had been provided for the sickest ones, and the physician daily took applications for admission. Spare and insubstantial rations evoked daily jeremiads on hunger. Of course, he who had money could buy (from the sutler) meat, bread, sweet potatoes, and other vegetables. But while the well-to-do feasted (meat and vegetables constituted a regal banquet), the majority starved on cornbread or mush and sorghum. Those repulsive dishes curb the appetite momentarily but do not satisfy long. How often did we hover with grumbling stomachs at the sutler's booth, looking with famished eyes at [loaves of] bread and cuts of meat![6]

Such experiences teach people to appreciate, forever after, the sufferings of the poor and the wretched, and even to excuse the poverty-stricken when, in moments of dire need, they stray from the straight and narrow.

After Semple the Speechifier relinquished command, Lieutenant Colonel [Robert S.] Means assumed it for a short while, then Major [Elias] Griswold of Maryland, one of old General Winder's most obsequious toadies. All these lords and masters were wardens to suit Jefferson Davis and his chief beadle, Winder.

The guards were militia from Georgia [and South Carolina]. The Georgians felt unhappy away from home and treated us nicer than did the South Carolinians.[7] In gray rags, unwashed, unkempt, this corps looked like footpads and highwaymen. They were of the last conscription, reserves, companies of boys and of old men with gray hair. The officers seemed to have much trouble with these undisciplined troops and often punished the recalcitrant hard, tying them to trees or stretching them on the rack. During one of the disciplinary sessions a mutiny broke out, which the officers quelled only with difficulty.

As surely as depravity of appearance marked them outwardly, so they shared a profound ignorance, these men forced into uniform by conscription. They belonged to the South's population of poor whites, who differed from Negroes only in the color of their skins, and stood lower than Negroes in the eyes of the slaveholding aristocracy. (A Negro was at least worth money and constituted an investment.) Born impoverished on tiny plots of land or to [other] low stations, these people get no education worth mentioning. They grow up ignorant and illiterate, they know nothing but a few practical skills of everyday living and some [local oral] traditions, and they assume the inferior status of their parents. Politically of course they were tools of the omnipotent aristocracy that fomented the Rebellion because of real or illusory threats to the aristocracy's material interests. The poor whites usually voted overwhelmingly for the aristocracy's candidates and, in the end, though they did not share the aristocracy's economic advantages, they took up arms for the aristocracy's way of life. The first hope, that the poor ignorant whites could be saved from their subhuman condition, dawned on the day of the Emancipation Proclamation, when the immortal Lincoln unlocked the shackles of the slaves.[8]

Thus the slave system was deleterious in three ways.

• It produced an aristocracy openly arrogant and essentially corrupt, an element dangerous to society in the Republic at large.

• It debased to pariahs a mass of [white] people once capable of education and culture.

• It damned the Negro to a disgraceful bondage: a scandal and a persistent stumbling block to the Republic.

Not only the men but also the officers of this militia were ignorant. I recall several instances of an officer's asking one of us to read him an order he had just received. To mask illiteracy, he would say, "The writing is too hard to make out."

As I've said, the Georgians were good-natured. The South Carolinians, however, could be nasty; there were those who obeyed with pleasure stern orders [against prisoners] and sometimes were harsher than they had to be. One evening, Lieutenant [Alvin] Young of the Fourth Pennsylvania Cavalry sat with a friend by the fire, talking. Young's enlistment had expired the day before. A shot rang out, and Young collapsed, mortally wounded. His friends buried him the next day.

"The gun went off accidentally," the sentry said, and there the matter ended.

One morning, at the hour appointed for wood gathering, Lieutenant Turbane of the Sixty-Sixth New York, ax in hand, walked to the deadline, intending to go out and gather wood. Here in Camp Sorghum, stakes marked the line. He reached them, the sentry opposite him fired, and he was a corpse.

In camp, uproar over cold-blooded murder. Yet insult would be added to injury. Yes, the murderer was relieved, but that afternoon he, an old, weather-beaten fellow named Williams, resumed his post. The next morning, as usual, a large detachment of guards attended roll call; he appeared in our midst, as if a plot was afoot to provoke us. Moreover, reserves stood in formation outside [our enclosure], and cannoneers were on station. A vulgar insult, that scene, but it characterized Major Griswold perfectly. While in our camp, however, the murderer must have heard words that ring in his ears even yet.

Several times, before and after that affair, sentries fired into our camp without provocation, fortunately hitting no one. Each time, it was said, the gun discharged accidentally.

So we were exposed to the malice of a savage soldier mob and unable to do anything about it. Even the most humble remonstrance would have gone unheeded. Or, at the worst, it would have prompted Major Griswold to act like Lord Gibbs in Macon and furlough and promote the murderer.

With so little reason to be happy in our proletarian town, we seized every chance to amuse ourselves:

- On pleasant evenings our "band"—of four players, like the true article at a local fair—played to our delight, even though the old favorites were repeated again and again.

- Now and then a cabin caught fire. At the cry—"Fire! Fire!"—the same hullaballoo erupted as would accompany a big-city conflagration.

- Pigs strayed in several times: welcome occasions for great excitement. "Halloo!" burst from every throat; craving [for meat] manifested itself, especially among men who had no money to buy such food; and the chase was on. Of course the poor beasts never returned whence they came. Slaughter was workmanlike, appetite immense, and the feasting worthy of the prince of gourmands.

- Another day, two bloodhounds paid a visit. Now, the bloodhound is an attractive-looking animal but savage when incited. At headquarters, six were always ready to be set after escapees. By chance, two of those six got loose and came friendly and innocent to us. Still wearing a small wooden yoke that kept them together, they were taken hold of and secured at once. A fellow prisoner and former escapee (bloodhounds had aided his recapture) pressed his case, and we decided that these two public enemies must die. An ax was brought, and in a moment they were killed and buried in a shallow grave in the center of the camp. They had been trained to their owner's horn, and now it blew again and again, louder and louder. This man—hounds were his trade—rode about, faster and faster, outside the camp and in the forest, seeking the lost ones. In vain. At last a detachment [of guards] entered the camp, sighted fresh blood, tracked it to the grave, and dragged out the carcasses. We heard that the owner, at sight of his dead pets and breadwinners, exclaimed, "For each of these dogs, more than one Yankee will pay with his life, and I shall personally collect." Who knows; perhaps he fulfilled that vow.[9]

- A sensation erupted the day we heard of gold, several nuggets, found at the sandy edge of the creek. Many prisoners actually let themselves be fooled into rushing there to scoop it up—in grand nuggets if you please. Truth soon prevailed: somebody or other had played a bad joke.

- We even held a presidential election. After proper notice, the senior officer set up ballot boxes on the appointed day, 17 October, one for each state [represented among the prisoners]. Results were loudly applauded when announced: Lincoln, 1,024; McClellan, 145 (for president); [Andrew] Johnson, 1,031; [George H.] Pendleton, 112 (for vice-president).[10]

More prisoners escaped from Camp Sorghum than from any other prison.[11] On dark nights many slipped across the deadline and past the sentries. Others bribed sentries. But escapes were most frequent during times of wood-gathering. On many a day, no fewer than thirty or forty disappeared, and their absence always ignited commotion among the Rebels at roll call. A Georgia lieutenant of militia, the one who persisted in passing us false news about exchange, did not know what to say or do one day when he learned at roll call that no fewer than two dozen were missing from one squad. Later, wood gatherers had to sign the parole, but just as many ways and means were found to dupe the Rebel officers and sentries.[12]

I believe that Camp Sorghum's runaways amounted to at least 400 and would have been significantly more had so many prisoners not lacked shoes and boots. Two-thirds of the runaways were recaptured, and some were shot while fleeing. How many reached Union lines has not been precisely determined. The ones returned [to Camp Sorghum] usually could tell us many interesting stories about escape and its adventures and dangers—from personal experience.

Most runaways headed for the mountains of North Carolina and eastern Tennessee; others aimed for our positions to the south; a few groups went toward Augusta; and some took boats down the Congaree River; but all agreed that escape was a perilous act of daring. In the first place, not only the militia, but especially the [white] civilian population (and *all* of them), were exceedingly vigilant. Furthermore, many patrols roamed those areas with bloodhounds. Fugitives, usually forced to hide in forests during the day, could press forward only nocturnally on their arduous trek through swamps and thickets. (Roads were almost always to be avoided.) Negroes provided the only aid. Whenever possible they sheltered hungry fugitives, gladly shared bread and meat, and gave directions where to go and how to find [other helpful] Negroes. Not a single Negro, so far as is known, ever willfully betrayed one of our fugitives. Reports [of that Negro aid, comfort, and cooperation] contributed greatly to an improved opinion of Negroes. For, even among us [Northern whites], not a few were prejudiced and held the lowest opinion of the Negro, even disdained him.[13]

The torrent of attempts to escape alarmed Rebel commanders. Major Griswold declared one day that he would greet us with grapeshot if this running off did not stop. Lieutenant General Hardee (who headed the Department of South Carolina, Georgia, and Florida) ordered reported to him the name of every fugitive and directed Union officers in captivity to sign a parole not to escape.[14] If they did not sign, he said, they—like captured Union enlisted men—would be clapped into a closely guarded pen. (As if any place, except perhaps the prison in Charleston, could have been worse than Camp Sorghum.)[15]

Two events prompted us again to discuss, thoroughly and painstakingly, the subject of exchange. (1) A special exchange of about a hundred officer-prisoners took place in November. (2) Soon thereafter we heard that our government had interdicted the shipment of packages [to us]. The second loosed a flood of diverse comments. A sure sign, some of us said, that a general exchange was imminent. Others growled that the government had cut off even this tiny comfort and therefore wanted to do its captured soldiers an ill turn. A third group, of a mind that the packages benefited none but thieving Rebels, calmly accepted what had happened.

After we had frozen and starved almost ten long weeks in Camp Sorghum, the order of 1 December transferred us elsewhere in Columbia. The next morning a number of wagons arrived. We loaded up our belongings, everything we could move, then set fire to most of the cabins. We did not want them left to possible Rebel advantage, perhaps as a camp [for their troops]. The fire raged two hours in the wooden town, destroying our homes that had cost so much trouble and work. We were carefully counted, the command rang out—"Forward march!"—and still the thick smoke surged and billowed.

Going the way we had come on 6 October, we passed the train station again and moved through the city's principal streets, headed for the garden of the insane asylum. Columbia is pleasantly situated on an elevation. We saw many fine summer houses and substantial buildings of stone. But in the chief commercial streets, evidence of ruin (a consequence of this Rebellion) manifested itself, too: many businesses securely locked, others empty and deserted, their broken display windows boarded up or papered over. A lady, on her balcony for a look at our column, waved her handkerchief as we neared. When she saw we were Yankees, she hastened back inside. We went a few more steps and some guy, who had obviously imbibed plenty of whiskey, tried to insult us with the filthiest talk. His wish, "May all Yankees go to Hell," was superfluous; we had been in Hell for a year and a half.

Arriving at the garden of the asylum, we had the pleasure of listening to Major Griswold speechify. He, standing on a platform used by guards, proclaimed various rules and regulations, then closed with the hackneyed promise that everything would be done to ameliorate our imprisonment. Not one of us believed a syllable of what he said.

A stone wall enclosed the garden, and a board fence of equal height (ten feet) divided it. Our half embraced two acres. A small ditch marked the deadline. On the west side a board covered holes in the fence that would admit the barrels of two cannon placed outside. To the north, just before the line, potable water was piped into six wooden troughs. The three lower ones were for washing and bathing. Cold water, often covered with ice, did not stop us; several times a day, to the amazement of our unwashed guards, we took advantage of this superb place to bathe. Never in their lives had they seen such "waterfowl" as these Yankees.

Immediately several groups took possession of the rooms in a two-story building near the gate, but soon they had to vacate because it was to be used as a hospital. A few steps beyond it, sick men had already been installed in a small, one-story building. Health here being as bad as in Macon and Camp Sorghum, both these hospitals were to be always overfull, and there were several deaths. No wonder: hunger and cold did their work.

Many of us found refuge under the two buildings; others contrived a tentlike shelter of blankets; and the rest camped beneath the sky with no protection whatsoever. Of course Major Griswold promised lumber, nails, and tools to build barracks. What he delivered did not suffice for barracks for all. Later he sent tents, also insufficient. We named the place after what it had been: Camp Asylum.

Barracks were intended each for thirty-six men; the same thirty-six built and lived in one. Barracks granted a measure of protection against wind and rain but we still suffered all the while. For, though it never snowed, it was either viciously cold or violently rainy, and we got little firewood. Inside we put up three-tiered bunks along the walls, like ships' berths. Prisoners who could afford it bought a few pounds of cotton to make a bunk warmer and softer. Each barracks had two fireplaces with chimneys. When there was enough wood, a warming fire burned of an evening and we sat on little benches in front of it and sang or told anecdotes and tales of the war—or we groused about our fate.

At the fireplaces, too, we cooked our mush or soup, or brewed that "coffee" of roasted cornmeal. Near the back door we fashioned an oven, better to bake bread than the skillets, with a saving of firewood besides. Prisoners able to buy meat also used the oven to prepare it.

Rations were as scanty and as bad as at Camp Sorghum. Yes, various foods could be bought from the sutler; but at sky-high prices: beef $4 and pork $7 a pound, butter $20, fat $15, sugar $10, and flour $3.50; bread $1.50 a loaf, sweet potatoes $45 a bushel, squash not less than $5 each, and one turnip $1; salt $2, mutton $5, and pepper $35 a pound. Other things were equally expensive: a pair of clumsy shoes, army style, made in England, $100; a pair of stockings $14; a ream (480 sheets) of writing paper $225; a pound of thread $150; a pound of tallow candles $20; and an ax $45. The sutler hauled in these wares in a two-wheeled cart under guard. Four or five officers sold them in a tent and turned a handsome profit. Yet, as a rule, a crowd surged there. You had to struggle through them and work to put your Confederate money into the seller's hand.[16]

Such currency was worth little—a dollar bill represented, at most, five copper pennies—but we paid dearly for it. One Potter, of Charleston, posing to us as a Union man, purported to act out of exceeding goodwill when he provided Confederate money against bills of exchange.[17] His customer and a witness would sign one, the senior officer of prisoners (here, Colonel Shedd of the Thirtieth Illinois) would countersign, and then this statement was added:

> This money was loaned to me while a prisoner of war at Columbia, S.C., for my own personal use, as a favor. I therefore desire it paid.

Potter gave two Confederate dollars for one pledged in greenback, and six for one in gold. How lucrative was his business? In the general market, one greenback dollar would get fifteen to twenty Confederate; and a dollar in gold, fifty Confederate. At that time in the North, however, a gold dollar would bring $180 greenback. So, for example, when we bought a pair of shoes for $100 Confederate, we were paying [in effect] $16.33⅓ gold or $30 greenback.[18]

A prisoner fared little better with money sent him from the North. It went not to him but to the Rebel quartermaster, who converted it at the so-called government rate. (The standard rate would have been far more favorable to the prisoner.) And then the prisoner received, not the Confederate money due him, but a draft on the sutler. So, after losing about two-thirds of his good money by the conversion, the prisoner had to pay the sutler's exorbitant prices. It was a double swindle.

Furthermore, Rebel officers kept some of the money sent us; a third swindle. Yes, the quartermaster did post a notice that these sums were to be paid. But when we applied to him, he said: "A printed conversion table is needed. I'll see to it." The table did not appear, and we never got our money.

As the Rebels were vile about money, so they were shabby about our letters to family and friends in the North. Everything we have learned about the mail leads us to believe that at least half of our letters were never dispatched. Rebels removed the stamps and forgot the letters while our people at home longed for them. The same situation obtained with letters for us. They reached us two or three times in Macon. In Savannah, almost never. In Columbia, about six or eight times.

At the cry—"Letters! Letters!"—the camp would erupt. Everybody, if not in the middle of cooking or baking or washing, ran to the place where names were called. Joyous was he who received word from relatives or friends. Depressed was he who left empty-handed. Letters had to be sent unsealed, so of course they lacked much we wanted to know. Here in Camp Asylum the adjutant called the names—hard labor for Lord Adjutant, who could barely read. He amused us when he tried to sound them out. Often he would put a letter aside, saying, "I can't pronounce *that*."

Late afternoons, whenever the weather was at all agreeable, the choir and the glee club did their best in singing us various songs. Instrumentalists and vocalists stood on the hospital veranda, and we formed a large circle around them. Here the now-famous "Sherman's March to the Sea" was first sung. One prisoner had written the lyrics and another the music. (It was agreeable and popular but too strongly suggestive of "The Red, White and Blue."). Enthusiasm beyond description greeted its initial performance; encore followed encore; and in every barracks and every tent, men learned it, practiced it, and sang it. Ladies and gentlemen often gathered on a platform outside the fence, to hear our concerts. Very soon such spectators got the chance to *see* Sherman's army and by the light of a grand fireworks.[19]

Every week, special exchanges intensified our general dissatisfaction. We often held meetings to discuss steps we might take to effect exchange. Prisoners caucused according to home state to compose letters to the respective governors. Prisoners captured at Gettysburg met and decided to write to two United States senators and ask for presidential intercession. Colonel Thorp addressed President Lincoln himself, requesting food and clothing. As far as I know, none of those letters was delivered.

The post of prison inspector called for someone at the rank of captain. One day the post changed hands, and a certain Latoure took it: an elderly man of mercenary appearance, who spoke a French-German-English patois. On his own initiative, he promised us his best—he would have straw delivered, for example—because (he said) he had been a prisoner himself, in Fort Delaware.[20] "I know from experience how it feels to be in prison." Regularly at about 9:00 P.M., he would make the rounds, wrapped in a huge coat and carrying a dark lantern. When he discovered a light in a barracks, he would enter and, in his inimitable dialect, announce: "Closing time!" Soon, however, he got drunk, had words with the Rebel physician (to our general amusement), and was relieved as inspector and arrested.

One day the inspector, the adjutant, and a detachment entered camp, went straight to the first tent on the east side, and started looking for a tunnel. In a few minutes they found one. Suspicion [among us] rose—"Somebody squealed!"—and settled on a fellow prisoner. Terrible threats were flung at him, and a committee was formed [among us] to investigate [his possible treachery]. Major Griswold heard of these things. In the afternoon this order was posted:

At the behest of General Winder, I inform the Union prisoners under my command that if tunneling does not stop, he will have all tents, barracks, and [permanent] buildings removed from camp. Let me add that I shall use force against force if any attempt is made to harm a prisoner suspected of having told headquarters about tunnels.

Griswold

Commandant

On 8 February we received word of an event of great interest. General Winder, the brutal commander in chief of Confederate military prisons, had died the day before in Columbia. When the sutler brought the news, infernal jubilation burst forth in camp. Cries, countless cries:

"The tyrant is dead!"

"He's already roasting in Hell!"

"The Devil's got Winder!"

Some of us waved hats and caps, or threw them into the air, while others leaped and danced. The sentries looked down from their platforms, amazed and alarmed, never having seen such tumult. The usual calm of circadian routine did not resume for several days.

In his last order, Winder had threatened to remove our barracks and tents. In them, after normalcy returned, his death continued to prompt frequent and diverse remarks. One of our worst enemies was dead. Thousands of imprecations and eternal curses followed him to his disgraceful grave. He, in cooperation with Jefferson Davis and Robert E. Lee, was the one who sacrificed our soldiers to suffering and starvation at Belle Island and in Richmond, Andersonville, Salisbury, and Florence.[21]

The effect of Winder's order was the opposite of its intent. Subterranean labors recommenced with even greater zeal. A tunnel began in the third barracks, which I shared with thirty-five other prisoners. We swore a common oath: we would put our united strength to the tunnel, we would pursue through thick and thin anybody who might betray our venture, we would see that person dishonorably discharged from the Union army, and we would flee together on one and the same night. Then we began inside, in front of the back door, digging straight down about six or seven feet and burrowing horizontally from there. Every night after 10:00 we set to it. Blankets over the windows prevented sentries' seeing our lights. The back door was bolted and a man put on watch at the front to prevent surprise by a patrol. Diggers one at a time observed two-hour shifts. Packed soil and poor tools meant tough going. Every half-hour, two soil carriers moved out what had been loosened, and temporarily hid it under the lower bunks. At dawn we stopped. As soon as the last man was out, a wooden trapdoor was shut and concealed with earth and ashes.

After much of the hard work had been done, we received the order to leave Columbia.

14

To Freedom

A few days after General Winder died, we heard that we would be exchanged, all of us, in a few weeks. We treated it the way we treated similar talk a hundred or a thousand times before: as a delusion sprung from a prisoner's overheated imagination, or a humbug cooked up in the cauldron of a Rebel's malice. But this time the glad tidings reappeared and persisted. Then Major Griswold confirmed that the "differences over exchange have been resolved." Sanguine prisoners rejoiced. But the "old fish" refused such bait; diligently they continued their tunnel.

Then one day the Rebel adjutant showed us a clipping. General Grant, it said, had informed [Ould's assistant] Captain Hatch at the Rebel exchange bureau: "Exchange shall proceed at once."[1] Excitement swelled among us. In a manner of speaking, the value of "exchange stock" skyrocketed.

At last, on 13 February [1865], the order to 600 of us: *Be ready for transfer to Charlotte* [North Carolina] *and from there to Richmond.* Delight, practically fanatical ecstasy, seized most of us. The doors of our cage might already be open, so joyous our songs in front of the hospital. Still the "old guard" would not be led astray by [false] hope. "It's all a cruel repetition of a hackneyed fraud," they said. "Sherman's closing in, so the 'Rebs' feed us this malarkey about exchange. They want to move us and keep us from trying to get away during the trip." As to our transfer to Richmond, it could easily be that the Rebels intended to return us there in order to put us again "under fire" as in Charleston.[2] Thus the old-timers of the Libby reasoned, coldly and skeptically, vexing the prisoners who hoped [for exchange].

Again [therefore] plans were laid and preparations made to escape during the transfer—all ruined by the weather. Rain began while we marched to the station. A chill followed, icing the streets. A storm broke during the night. Rebel sentries, nearly freezing on the roofs of the cars, could easily have been overpowered. But an attempt to escape on this cold, rainy, blustery night would have had to be called *madness.* A few dashed off anyhow, to be soon caught, half-frozen. How cold we were, in those old, drafty cars—how very cold![3]

In the afternoon of 15 February we arrived in Charlotte and marched at once through rain and mud to a field about a mile from the city proper. Near trees and an old barn we pitched camp, one of our worst. The weather was raw and rainy, the wind colder and sharper during the night, and the ground wet. We had to drink the muddy yellow water of a pond in a swale about a hundred paces off. Food consisted of pork and cornmeal, quantity small. Guards, demoralized, did little to stop prisoners who attempted escape. (At least a hundred got away during our stay here— proof that the news of exchange had been scarcely believed.) The rest of the prisoners arrived from Columbia the next day, after barely missing an accident on the railroad. During our second day the Rebel captain, Stewart, who commanded the guards, told us what he had learned from the commandant of Charlotte, Colonel [Robert F.] Hoke: "Yes, you are on your way to the exchange point." Hoke himself arrived in the afternoon and confirmed Stewart.

On 19 February, 200 of us left Charlotte. The next day we reached Greensboro, where Captain Barth, a Floridian, took charge. One of the most humanitarian Rebel officers in our experience, he endeavored (sometimes with pain to himself) that we get enough food. We stayed about a day and a half, waiting in an open field near the road. Many people came from the city to see and talk to us. We spoke German with two young Germans who gave us tobacco and bread. These youths had been drafted into the Rebel army but wanted no part of active duty—did we know how they might skip to the North? [We pointed to] several hundred Union enlisted men (prisoners) near the railroad, about fifty yards from us. (They had arrived the prior evening.) "Lose yourselves among those Yankees," we advised our loyalist Germans. "Leave with them." They said they would. I don't know whether they succeeded or failed.

Our transfer to the North Carolina capital of Raleigh, begun 12 February, proceeded so slowly that we did not arrive until early the twenty-second. We spent the morning beside the station, guarded by Hillsborough military academy cadets. There we could study several hundred of our enlisted men who had spent months suffering in prison. We saw skin blackened almost to Negroid (they had been given no soap). We saw countenances distressed, faces haggard, bodies emaciated. What they had on their backs and called clothes looked worse than the rags we wore!

In the afternoon we marched away, along the tracks, to a place near the city, where a group of prisoners joined us a day later. Several Raleigh loyalists visited. With sympathy they asked about our condition and assured us that, as far as they knew, we would be exchanged. Some of them almost wept at the old patriotic songs, which they had not heard for years.

We expected to leave Raleigh soon. Sure enough the order arrived forthwith: *Be ready to move.* But the platform cars, intended for us, stood not on the Goldsboro but on the Gaston line. When, in addition, Captain Barth told us we would encamp, our hopes dissolved. We believed we would not be released soon; we imagined ourselves once more involved in pitching a camp; we dreaded a stay of weeks and months. Six hundred of us boarded the cars. Scarcely beyond the city's outermost houses—a jolt—and the train stopped dead. Many of us jumped. Some fell off, wrenching knees and spraining wrists. Hurrying to the engine, we found it beside the tracks, wheels deep in the ground. Had it gone one step farther, every last car would have plunged off the fifty-foot embankment, no doubt about it. The opened switch that caused the mishap provoked immediate suspicion of [malicious] intent. They who could plot arson to burn Northern cities, they who could scheme [a kind of germ warfare] of yellow fever spread through contaminated clothing, they who could contrive to murder the president—they could also have hatched the idea to bury 600 prisoners under the wreckage of a train.

Leaving the hapless train, we walked the remaining three miles (or so) to the small, dilapidated, desolate, forest-ringed barracks on the left side of the tracks. Camp Holmes had been temporary billets for Rebel regiments. The dirty huts would not hold us all; some must stay outside under the firs. Though tall, they afforded scant shelter. A downpour the first day, then freezing temperatures, and we suffered. Captain Barth drummed up what few rations he could. We rejoiced that at least our captain did his best to provide us necessities. We knew nothing of our situation or our future, however, and the ignorance turned our suffering into torment. In Raleigh we had complied with a condition of exchange by signing a parole. Captain Barth repeatedly assured us, "All arrangements for exchange have been made. The only thing lacking is transportation." Still we suspected the worst. "A humbug, this whole affair," we said.

Captain Barth received an order at last to return us to Raleigh. We hastened on a train from sad Camp Holmes straight to Goldsboro [North Carolina] without pausing in Raleigh, stopped an hour [in Goldsboro], and rolled again, five miles or so, to the middle of a forest. Used to Rebel mischief, each of us, without complaint, took up quarters under a tree. Soon our many fires blazed, fed and maintained with dry twigs and branches lying everywhere. Cornmeal and smoked meat arrived presently. The next day we signed the parole again; the first had been declared void. In the morning a cart, sent by a Goldsboro group of loyalist women, drove up with a load of all sorts of foods: staples and delicacies.

Though ecstatic over this unexpected kindness, we decided not to use the gifts ourselves. For, hunting fuel in the surrounding woods, a few of us stumbled on a small clearing and several hundred Union enlisted prisoners. Were they in a state! Sick unto death, without medical care, nearly naked in cold weather, unfed for nearly a week, the poor devils lay on wet frigid ground and shivered. They were the so-called worst cases, or the sickest of the sick, they could not be moved anymore, so the Rebels brought them here and left them helpless. Our men, the ones who found them, hurried back in alarm and described the sight. At once and unanimously we determined what to do with the food. Those of us who could spare clothing sent it along. A committee charged with the task in a few minutes led the cart the short way to the miserable spot. Many of these victims of incredible barbarity, the starved and the moribund, were beyond help. A few, languid, could no longer put food in their own mouths. Sickness so racked others that they swallowed food one minute and vomited the next. Some, bereft of sense, stared at our men with the blank, fixed gaze of the idiot. One, nearly rigid with cold, dragged himself to the remnants of a newly dead fire, collapsed into them, and lay motionless, his head in hot ashes. Another, naked above the waist, cowered beside a tree, teeth chattering. We never learned whether all or any of those wretches reached Union lines.

We left Goldsboro on 28 February. The next morning the train stopped in a forest twelve miles from Wilmington [North Carolina], at the farthest of Rebel outposts.[4] We anticipated developments anxiously; we still feared something unforeseen that would intervene to block exchange. A half-hour wait, then a train roared up. The engine flew a white flag. Hatch, a Rebel exchange agent recently promoted to colonel, had arrived. In a few minutes an order for us: *Dismount*. Rebel guards stood at one side of the railway while a Union company formed a cordon at the other. The two agents [Union and Confederate] stood before the cordon, we passed them, and they counted us: 1,001. The Union troops presented arms.

Silently we walked a few steps. When the last of us passed the cordon, we stopped. A scene began; it almost beggars description. For sure, and the fact could not be denied, our yearning would be gratified at last. Our every doubt had evaporated. After such protracted imprisonment, finally, we had regained freedom. Tumult erupted. Joy produced *hurrah* after spirited *hurrah*. We flung used cornmeal sacks high into the air and stood in a shower of meal. Every possession that could be thrown we hurled into the woods. We embraced one another, waved hats and caps, leaped like ballet dancers—in a word, we surrendered to *bliss*. Adjutants and staff officers rode past bareheaded, and we greeted them: a thousand voices booming with delight. "Hurrah for the Union! Hurrah for Abraham Lincoln! Hurrah for General Grant!" And *hosannah* to the first day of March—when springtime sunshine beamed again on our freedom—our unforgettable day, the one we shall remember until death. How long, and with what ineffable longing, we had contemplated the moment of salvation!

The moment had arrived. Our happiness knew no bounds. A day cold, dark, and rainy [after early sunshine]? So what! In our joy we asked nothing of the weather! Our feet bore us, as fast and easy as birds on the wing, to the Cape Fear River. A muddy trek, the way partly under water, but we went as if promenading on the sidewalks of a boulevard.

We reached the pontoon bridge. On the opposite shore a band broke into a national tune. Up went a triumphal arch of freshly cut boughs, the inscription framed in evergreens: *Welcome Brothers.* Seeing it, as if on command, we exploded into unanimous exultation that wanted to continue forever. We crossed the bridge, mounted the high bank, and *there* we beheld again what we had missed since capture: the American flag. We bared our heads. A veteran captain strode weeping to the flag and kissed it. Union troops greeted us with a lusty cheer. Every band played. Flag bearers waved the Stars and Stripes. The reception could not have been heartier or more sublime.

We marched the brief way to the supply depot and sang the Sherman song ["Sherman's March to the Sea"] to the lieutenant colonel in charge. Then something appeared that aroused equal enthusiasm. Expecting famished guests, the quartermaster had slaughtered and roasted a few fat oxen. Soldiers [acting as waiters] brought cuts of meat, good crackers, and coffee. Follow custom, stand upon ceremony, and wait to be asked? Perish the thought! We helped ourselves and dug in at once and feasted and feasted, pleasing the soldiers who watched. We tried as hard as we could but could not devour everything. (Uncle Sam's table had been too sumptuously laid.) What a meal—a blowout such as we had not known for twenty months—a banquet festive, voluptuous, and fit for a king!

At last we hit the road. Nine miles remained to Wilmington [North Carolina]. We amused ourselves en route and arrived in the afternoon. Blockade runners had headquartered here for several years; and the city had only recently come under Union control. It is a city of size, with broad streets and a number of new and elegant buildings, as well as many old dilapidated affairs that must date to some century before this one.

We stopped on the main street in front of a large and beautiful private house, now headquarters of General [John M.] Schofield, commandant [of the Department of North Carolina]. Schofield himself, ill, could not attend, but other generals and officers came and listened to us. Astonished by how pitiful we looked, they fulminated against Rebel vulgarity and coarseness.[5]

People passed us as we stood there. A Negro stopped and asked one of us, "Massa, haven't I seen you before?"

"Where?"

"In Raleigh, sir."

"And how did you get there?"

With a knowing grin, tugging his old black hat to one side, he said: "Sir,

I was 'fireman' on the engine. You took care of Yankees—you were in Raleigh, standing along the tracks, I saw you."

"Very well. But how did you get *here*?"

"When prisoners were exchanged out there in the bush, I jumped off the engine and joined the Yankees. They crossed the line and I sneaked over, too, along with them."

Amid booming laughter and with grand mugging he ended his story: "You no longer have a fireman, no fireman anymore."[6]

We waited quite a while in front of headquarters, then got assignments to churches and various other buildings, where we billeted until we left Wilmington. The commissary served us superb meals. At noon the next day we departed aboard a Federal steamship, passed Fort Fisher, and hit the high seas twenty-four hours later. Most of us fought seasickness during the three-day voyage. We landed in the Maryland capital, Annapolis, and received greetings by a band together with officers and men stationed there. After our names had been recorded, we hunted up quarters for ourselves in the city and then addressed our first and foremost need, something we sorely lacked: clothing. Shopkeepers extended unlimited credit and we nearly exhausted inventories. In a few days we got plenty of money [back pay] and could settle the debts. Having shed our old rags, we felt like new men.

Several transports docked a short while after ours. Like us, their cargoes of Union soldiers had been brought straight from prisons to Wilmington. Most could leave the ships only with the help of hospital orderlies. So weak, and verging on death, many had to be moved on stretchers to nearby hospitals. The heartrending appearance [of the invalids] shocked military and civilian bystanders who watched the poor devils carried past. (Much had been heard and read of how Rebels treated prisoners but [until now] people did not know that the treatment had been so vicious.) Many of the moribund died on the short trip from pier to hospital. The best care could not save the rest of the doomed; emaciation, exhaustion, and mutilation had damaged them beyond help. One sad case on a stretcher seemed unaware of his doom. (His frostbitten feet had rotted off.) He lay in apathy, eyes open but fixed and glazed, hair nearly gone (fallen out), countenance like a death mask, body in scanty rags and wasted to a skeleton. Nearly all victims looked like specters straight out of the grave, subject again to putrefaction and beginning to putrefy. None talked, none groaned, and all seemed to have reached the end. They appeared to have lost emotion and to lack awareness. Bodies twisted and ravaged by sickness and suffering, bodies from which a last spark of once-sturdy life yearns to escape, such bodies create a spectacle that must ignite supreme compassion.

On a clear and beautiful Sunday morning, in mild and springlike weather, the dome of the old capitol gleamed under bright sunlight. Church bells rang with measured strokes. In shrubbery picturesquely surrounding the nearby military cemetery, birds sang their first songs of spring. Far away, now louder, now fainter, a dirge registered sublime tones. A long cortege moved down the street toward the cemetery, where grave-diggers had just finished the fortieth. The cortege halted at the gate. The music died. In came forty coffins of forty skeletons of forty Union soldiers, martyrs. Those victims of the "noble South" died between ship and hospital. The land of freedom could provide them nothing anymore, only a grave. Earth rumbled on wooden boxes that held human forms. Once, aflame with patriotism, they surged into battle to save the threatened Republic; now they rested in peace. They fell, not to an enemy's deadly fire, but to misery inflicted by calculated malice of barbarians. They suffered the worst, the most excruciating of deaths.

But the genius of freedom has planted immortelles on the martyrs' graves. Let their names be recorded with due honor in the nation's annals.

Appendix

The Escape from the Libby

by Albert Wallber[1]

At first, in that hellhole [the Libby], hope for exchange cheered and sustained us. Gradually, the hope faded and another replaced it: to free ourselves. In November 1863, officer-prisoners here laid the plan to conduct their own exchange. A number of them, after discussion and debate, decided to start digging behind the fireplace in the cellar under the hospital, and to dig to the sewer, which led to the canal behind the prison. The fireplace's chimney went up through [the hospital and] the prisoners' rooms above it. Conspirators contrived a rope ladder to let moles down the chimney and they dug zealously and with success.[2]

They compacted the excavated soil and hid it under the straw and other junk down there. As work progressed, carrying out the soil by the handful grew too difficult. A spittoon from one of the rooms served instead. A rope lowered the spittoon empty and raised it full, and the straw hid the soil, as before.

Knives, chisels, and fingernails, the available tools—and nasty toil— pushed the tunnel a distance. When the diggers hit piles (sunk from [the building] above and at least a foot in diameter), they did not lose heart; they attacked with penknives. Chips flew. After many days (actually, many *nights*), digging resumed; the piles had been cut. Diggers soon struck the sewer and another unexpected obstacle: stench. Noxious vapors gassed several diggers, and they had to be brought out half dead. Work could not continue in that direction. The small circle, those who knew the plan to escape, shared it with others now.

The larger group sized up the terrain and elected to burrow to the empty yard beside the prison, hoping to exit in a kind of coach house on the far edge. The new tunnel, commencing on the opposite side of the fireplace, hit a stone wall. Undaunted, we diggers addressed it with knives and chisels. In nineteen days we pierced three feet of stone. Again [mere] earth lay before us.

Work proceeded apace. Once more the spittoon must serve as hod.

After days of digging around the clock, we believed we neared our destination. One of us asked the officer of the day, "May I go to the building across the street? I think there's a package for me. I want to look for it." (Packages for us from the North were stored there.) Permission granted, our scout crossed the street under guard, pacing off the distance as accurately as he could. Sixty feet.

On 6 February, believing we had bored far enough horizontally, we headed upward. At our objective, sentries patrolled outside a high fence. Nearing the surface, we heard them talking, which told us we had stopped three feet short of the fence. Suddenly a section of pavement collapsed [into the tunnel]. The sentries asked each other what had caused the noise. When no more followed, they took nothing amiss and resumed their rounds.[3] We plugged the hole with an old pair of pants stuffed with straw and held in place by boards beneath, then dug another six or seven feet horizontally.

On the evening of 9 February: success. The diggers broke through to the surface, and word went to fellow inmates: "There's a way out."

At 8:30, Colonel [Thomas E.] Rose began the escape. Groups formed of three or four men each. [Descent to the cellar would be by] the rope ladder, put into the chimney now. Groups decided, among themselves, which of several routes to follow to the nearest Union lines. The diggers left [first], an hour before the next group. A few of us, familiar with the tunnel, guided those ignorant of it, or remained behind as rear guard. Looking out the window, we [of the rear guard] could see our comrades [emerge] on the other side of the coach house and slip one after another through the gate.

About midnight an alarm sounded. What trouble for prisoners [still in the building] to get back to quarters!

[The alarm was false.] Guards suspected nothing. Flight soon continued as before. Several escapees walked [heedlessly] under the gaslight [outside, on the corner], vexing the prisoners watching from the window. But those careless ones provoked no [Rebel] misgivings; many guards wore stolen Yankee uniforms, and escapees wore some civilian clothes. Street lights went out between 1:00 and 2:00. Escape continued at less risk.

Only one at a time could exit the tunnel's tiny mouth.[4] (The tunnel itself, miniature in scale, had to be negotiated on the belly at a crawl, like a snake.) Crawling, Colonel [Thomas E.] Rose of the Fourth Missouri Cavalry [actually, the seventy-seventh Pennsylvania Volunteers], Major [Alexander von] Mitzel of the seventy-fourth Pennsylvania Infantry, and I emerged about 2:00 A.M., 10 February. I listened: not a sound. Then, a few steps away, the sentry called: "Post Number Six—all well." He turned his back on me and I ducked around the corner to freedom. (My compliments to the sturdy fellow for his dubious report on things at his post!) I awaited my comrades. They, too, slipped out unnoticed.[5]

Free, rid of the shackles that had held us so long, we breathed deep drafts of night air and shouted: "Thank God, free at last!" From the bottoms of our hearts we resolved to die rather than return to that dungeon, should we meet anybody in flight who would recapture us.

Time being of the essence—"Let's go!" or "Out of this hellhole as fast as possible to the land of freedom!"—and away we went double quick. We jumped fences, crashed across gardens, raced down boulevards, hustled through alleys, and startled dogs that barked at us because we disturbed their nocturnal peace and quiet. Evading Rebel patrols that prowled the streets at night, we reached the fortifications [on the city's edge] without incident. Circumstances favored escape here also. A depression between two tall earthworks let us out unseen by sentries pacing the ramparts. Soon we gained the tracks of the York River Railroad, a happy find for us.

Briskly we followed it single file. We had not gone far when a nearby *hiss* stopped us. We called out. A pair of comrades appeared beside us. They too, had just escaped. We exchanged greetings, agreed on procedure, and resumed the march along the railroad. At daybreak we turned to the right and took shelter in a piny woods. A lieutenant of the Forty-fifth New York, thinking it dangerous to rest here, pushed ahead [alone]. A half-hour later we heard a train approach.

Then a horn sounded: a signal (we learned later) to assemble farmers so they could be told of the escape. In a little while two baying bloodhounds emerged with their master. He carried a rifle. Though tired, we must clear out; we had no desire to meet those beasts. Away we ran as fast as our legs could carry us, in the footsteps of the lieutenant who had left us earlier. The hounds set upon our scent as we raced off but we confused them after three-quarters of an hour of crisscrossing our tracks. Soon, hearing their baying grow ever more distant, we surmised they had found the lieutenant's trail and left ours for it. Having won a respite, we [paused and] listened: the baying dimmed and faded. Then, silence. We had lost the bloodthirsty beasts; we were safe—for now.

We allowed ourselves a rest. A noise shortly put us to flight again, through the same forest. Leaving it [at last] near evening, we saw a line of Rebel pickets. A "Halt!" thundered, and we turned back. The Rebels fired a few unsuccessful shots in farewell.

We rested unhurt in the densest of thickets and deliberated in whispers: "What now?" Not knowing which way to go, we could not decide what to do. Nothing remained but to choose a course at random. We wandered all night, seeking a direction out of the forest and a solution to our predicament. But Rebels ringed the forest, ever eager to spot us again. They must have assumed, however, that we could not elude them; they did not [enter the forest itself in] pursuit of us.

Exhausted, we lay down [to rest] on the cold, damp ground. We huddled together to protect ourselves from the night's icy chill. Yet even here we did not long indulge fatigue. We must be pushing on, ever forward, lest we be surprised, for we could be recaptured at any moment. But we failed to find a way out [of the forest]. Troops had shut the location tight.

When night had become day, we stumbled on a creek, a tributary (we thought) of the Chickahominy River. We followed the creek's twists and turns. The moment the sun rose above the canopy, we descried an open flat and, beyond, forest again. We felt like the discoverers of America who, sighting a new continent from their ships, shouted "Land! Land!" With us, at the edge of another forest, it was "Trees! Trees!"

But how to get there undetected? To our right we saw a Rebel earthwork. A bugler, standing on a rampart, sounded reveille. *We must risk it!* When he ended his ode to morning, we bent low, moved out slowly, and gained that forest.

The creek, our guide during the night, became a river. Our course demanded that it be crossed. Luck favored us again when, searching, we discovered a tree knocked athwart the river by lightning or wind. We shambled over it on our hands and knees to the other shore.

We hid for the day in a nearby swamp and slept. Watch rotated from man to man: someone always on guard to protect all from surprise.

At dusk we set off again and walked briskly the whole night, our second [on the move]. As we must shun roads and even houses, so we must proceed without a compass by taking directions from the sun and the stars. The way led through swamps and morasses where few people had been before. Every five minutes we [paused and] listened for anything suspicious.

Poorly fed for a long time [in prison], we now suffered so many hunger pangs that we wanted to risk getting food. (I had left captivity with only a scrap of hard Libby corn bread in my pocket—and lost it while crawling through the tunnel.) So we knocked at the door of a little Negro shack, and shook it and pounded at it, before we heard the voice of the Negress.

"You can't come in. Go away!"

Surprised and almost in despair, we turned to go. Then the Negress popped her head out the window and asked us not to think ill of her insolence.

"My mistress is in the next room. I know who you are—you're escaped Union officers, no less. I spoke rudely in order to mislead her."

We wanted food, did we? Well, she could spare nothing to relieve our misery.

"I've barely enough to keep myself alive."

But, able to help in another way, she informed us of Rebel positions hereabouts and told us what route to take.

Using her counsel to advantage, we walked the night through without rest. Toward morning we rejoined the Chickahominy, nothing short of a quarter-mile wide here. We discussed [the alternatives]. Build a raft or swim? Risky, a raft, because farmers might hear the noise of our cutting the materials: we'd be discovered. Dive and swim? Yes, had the water not been so cold. After some scouting, we saw an armed Rebel in a boat, rowing toward us. He landed, secured the boat, and disappeared. We seized the opportunity, snatched up fallen limbs to aid propulsion, leaped into the boat, crossed, shoved the empty boat back into the current, and climbed the hill that crowded the shore. Looking around on top, we spied the Rebel on the opposite side taking aim at us. He fired and missed. Seemingly out of ammunition, he shot curses at us instead. His behavior brought a roar of laughter from me, despite our distress. He could no longer see us when we headed into the shade of the trees and left him to find his own way home.

We fled like hunted animals. Soon we met a Negro at work in a field. He told us, "You're about five miles from New Kent Court House. Don't go there." He thought we should make for the "settlement of free Negroes" about two miles away; we would get protection and aid there. He explained how the Rebels had set up a strong outpost of pickets, trying to stop desertions [of their own men] to Union lines. We must be near friendly troops, we decided, especially since the [Union] raid on Bottom's Bridge [had shifted them in our favor on 6–7 February 1864]. Therefore we did not heed the Negro. His offer alone sufficed to cheer us.

We covered five times the expected distance, the sun registered high noon, yet we saw nothing [of our presumed destination]. Amid silence and desolation we heard only the crackle of brush under our feet. The sound urged us to continue to care and to struggle. But, lacking evidence that we neared our goal, our hopes for speedy deliverance gradually vanished. Again and again we lost our way in the forest. At last we could endure no longer the exertion, hunger, and pain. We collapsed, stiff with cold and weak, one after the other as if by electric shock. We lay in a grimy heap of misery and distress incarnate: hair long and disheveled in our faces, clothing tattered, feet slashed by thorns and bleeding. Sleep closed my lids. I feasted my mind's eye on the most refreshing scenes—tables laid and loaded with delicacies appeared from memory—and all the [recollected] joys of dining exacerbated my pain.

Awakened from such dreams by hoofbeats, we heard them approach and saw a cavalryman hunting escaped prisoners. We cowered behind a stump until he passed. He did not notice us.

Our way led us again to the Chickahominy. Suddenly the man a few paces in the lead came running and holding high in one hand what he had found: a clam. We all started looking and brought a few more out of the water. They smacked of train oil but, our first food in three days, they tasted delicious.

One of our party, a comrade with us from the beginning, meanwhile wandered along the river, seeking more. In vain we waited his return. We hunted, we shouted and shouted, to no avail.

Three of us remained together and continued the trek. Toward evening we met another Negro at work on a plantation. We called to him. He looked at us with astonished eyes, unable to conceal amazement at men who could come so far from Richmond and suffer no mishap. He told us what his master had told him: a hundred [Union] officers, and more, had escaped; their guards were locked up [afterward]; and many escapees had been [caught and] brought back. "Stay here in the woods until dark," the Negro said [when he left us]. He returned at the appointed time with a basket and distributed bacon and warm fresh-baked corn bread. [Famished] after four days of strenuous hiking, we devoured both. We gave him $6 Confederate for his trouble. This gratuity, every last cent we could shake out of our pockets, so delighted him that he declared one good turn deserved another. He pondered how he might best help our escape, then led us about two miles and asked us to wait until he came back. He reappeared with another Negro and introduced him as his friend. The friend suggested we accompany him to his place to discuss what could be done to aid our flight.[6]

Kind hearts welcomed us to the small, modest cabin, their humble home. [Enjoying] our first offer of hospitality after days afoot, we sat by the hearth and warmed ourselves at the cheery fire.

"I'm a free Negro," our host said. "Name's George Washington."

I trusted him even before he stated his name, but it justified my trust (and time confirmed it). He took keen interest in our stories of suffering in prison. His face confessed determination to help us any way he could and thereby overreach the Rebels. During the conversation the woman of the house served corn bread and bacon, graced with a cup of hot coffee. We took leave of these honest folk, carrying with us their wishes that our flight end happily.

The cabin being on the Chickahominy, our host rowed us in his small boat about eight miles to Jones Farm [or Jones Bridge]. He had brought us as far from his home as his personal safety allowed. We said good-bye and gave him a small gift for his trouble. He left us to our fate.

Our fate promised nothing good, for we still did not know when, where [or how] we could reach our lines. A precarious situation!

I had removed my shoes at the fire, the better to warm my feet. The wet shoes had shrunk so that I could not get them back on feet bloody and swollen. But (as the proverb teaches) necessity knows no law. I removed my coat collar with one cut of my knife, halved it, wrapped a half around each foot, and walked the whole night.

We stumbled onto a trail in the forest. By morning the trail had led us to the road. We trotted along it so fast that, when fortune brought us to another Negro, he said we were but fifteen miles from Williamsburg [Virginia], our destination. Our fondest expectations had been exceeded; we did not think we had approached so near our lines.[7]

Still in danger, however, we could yet be captured by a Rebel patrol or shot by a guerrilla from ambush in the forest. For safety we exacted precautions, hid the entire day in a thick grove of firs, and reconnoitered all around. We sneaked near the house of a secessionist officer and watched him peacefully cultivate his fields. At dusk he entered the house, [came out] armed, mounted a horse, and galloped away, presumably to hunt escaped Yankees. A verse popped into my head as I observed the scene from behind a tall hedge:

> You search so far and wide.
> But look: your prey, the prize, is at your side!

At last the sun went down, and we took up the march again. Soon we saw light in the distance. Hope brightened in us. *Let it be the fires of our outposts.* The thought of reaching the end of our trek cheered us. We neared the light and discovered—a forest fire! Swelling, it drove us, disappointed, out of the cover of trees and onto the road. Illuminating the darkness [it would expose us to enemy eyes]. So we rushed off as fast as we could. [We also fled because] McClellan's troops, camping hereabouts, had felled the trees on either side of the road, to our disadvantage had we been chased. Fortunately the sandy soil provided traction underfoot, else we would have had trouble getting away from there.

The road brought us through a skimpy forest. Meanwhile darkness thickened until we could not distinguish even the things near us. So we did not see the cavalry detachment come around the bend. They startled us with a thundered "Halt!" We dispersed fast into the trees, threw ourselves to the ground, and expected the intruders to leave when they lost sight of us. But they marked the spot [where we entered the trees], rode after us, drew up abreast, and cocked their carbines. In a moment they surrounded us (so quickly it made our heads spin) and issued an order in a tone that would brook no contradiction.

"Come out with your hands up or we'll shoot!"

Unable to find a hole, we could only surrender and accept fate.

A gruff voice demanded, "Who are you and what are you doing here?"

"We're farmers, we live around here."

"You lie," said the commanding officer. "The truth *now* or you'll hang from that tree in a minute."

He called his men to attention and ordered them to dismount. They grabbed us and searched us for weapons.

"So [we confessed] you want the truth? Well, we're Union officers. Yes, officers who escaped from Richmond."

"Just the people we're looking for."

(We would soon learn what the last speech meant.)

"State your corps, regiment, and rank."

We complied.

They shouted: "You're in good hands. We're the Eleventh Pennsylvania Cavalry!"

What? *Pennsylvania* cavalry? They could not be Rebels. Union forces, *our* men, greeted us with glee. Saved! Friendly troops had set us free! To witness their happiness, to receive their sympathy, meant more than any money to us.

Truly the moments when sadness changes to happiness, and happiness to sadness, if brief, pass too fast to seem more than illusions. Only life's [grand] times, those [long enough to] pour over us a cornucopia of delight, endure in memory and [while they last] blot out recollections of days of misery and pain.

My own experience confirms what I have just said. Brought to Richmond a prisoner from Gettysburg's bloody fields, I managed to elude the enemy's jailers after eight months, and escape to a long-desired freedom. Yet when those friends [the Eleventh Cavalry] gathered around, I forgot the horrors of prison and the dangers of flight. I relished the moment in bliss. Nor shall I forget the scene when battle-hardened veterans, used to the abominations of war, could find no words to express their feelings. Tears rose to their eyes [instead of words to their lips] at the sight of us, and they wept without shame. The tears, which signified indignation and rage at the myrmidons [who abused us], also proclaimed joy at meeting us here. What a happy circumstance! The storms of time can never erode my memory of the moment, so firmly is it fixed forever!

Earlier that day, two [other fugitives from the Libby] had fortunately reached General Butler's lines, bearing news of the escape. Butler, commandant of the [Union] Department of Virginia, immediately ordered this 300-man detachment of Colonel [Samuel P.] Spear's Eleventh Pennsylvania to ride out, meet us, and prevent our recapture. And so we met them at midnight of our fifth day [in flight], six miles from Williamsburg.

When the detachment realized our state—hungry, thirsty, and exhausted to the point of collapse—they gave us their food and drink, put us on their horses, and trotted beside us. We had been integrated into the column because guerrillas imperiled the route back to Union lines.

A sudden "Halt!" stopped the column; several more of us had been picked up. We [escapees already in the column] did not see them until later. At last in camp for the night, fires built, we greeted the newcomers: lieutenant colonels [T. S.] West [Twenty-fourth Wisconsin Volunteers] and [H. C.] Hobart [Twenty-first Wisconsin Volunteers].

Early the next morning the bugler sounded departure and the column rode again. Guidons flew a friendly sign to any [escapees] hidden in the forest. None appeared. Unwilling farmers [meanwhile] complied with a forcible requisition and surrendered several two-wheeled carts and some young mares to pull them. We [Libby fugitives] rolled into Williamsburg in triumph.

Without delay, Colonel West, commandant of the garrison, made a place in his barracks, laid an excellent dinner, provided footwear, served port wine (a treat!), and in a fatherly way did everything else [to welcome and comfort us]. As a result I got tight (I humbly confess) for the first time in a long while. Questions and stories seemed unending. Then to bed—with a hearty "Good night!"—in lodgings prepared expressly for us.

At 5:00 the following morning, after breakfast, we got into an ambulance that took us to Yorktown, a two-hour ride. There we joined six or seven of our comrades aboard a steamboat to Fortress Monroe. Every face registered emotion, but nobody said anything and no one put an arm around anyone. Neither word [nor gesture] could have expressed what the long, firm handshake meant.

We told our story to the few civilian passengers. They listened in suspenseful excitement. One of us had by chance kept a bit of Libby corn bread. The civilians accepted crumbs to preserve as relics. In our never-ending struggle against boredom [in the Libby] we had made knives, crosses, needles, and other such things. Accepting them as relics, too, the civilians marveled that we contrived such [conversation pieces] out of mule bones.

In the afternoon we reached Fortress Monroe and reported as ordered to General Butler. Each shook his hand and stated regiment and rank. Welcoming us with a short speech, he expressed pleasure in seeing so many escaped officers. One of us observed that he, Butler, had delayed exchange so long that we could meet him only after having to hazard escape through a sixty-foot tunnel.

The old man [Butler] sent us to a hotel, where each could avail himself of its services to his heart's content. The barber cut hair and beards. Thus groomed, looking a little more human, we marched in formation through the streets. Of course the inevitable reporters set upon us. Details of our hegira appeared in the next day's newspapers. Then a train conveyed us to Washington, and we lodged at the National Hotel. Heroes of the hour and lionized, we brought profit to the owner as people crowded in to see us.

With alacrity we accepted our [back] pay [for the time in prison]. Those who needed medical care received it in hospitals. Then we parted, each hurrying home. I separated from, perhaps never to see again, men who had shared [and become friends] amid hardship.

Of the 104 who escaped, about half reached Union lines. With sorrow we learned of brutality inflicted upon comrades [the recaptured or those left behind in prison]. The end of the war, which came soon, brought them freedom, too.

All who endured shall never forget [the hardships of imprisonment, the dangers of breakout, and the rigors of flight]. Reminiscences will cast shadows across many a face. But stories [of captivity and flight] will shorten the hours at the fireside. And renewed by the salutary peace that now prevails, we can [again] indulge the gentler side of our natures.

The beacon of the future beckons with brilliant light! Let us weigh anchor and sail bravely into new and better times!

Belle Island[1]

[by Joseph Arnold]

The battle [in the morning] of 1 July 1863 took place on an open field [along the Chambersburg Road, west of Gettysburg]. The First and the Eleventh Corps withdrew to the town, where I was taken prisoner. The next day I joined Captain Domschcke [and other prisoners]: Adjutant [Albert] Wallber, eight soldiers of Company A, three of C, one of D, seven of E, six of F, one of G, three of H, six of I, and one of K—all of my regiment [the Twenty-sixth Wisconsin]. I shared leftover crackers with the captain and the adjutant, and made and served them a little coffee, my last. Afterward our captors separated the officers from [us] enlisted men.

Then we [enlisted men] faced the question, *Should we accept parole?* We requested and got permission to discuss it with our officers. I consulted with Captain Domschcke. He told me our government would not recognize such parole. If we accepted it, we must assume responsibility for the consequences. "We officers [he said] are going to Richmond. I advise you men to do likewise." I returned to my fellow prisoners, men of my regiment, and told them what the captain said. We agreed to go to Richmond. Members of other regiments did accept parole, but not an officer or an enlisted man of any Wisconsin regiment accepted it.

On 4 July we began the march to Virginia, and on the eighteenth reached Staunton, 175 miles from Gettysburg. Rations during the march, mainly meat and flour, could not appease our hunger. In Staunton the Rebels made us line up single file, searched every last one of us, and took money, rubber blankets, canteens, and other things. Then we went under guard to an open field [and stayed] without protection from rain or the heat of the sun.

On 19 July 700 of us left for Richmond; on the twentieth, 1,000; on the twenty-first, 600; and on the twenty-second, 800. On the twenty-eighth a number of [other] prisoners, including several officers, joined us. Hearing that they would be robbed of personal effects, they tore up their greenbacks and smashed their watches with stones. The Rebels flew into a rage and clapped the officers in irons. The next day, eight [enlisted men] escaped. On the thirtieth several slave catchers appeared with some [captives] to be shackled: Negroes, fugitive [slaves] from the South, caught near Washington. On the thirty-first the Rebels searched our clothing again but found little except $100 an Italian had hid in his socks—money the Rebels grabbed with glee and never returned. Packed into freight cars, we left Staunton on 4 August and arrived in Richmond the fifth.

We waited several hours at the station. Then [the Rebels] took us to opposite the Libby, put us in a warehouse, and confined us to a space so tiny that we could barely lie down. In surroundings hot and close, we nearly choked. The Rebels searched us again and took our last possessions: backpacks and haversacks. Hours passed. Then we had to leave and march to Belle Island in the James River between Manchester and Richmond.

A building on the island's southern end had been a foundry, and a few houses occupied the northern end. A place [in between] had been designated a prison camp: two acres of tents for about 3,000 inmates, enclosed by an earthwork, a ten-foot-wide ditch, and sentries pacing to and fro outside.

Our names went into the roll book, and we divided into hundred-man squads. I headed the thirty-fourth squad, all Wisconsin men.

I appealed to the lieutenant in charge: we had gone without food since Staunton. He replied gruffly, "You'll get rations in the morning. Not before." We lay down tired and hungry on the ground. A sentry shot at one of us for approaching too near the ditch. We had not been told to avoid the ditch, but he up and fired anyway. On 14 August a sentry shot into the camp for no reason, killed a prisoner, and wounded two others.

Rations [in the morning] consisted of three ounces of bread and an ounce of beef; in the afternoon, another three of bread and a half-pint of thin soup. Famished women of Richmond [thereafter] would set upon food being sent us. Often they stole bread, which meant even more hunger for us.

Almost every day, new prisoners arrived. At the end of August, meat began to diminish. A little cornmeal came but every other day. On the twenty-seventh, Rebels tested cannon with rounds fired over the camp. One missile exploded [above us] and shrapnel fell among the tents, fortunately hurting no one. A prisoner, nearly without clothes, ripped up a tent to cover his nakedness. The commandant ordered him bucked, then hung by the thumbs, then set on a fence post. Physicians had no medicine, illness flourished, and every day a few of us died. In September, meat stopped. From then on, we got only bad corn bread baked without salt. Occasionally the Rebels brought sweet potatoes, but fewer than one per man, and no wood to cook them. Hunger racked us to madness. We suffered from cold because the Rebels brought scanty wood: three pieces every three or four days—for twenty men. In November a prisoner from the Libby visited us, General Neal Dow. We told him our troubles. He said that he and his fellows there received equally meager rations. He said that our government would send clothes. On 10 November a few did arrive and with them our first soap since capture. When winter began, hunger grew to starvation. We ate dogs, mice, and rats.[2] The lieutenant in charge [of a section] arrived to see *his* dog being skinned after prisoners had caught and killed it. He forced them to eat the flesh of his pet raw. (They ate it without complaint.) One day a sick man swallowed his bread and vomited. Another man hurried there, gathered the regurgitated bread out of the sand, and ate it. (I witnessed this abomination that day and another time [later].)[3] A number of the mortally sick lay where they had been put: behind the hospital tent about forty feet from us. There they remained for days, alone and helpless, the pitiful wretches. Hogs chewed the faces of some of them.[4] Every morning we found comrades frozen to death or dead by starvation. The dead littered the ground a long time before the Rebels deigned to bury them.[5]

After we endured that deplorable existence—after hunger, cold, and sickness devastated our ranks—we were transported at last to City Point and exchanged, 7 March 1864.

German[-American] Officers Imprisoned, 1 May 1863 to 1 March 1865 at Richmond, Danville, Macon, Savannah, Charleston, and Columbia

[Unless an exception is noted, the first date after a name is that of capture; the second, of exchange. Deviations from alphabetical order are Domschcke's.]

Lieutenant Colonels and Majors

Helmerich, Gustav von—Lt. Col.—4th Mo. Cav.—29 June 1863 (Independence, Tenn.), Apr. 1864; captured again, June 1864; exchanged 1 March 1865.

Schrader, Alexander von—Lt. Col. & Insp. Gen. XIV Corps—19 Sept. 1863 (Chickamauga), [?] Mar. 1864.

Mitzl, Alexander von—Maj.—74th Pa. Inf.—1 July 1863 (Gettysburg); escaped from the Libby, 9 Feb. 1864.

Muhlmann, J. B.—Maj. & Asst. Adj. Gen.—20 Sept. 1863 (Chickamauga), 1 Mar. 1865.

Kowacz, Stephen—Maj.—54th N.Y. Inf.—1 July 1863 (Gettysburg), Apr. 1864.

Captains

Biebel, H—6th Conn. Inf.—14 May 1864 (Drury's [Drewry's] Bluff, Va.), 1 Mar. 1865.

Busch, J. T.—16th Ill. Cav.—in the Libby from autumn 1863; 1 Mar. 1865.

Dietz, Heinrich—45th N.Y. Inf.—1 July 1863 (Gettysburg), 1 Mar. 1865.

Dircks, C. S. F.—1st Tenn. Inf.—26 Jan. 1863 (Nashville), 1 Mar. 1865.

Domschcke, Bernhard—26th Wis. Inf.—1 July 1863 (Gettysburg), 1 Mar. 1865.

Fiedler, J.—Engineer.—7 Aug. 1864 (Jonesboro, Ga.) 1 Mar. 1865.

Frey, Ernst—82d Ill. Inf.—1 July 1863 (Gettysburg), [?] 1864.

Goetz, Joseph—22d Mich. Inf.—20 Sept. 1863 (Chickamauga), 1 Mar. 1865.

Haack, Adolph von—68th N.Y. Inf.—1 July 1863 (Gettysburg), 1 Mar. 1865.

Heil, J.—45th N.Y. [Inf.]—1 July 1863 (Gettysburg), 1 Mar. 1865.

Heltemes, J. B.—18th Ky. Cav.—23 June 1864 (Dalton, Ga.), 1 Mar. 1865.

Hendrick, F.—1st N.Y. Cav.—14 June 1863 (Winchester, Va.), 1 Mar. 1865.

Herzog, R. H. O.—1st N.Y. Cav.—23 Apr. 1864 (Shenandoah Valley), 1 Mar. 1865.

Irsch, Franz—45th N.Y. Inf.—1 July 1863 (Gettysburg), 1 Mar. 1865.

Krause, J.—3d Pa. Arty.—24 Apr. 1864 (Plymouth, N.C.), exchanged at the end of 1864.

Kronemeyer, C.—52d N.Y. Inf.—8 May 1864 (Spotsylvania Court House), 1 Mar. 1865.

Memmert, F.—[?]—5th Md. Cav.—[?] June 1863 [?]—[?] Mar. 1864.

Ritter, H.—52d N.Y. Inf.—22 June 1864 (Petersburg, Va.), 1 Mar. 1865.

Rose, Carl—4th Mo. Cav.—10 July 1863 (Union City, Tenn.); escaped from the Libby, 9 Feb. 1864.

Syring, Wilhelm—45th N.Y. Inf.—1 July 1863 (Gettysburg), 1 Mar. 1865.

Thoenssen, B. C.—9th Ohio Inf.—20 Sept. 1863 (Chickamauga), 1 Mar. 1865.

Ulfers, H. A.—Asst. Adj. Gen.—[?]—6 June 1864 (Bethsaida [Bethesda] Church, Va.); escaped from Columbia at the end of 1864.

Van der Hoof, J.—45th N.Y. Inf.—1 July 1865 [i.e., 1863] (Gettysburg), 1 Mar. 1865.

Zeis, Heinrich—80th Ill. Inf.—3 May 1863 (Rome, Ga.), 1 Mar. 1865.

Lieutenants

Ahlert, J. H.—2d Lt.—45th N.Y. Inf.—1 July 1863 (Gettysburg), 1 Mar. 1865.

Altstädt, C. L.—1st Lt. & Adj.—54th N.Y. Inf.—1 July 1863 (Gettysburg), 1 Mar. 1865.

Bader, Hermann—1st Lt.—29th Mo. Inf.—27 Nov. 1863 (Ringgold, Ga.); escaped, 1865.

Bath, H.—1st Lt.—45th N.Y. Inf.—1 July 1863 (Gettysburg), 1 Mar. 1865.

Bath, W.—2d Lt.—132d N.Y. Inf.—2 [sic] 1864 (New Bern, S.C.); escaped at the end of 1864.

Bülow, H. von—1st Lt.—3d N.Y. Cav.—6 July 1864 (Williamsport, Md.), 1 Mar. 1865.

Candler, Hugo—1st Lt.—45th N.Y. Inf.—1 July 1863 (Gettysburg), 1 Mar. 1865.

Cohn, M.—1st Lt.—4th Ky. Cav.—23 Apr. 1863 (Lookout Mountain), exchanged?

Cramer, C. P.—1st Lt.—21st N.Y. Cav.—1 July 1864 (Petersburg, Va.), 1 Mar. 1865.

Cloedt, A. von—1st Lt.—119th N.Y. Inf.—[1] July 1863 (Gettysburg), 1 Mar. 1865.

Curtis, Rudolph—2d Lt.—4th Ky. Cav.—21 Sept. 1863 (Lookout Valley, Tenn.), 1 Mar. 1865.

Dieffenbach, Adam—1st Lt.—73d Pa. Inf.—5 Nov. 1863 (Mission[ary] Ridge), 1 Mar. 1865.

Diemer, Michael—2d Lt.—10th Mo. Inf.—16 May 1863 (Jackson, Miss.), 1 Mar. 1865.

Fischer, Robert—1st Lt.—17th Mo. Inf.—27 Nov. 1863 (Ringgold, Pa. [i.e., Ga.]), 1 Mar. 1865.

Gareis, A. J.—1st Lt. & Adj.—1st Md. Cav.—9 June 1863 (Brandy Station, Va.) 1 Mar. 1865.

Gerhardt, Hugo—1st Lt.—24th Ill. Inf.—20 Sept. 1863 (Chickamauga), 1 Mar. 1865.

Gerson, Otto—2d Lt.—45th N.Y. Inf.—1 July 1863 (Gettysburg); murdered by a Rebel sentry in Macon, 12 June 1863.

Gross, Theodor—2d Lt.—21st Ill. Inf.—20 Sept. 1863 (Chickamauga), exchanged?

Gutland, Ch[arles] F.—1st Lt.—124th N.Y. Inf.—1 July 1863 (Gettysburg), 1 Mar. 1865.

Hallenberg, Gustav—[?]—10th Ill. Inf.—20 Sept. 1863 (Chickamauga), exchanged?

Hauf, Adam—1st Lt.—45th N.Y. Inf.—1 July 1863 (Gettysburg), 1 Mar. 1865.

Hepp, Eugen—1st Lt.—82d Ill. Inf.—1 July 1863 (Gettysburg); escaped from Charleston, 5 Oct. 1864.

Herzberg, F.—1st Lt.—66th N.Y. Inf.—17 June 1863 (Gettysburg, Va.), 1 Mar. 1865.

Kost, R.—1st Lt.—6th Conn. Inf.—8 July 1863 (Fort Wagner, S.C.), 1 Mar. 1865.

Krüger, Wilhelm—1st Lt.—2d Mo. Inf.—23 Sept. 1863 (Chickamauga), 1 Mar. 1865.

Kühn, A.—1st Lt.—5th Md. Inf.—15 June 1863 (Winchester, Va.), exchanged?

Kunkel, Edward—2d Lt.—45th N.Y. Inf.—1 July 1863 (Gettysburg), 1 Mar. 1865.

Leydecker, Jakob—1st Lt.—45th [N.Y.?] Inf.—1 July 1863 (Gettysburg); died in Savannah at the beginning of Sept. 1864.

Lindmeyer, Louis—1st Lt.—45th N.Y. Inf.—1 July 1863 (Gettysburg), 1 Mar. 1865.

Mayer, Leopold—1st Lt.—12th Pa. [?]—17 June 1863 (Point of Rocks, Md.), 1 Mar. 1865.

Muri, Kasimir—2d Lt.—15th Mo. Inf.—20 Sept. 1863 (Chickamauga), 1 Mar. 1865.

Mussehl, Otto—1st Lt.—68th N.Y. Inf.—2 July 1863 (Gettysburg), 1 Mar. 1865.

Mylius, Victor—2d Lt.—68th N.Y. Inf.—1 July 1863 (Gettysburg), 1 Mar. 1865.

Newbrandt, J. F.—2d Lt.—4th Mo. Cav.—10 July 1863 (Union City, Tenn.); escaped, Feb. 1865.

Niedenhoffen, C.—1st Lt.—9th Minn. Inf.—12 July 1864 (Brie's Cross Roads, Va.), 1 Mar. 1865.

Niemeyer, Bernhard—2d Lt.—11th Ky. Cav.—22 Oct. 1863 (Philadelphia, eastern Tenn.), 1 Mar. 1865.

Pentzel, D.—1st Lt.—4th N.Y. Cav.—16 Sept. 1865 [i.e., 1863] (Raccoon Ford, Va.), exchanged?

Reinecke, G.—1st Lt.—5th Pa. Cav.—29 June 1864 (Petersburg, Va.), Mar. 1865.

Rothe, H.—1st Lt.—15th N.Y. Arty.—15 May 1864 (Spotsylvania Court House), [1?] Mar. 1865.

Sachs, Johann—1st Lt.—5th [?] Cav.—[?] June 1863 (Winchester, Va.), [?] Apr. 1863.

Schroeder, Hugo—2d Lt.—82 Ill. Inf.—[?] July 1863 (Gettysburg), 1 Mar. 1865.

Schroeders, Edgar—2d Lt.—74th Pa. Inf.—1 July 1863 (Gettysburg), 1 Mar. 1865.

Schühle, Georg—2d Lt.—45th N.Y. Inf.—1 July 1863 (Gettysburg), 1 March 1865.

Schweinfurth, Fr[anz?]—1st Lt.—24th Ill Inf.—23 Sept. [1863] (Chickamauga), 1 Mar. 1865.

Spindler, G.—1st Lt.—73d Ill. Inf.—23 Sept. 1863 (Gettysburg [Chickamauga?]), exchanged?

Sutter, Carl—1st Lt.—39th N.Y. Inf.—2 Dec. 1863 (Germania Ford, Va.), 1 Mar. 1865.

Veltford, G.—2d Lt.—54th N.Y. Inf.—1 July 1863 (Gettysburg), 1 Mar. 1865.

Wallber, Albert—1st Lt. & Adj.—26th Wis. [Inf.]—1 July 1863 (Gettysburg); escaped from the Libby, 9 Feb. 1864.

Wassow, F.—2d Lt.—54th N.Y. Inf.—1 [July] 1863 (Gettysburg), 1 Mar. 1865.

Wieser, Louis—2d Lt.—1st Md. Cav.—9 June 1863 (Brandy Station, Va.); autumn 1864.

Zobel, C.—1st Lt.—15th N.Y. Arty.—6 May 1864 (Wilderness, Va.), 1 Mar. 1865.

English Words and Phrases
Used in the Original Text

This list of English used spontaneously in the German text omits the English of deliberate quotation, especially of someone Domschcke heard speaking, including commands and conventional expressions: *good-bye,* for example, or *Pack up!* Specialized English, quoted because it defied translation into German, is also omitted here: such as *Yank, Reb, fresh fish, deadline,* or *greenback.* All nouns are singular below, but nearly all are plural in the text.

bill of exchange (a promissory note)
blanket
broker
bunk (a bed)
bushel (the unit of measure)
clam (the shellfish)
clerk (noun)
clown (a comic performer)
comfort (noun)
commissary, chief commissary (a person in charge of supplies)
cracker (the food; hardtack)
double-quick (speed of personal locomotion)
Dutchman (misnomer for German)
dysentery
exchange stock (shares of ownership publicly bought and sold)
excitement
farce
flag of truce
general hospital
hazard (the game of dice)
hurrah
long roll (the drum signal)
mess (arrangements for eating and the eating itself, esp. in the military)
mush (the cornmeal dish)

office (a place for conducting business)
parole (the release of a prisoner, with conditions)
pint
quart
raid (noun)
ream (the unit of measure of paper)
retailer
roll call
sanitary goods (anything for prisoners' aid, sent or provided by the
    Sanitary Commission)
shed (a building)
siesta
sink (a cesspool)
skillet
skylight
sorghum (the syrup from the plant of the same name)
soup (the liquid food)
special order
squad
stockade
sutler
tierce (the unit of volume: 42 gallons)
under fire (the state of being exposed to bombardment)
worst cases (the critically ill)
yard (three feet)

Notes

Preface

1. See Lonn, *Foreigners in the Confederacy* and *Foreigners in the Union Army and Navy.*
2. Lonn, *Foreigners in the Union Army and Navy,* 94. See also Kaufmann, *Die Deutschen,* and Rosengarten, *The German Soldier.*
3. See Heinrici, *Das Buch der Deutschen,* and Zimmermann, *Deutsch in Amerika.*
4. Faust, *The German Element,* 2:365–72. See also Arndt and Olson, *German-American Newspapers,* and Wittke, *The German-Language Press.*
5. Arndt and Olson, *German-American Newspapers,* 568.
6. Chukovsky, *High Art,* 6, 89.
7. Tribe, "Notes on Translation," xix.
8. Ibid.
9. Amis, "Broken Lances," 106.

Introduction

1. Boyd, "In Search of the South," 91.
2. Powell, "An Old Dispute."
3. Nevins, *War for the Union,* 3:196–97.
4. Wright, *A Study of War,* 67; Abdill, *Civil War Railroads,* 5.
5. See Ropp, *War in the Modern World,* 143.
6. Quoted by Grebner, "*Die Neuner,*" 140.
7. Walker, *History,* 1:1–195 passim, esp. 55.
8. Nussbaum, *Concise History,* 52, 318.
9. *De jure et oficiis bellicis et disciplina militari.* See Walker, *History,* 1:247–49.
10. Walker, *History,* 1:249–50, 252–63.
11. Ibid., 383–84, 318, 320.
12. Nussbaum, *Concise History,* 224.
13. Bk. 15, sec. 2 (Nugent trans., 1:236).
14. Ruddy, *International Law,* 246–47.
15. Bk.3, secs. 151–54; see Gilmore, *Notes,* 200–203.
16. Bk. 4, chap. 4, in *Political Writings* (Watkins ed., 10).
17. "The Civil War [for example], fought by every element in the Northern and Southern population, was a people's war . . . in a fuller sense than any earlier conflict of modern time" (Nevins, *War for the Union,* 1:v).
18. Due to the war, America became ordered "on a national scale," an organized society in the modern sense (ibid., 4:395; see also 2:viii).
19. Harwell, in Cooke, *Outlines,* xi.
20. Winston, *Lee,* 206.
21. Kniffin, "Battle," 630–31.
22. Grant, "Battle," 479.
23. Lewis, *Sherman,* 415.
24. Ibid., 636.

25. On the Civil War's being a new kind of war, and of massive proportions that fore-shadowed and influenced future wars, see McElwee, *Art of War*, 147–83.

26. Cf. the 165,000 engaged and the more than 50,000 casualties at Gettysburg in 1863.

27. Nussbaum, *Concise History*, 224–26.

28. Montross, *War*, 591. See also Connelly, "Civil War," 222, 224.

29. Freidel, *Lieber*, vii.

30. Ibid., 323.

31. Ibid., 334. In composing the code, Lieber consulted his predecessors and seemed to like Grotius but "scorned 'old' Vattel" (ibid., 333).

32. Ibid., 334–41. See also Harley, *Lieber*, 149–54. For the text of General Orders No. 100, see Lieber, *Lieber's Code*, 45–71.

33. Articles 15, 49–61, 67, 71–80, 105–110, 119–33. See also article 16: "Military necessity does not admit of cruelty"; and article 68: "Unnecessary or revengeful destruction of life is not lawful." Echoes of Lieber's predecessors, from Caliph abu-Bakr through Rousseau, are strong in those phrases.

34. Robertson, "Scourge," 184. See also Hesseltine, *Civil War Prisons*, 52–53, 99–204. Cf. Murphy, "A Confederate Soldier's View," 101–11, an atypical memoir that speaks of prison as fairly comfortable. In February 1863, 10 percent (387 of 3,884) of the inmates died in Camp Douglas near Chicago, "a mortality rate for one month not exceeded by any other large prison during the war" (H. Thompson, *Prisons and Hospitals*, 73).

35. The story has been often and extensively told. Hesseltine, *Civil War Prisons*, 133–58, is authoritative.

36. Ibid., 114–32, 159–71.

37. Perry-Mosher, "Rock Island," 30.

38. W. C. Thompson, "From the Defense," 43, 44.

39. Shewmon, "Amazing Ordeal" (April), 45.

40. Destler, "Andersonville Prison Diary," 57.

41. Moore, "Reminiscence," 454.

42. Heslin, "Diary," 261.

43. In honesty, it should be noted that, in spite of the evidence arrayed against him, the case was not open and shut; he has had his defenders (Hesseltine, *Civil War Prisons*, 238–58).

44. See Luttwak, *Dictionary*, s.v. "Geneva Convention."

45. Scott, *Military Dictionary*, 470.

46. Nevins, *War for the Union*, vol. 2; caption to frontispiece.

47. Coblentz, *From Arrow to Atom Bomb*, 340. See also Custance, *Study of War*, 3–4.

48. Grant, *Papers*, 4:281.

49. Ibid., 10:422.

50. Ropp, *War in the Modern World*, 161, quoting Henderson, *Science of War*, 213–14.

51. Ibid.

52. Eaton, *History*, 105–6.

53. *Official Records*, 2d ser., 7:685.

54. Ibid., 614–15. See also ibid., 606–7.

55. Nevins, *War for the Union*, 2:viii. See also 4:395.

56. Wilde, *Letters*, 568–69.

57. Melville, *Billy Budd*, chaps. 21, 22, 25 (Hayford and Smealts ed., 110–13, 115, 123). Vizinczey, "Engineers of Sham," 71–72.

58. Porch, Review of *On Writing*, 9.

59. Winston, *Lee*, 236.

60. Freeman, *Lee*, 4:254–55.

61. "Order of Retaliation; or, General Orders No. 252," in Lincoln, *Collected Works*, 6:357.

62. "In tactics as well as weapons this struggle is the first in history which can readily be identified with the warfare of the present day" (Montross, *War*, 591).

63. Nevins, Robertson, and Wiley, *Civil War Books*, 1:v. See also 2:v.

64. Byrne, "Prisons," in ibid., 1:185–206.

65. See also Hesseltine, "Civil War Prisons," 117–20.

66. Schlicher, "Domschcke," 319–20. For Domschcke's biography, see ibid., 319–32, 435–56, and *Dictionary of Wisconsin Biography*, s.v. "Domschcke, Bernard [*sic*]."

67. Koss, *Milwaukee,* quoted by Schlicher, "Domschcke," 329.

68. On Germans and the Republican party, see Lonn, *Foreigners in the Union Army and Navy,* 43–46.

69. They joined the Twenty-sixth Wisconsin Volunteers, an infantry regiment made up almost entirely of men of German birth or parentage. Domschcke began as a 2d lieutenant. On 17 September 1862 the Twenty-sixth mustered in and went to Washington, D.C., and then to Fairfax Court House, Virginia, where it became part of Sigel's Eleventh Corps and saw its first significant action at Chancellorsville, 30 April and 1 May 1863 (Love, *Wisconsin in the War,* 396–400).

70. His book is especially useful because "the historian of Libby is impoverished by the lack of primary sources undebased by subsequent revision" (Byrne, "A General behind Bars," 164). Among the first to publish a full-length memoir (1865), Domschcke did not have time to debase it by subsequent revision.

71. Cf. e.g. Armstrong, "Cahaba to Charleston," and Glazier, *The Capture.*

72. Schlicher, "Domschcke," 456.

Chapter 1

1. Domschcke may say "wretched" because the Union loss at Chancellorsville was blamed "on the Eleventh Corps in general and the Germans [in its ranks] in particular" (Trefousse, *Carl Schurz,* 134). The divisions under Schurz, Steinwehr, and Devens allegedly lost their nerve and ran without a fight. The quality of German courage became a scandal of the war, and the rehabilitation of German honor a cause célèbre afterward.

2. General George Gordon Meade, now in command of the Army of the Potomac, was moving to deal with Lee.

3. Domschcke's freethinking skepticism in religion, which he shared with other Forty-eighters, expresses itself here and in other places in this book.

4. The Twenty-sixth crossed the Maryland-Pennsylvania border, heard artillery, and saw Gettysburg and "beyond it the smoke of battle." The enemy "very hotly engaged" the Twenty-sixth on the other side of Gettysburg. The Twenty-sixth "checked the enemy's advance" and held the position until flanked and driven back "over open fields and under the fire [that] proved fatal to many." After a second engagement on the town's outskirts, only four officers remained with the regiment and unhurt. Domschcke was among the captured (Love, *Wisconsin in the War,* 417–18).

5. Perhaps Domschcke refers here to the tax in kind of 24 April 1863, assessing one-tenth of the land's produce for the year, or to the impressment-of-property act of 26 March 1863, authorizing seizure of forage and other goods, chattels, and slaves for use by the army.

6. Paroles and exchanges, to be regulated and enforced, were not forbidden absolutely. General Orders No. 207 was issued, not by Halleck, but "by order of the Secretary of War" (*Official Records,* 2d Ser., 6:78–79). See also Hesseltine, *Civil War Prisons,* 99.

7. The order did not mention countersigning.

8. The dapper Pickett wore shoulder-length hair perfumed and in ringlets (Boatner, *Civil War Dictionary,* 652).

9. "Pickett's Charge" of three brigades, broken and repulsed near Emmitsburg Road, withdrew beaten and devastated at the end of the battle but won immortality for Pickett though he neither commanded the Confederate forces nor led the majority of troops (ibid., 651).

10. It was the decisive engagement, beginning with a massive exchange of artillery and ending with the failure of Pickett's Charge.

11. For his German-language readers, Domschcke, here and throughout this book, specified "American" to distinguish the speaker from the many German-Americans around Domschcke. He refers to them as "Germans."

Chapter 2

1. When a prisoner of war signs a parole, "he [promises he] will bear no arms against the captor, will not visit certain localities, or will not give aid and comfort to the enemy," and

goes free, subject to those restrictions (Hesseltine, *Civil War Prisons*, 1). Hence the prisoner acts on his own initiative and pledges his word of honor; the offering and accepting of parole is up to captor and prisoner. When a prisoner of war is exchanged, he becomes an item of barter, usually traded "grade for grade, and man for man" (ibid., 2) by governments or commanders, without the prisoner's having any say in the matter. Thus Domschcke speaks here of prisoners deliberating and deciding whether to accept parole. Had it been a question of exchange, they would have had no voice in the outcome.

2. "Halleck's order" is General Orders No. 207, issued by the secretary of war, 3 July 1863, limiting paroles and exchanges (*Official Records*, 2d ser., 6:78–79). See Hesseltine, *Civil War Prisons*, 99.

3. Domschcke's garbled sentence has been adjusted in the translation, with reference to General Orders No. 207 (*Official Records*, 2d ser., 6:78–79).

4. The distance, at least thirty miles, seems too great to have been covered in one night by a concourse moving at a crawl.

5. Domschcke quotes the woman's words in English.

6. Probably a pie, sour because of a war-induced lack of sugar. See Starr, "In and Out of Confederate Prisons," 72.

7. A crowd of sympathetic and hostile onlookers created a stir. Guards "roughly warned away" the sympathetic who inquired "after friends in the North." The hostile shouted: "We all love you all and are going to keep you with us. . . . Now you have got to Richmond, we hope you will like it. . . . You won't be lonesome long, for General Lee will bring in all your friends to see you. . . . You'uns is fools to fight we'uns." In addition, "epithets too vile to mention were hurled at us, often by women, too, and menaces were made" (Isham, "Experience in Rebel Prisons," 29).

8. The *Examiner*, an outspoken paper, urged extreme positions during the war, after saying on 8 May 1861 that to win "we need a dictator" (Long, *Civil War Day by Day*, 71).

9. It seems strange that doubt arose. Large signs on the building's north and south sides identified "Libby Prison" (*Official Atlas*, 126, pls. 2, 3).

Chapter 3

1. In addition to the Libby for officers, Richmond's wartime prisons included Castle Thunder and several other buildings near the Libby, mostly for political prisoners and enlisted men, and Belle Isle on the island of the same name in the James River, chiefly for enlisted men. The Libby, "a large three-story brick building, old and somewhat dilapidated" (Glazier, *The Capture*, 42), stood near Twentieth and Cary streets, hard by the Lynchburg Canal and near and in full view of the James (Earle, "In and Out of Libby Prison," 257). "A great white sign extended across the sidewalk, from the west wall to a column. On it were painted these memorable words, 'Libby & Son, Ship Chandlers and Grocers' " (MacCauley, "From Chancellorsville to Libby Prison," 201). At various times during the war, the Libby contained 1,000 and perhaps over 1,200 Union army and navy officers, as well as a few civilians (Cavada, *Libby Life*, 69; Hobart, "Libby Prison," 397; Starr, "In and Out of Confederate Prisons," 75). Though less infamous than Andersonville, "the very name of Libby has become synonymous with that of *terror;* it carries tyranny and oppression in its very sound" (Kellogg, *Life and Death*, 358–59).

2. Streight and his 1,700 cavalry raiders intended to destroy Confederate railroads. Tired and discouraged by increasing trouble, the raiders surrendered to Nathan Bedford Forrest at Cedar Bluff, Alabama, on 3 May (Long, *Civil War Day by Day*, 337, 339, 348).

3. Imboden left Monterey, Virginia, on 20 April 1863 in a joint raid with General William E. ("Grumble") Jones, against the Baltimore & Ohio Railroad in West Virginia. The raid ended with partial success on 14 May (ibid., 340; Boatner, *Civil War Dictionary*, 445). During these operations, the raiders "plundered" Domschcke and his fellow prisoners at Staunton. Domschcke discusses the incident in Chapter 2 above.

4. "Money and other valuables on the person of a prisoner . . . are regarded by the American Army as the private property of the prisoner, and the appropriation of such valuables or money is considered dishonorable, and is prohibited" (Article No. 72, "General Orders No. 100" [Lieber's Laws of War] in Lieber, *Lieber's Code*, 45–71). Union prisoners

typically reported, however, that Confederates searched them everywhere and took anything of value. Shoes were taken and not replaced or were exchanged for "fragmentary apologies for shoes" (Putnam, "An Experience in Virginia Prisons," 211). All of Joseph Moody's clothes were taken in return for a grab-bag of others that fit badly. Moody put a $20 bill in his mouth to save it, leaving a $5 bill "in the pocket-book to divert the suspicion of having money hidden" (Moody, "Life in Confederate Prisons," 351). Thus, captives had to "run the gauntlet" at each prison when transferred. Searchers often used force. Prisoners early in the war surrendered valuables freely, thinking that they would be returned. Later, having learned otherwise, "our men [tried] to conceal their valuables, before or after capture." Conceal- ment, when discovered, meant "punishment of a cruel and sometimes of a revolting character," including "beating and other personal violence." Jailers "at Richmond, as shown by the testimony, became by practice specially expert in searching and robbing prisoners and detecting concealment" (Congressional Committee on Treatment of Prisoners Report, 25).

5. Office decorations would elevate jailers' morale and further depress that of prisoners called in there. Captured Union regimental flags hung upside down on the walls (Galloupe, "Reminiscences of a Prisoner of War," 507).

6. Libby memoirists usually mention the cells. The "dungeon" meant the entire Libby below street level. Some of its cells boasted barred windows that looked up at the street if they had not been boarded shut. Interior cells, impregnable on every side, became autono- mous hells: four men in twelve square feet; an open tub for excrement, not removed for days, producing an atmosphere "most noisome"; no letters in or out; and a "scanty, filthy ration," eaten in the guard's presence. A prisoner sick in a cell had to recover on his own or die (Isham, "Experience in Rebel Prisons," 34–35).

7. Prisoners extended this sarcasm and referred to the "*Hôtel de Libby*" (Chamberlain, "Scenes in Libby Prison," 351).

8. This Turner lived at the home of Richard R. Turner in Richmond. Though friends, companions, and colleagues at the Libby, the Turners seem not to have been related. Richard's son William remembered Thomas as "an undersized man, very quick and active"; voice "sharp and decisive"; and "very kind, but very positive" (Turner, "War-Time Recollec- tions," 620).

9. This "stern, dark-complexioned man" (Moody, "Life in Confederate Prisons," 352), once had Robert Ford, a black teamster who carried letters between prisoners and the outside, laid over a barrel, and while four men held him, lashed him 500 times. Long after Ford lost consciousness "the brutal Turner continued to whip his insensible form" (Congres- sional Committee on Treatment of Prisoners Report, 233). Turner's son remembered a man called the Libby Lion, dark of hair and strong of hand, with "eyes so mild and blue, and such a merry twinkle when he laughed! But [angry] they turned dark . . . and flashed. His hand was so soft yet so very strong that when it held mine I felt I was safe from every evil on earth." When Union forces took Richmond, they turned the Libby into a prison for Con- federates. Turner, imprisoned there, "experienced all the terrible sufferings which the Union soldiers had endured in the same place," including hunger, rags for clothes, and maggots in a bayonet wound. His son saw him once reach an emaciated arm through the bars for a scrap of food dropped by a tourist (Turner, "War-Time Recollections," 620, 621).

10. "Little Ross, the prison clerk," was "none of the brightest, because he could not count a thousand Yankees" (Glazier, The Capture, 86). "I saw a man ["Ras" Ross] with a book in his hand, and he kept hollerin' out something, and all the Yankees would holler back at him"; some "would say 'Here'" and "some would say 'Present'" (Turner, "War-Time Recollec- tions," 620–21). Ross would snap, "Fall in, yer Yanks, in four rows." To confound him, they would drop out of line after being counted on the right, and fall in again on the left. Or, when each prisoner passed before Ross in a count, some would crawl out a scuttle in the roof, reenter behind him, and pass by another time. Again, one prisoner would answer to the name of another who was digging in the escape tunnel. The first would not reply to his own until he was called specially, and he would say he did not know roll call had occurred—leaving the exact number of prisoners uncertain (Earle, "In and Out of Libby Prison," 260–61). Ross became a clerk at the Spottswood Hotel in Richmond after the war. When the hotel burned in the mid-1880s, he died in the flames (Moody, "Life in Confederate Prisons," 352–53).

11. This old soldier had fought with a Pennsylvania regiment in the Mexican War. At the

Libby his principal work was to communicate orders to prisoners (Chamberlain, "Scenes in Libby Prison," 349–50).

12. Greenbacks (the popular name for United States notes issued after 1862) remained standard in commerce for years. Because both sides printed money with nothing behind it, values fluctuated continually, in the abstract and in a comparative sense. But change always went toward less and less purchasing power for more and more dollars. The greenback remained greater—usually a great deal greater—in value than the Southern grayback. In May 1864, for example, an orange cost $20 Confederate in Richmond. So Southerners sought always to acquire Northern money, while both sides preferred gold over paper (see Milton, *Conflict,* 183–93, esp. 184–85).

13. Another prisoner called him "Old Newsboy 'Ben,'" a "jolly old negro" who "goes along past the prison crying, 'Great tallyraphic news in de papers! Mighty news from de Army of Northern Virginy! Great fightin' in de Souf-west!" (Glazier, *The Capture,* 56–57).

14. He carried embers and burning tar through the rooms to fumigate them. "Bery beneficial to the gemmen," he would say, "kase it was a Union smoke" (Earle, "In and Out of Libby Prison," 259).

15. Rumors of exchange grew into "a frightful epidemic of that alarming malady known as 'Exchange on the Brain'" (Cavada, *Libby Life,* 128).

Chapter 4

1. Confusing *Dutch* and *Deutsch* (German for "German"), and finding *Dutch* easier to pronounce, Americans since the eighteenth century have referred to Germans as Dutch, as in the misnomer "Pennsylvania Dutch."

2. Domschcke here refers again to the allegedly cowardly German divisions of the Eleventh Corps who, the report claimed and anti-Germans maintained, fled without a fight at Chancellorsville, causing the Union defeat. See Chapter 1, note 1, above.

3. In another pastime, audiences would gather around a fellow prisoner skilled in story-telling. Reading also helped pass the time. To share the few books available, prisoners would "club together" and pass around a book that belonged to one of them. "Many a time in the bright Southern starlight, have I read and reread and committed to memory passages from some favorite author, many of which I have never forgotten, as the associations have firmly fixed them in my mind" (Mattocks, "In Six Prisons," 169).

4. Cavada was born in Cuba of a Spanish father and an American mother. After education in Philadelphia, he became a lieutenant colonel leading Pennsylvania volunteers in the Civil War. In the first Cuban war of independence, he was a major general and the commander in chief of Cuban forces. In 1871 he died before a Spanish firing squad (Jova, prefatory matter, in *Libby Life,* by Cavada, pages not numbered).

5. The reference is to the enthusiasm of revivalism that flourished, with all manner of passionate expression, during the first half of the century in America (Sweet, *Story of Religions,* 332–34, 396). At a Methodist camp meeting in Allen County, Indiana, in 1852, amid "paroxysms of laughter and cataleptic trances," preachers "rave like maniacs and foam at the mouth until their voices degenerate to hoarse roaring, their teeth rattle, and their arms fall lifelessly at their sides" ("'Life in the Wild,'" 159).

6. "Edited by a witty and intelligent chaplain" (probably Bouldrye), the *Chronicle* "descants with considerable acumen upon the various occurrences of our prison-life." Articles were written on slips of paper, Cavada reported further, with "publication" being when the editor would read the slips aloud to an audience sitting on the floor around him (Cavada, *Libby Life,* 36).

7. With "numerous early lives of Jackson" (*Dictionary of American Biography,* s.v. "Jackson, Thomas Jonathon"), Domschcke's references to this one are too few and too general for it to be identified.

8. Domschcke could have based this discussion of Jackson on one or several biographies, on newspaper accounts, on word of mouth, or on all of these sources.

9. According to Boatner, they called him "Tom Fool Jackson" (*Civil War Dictionary,* 433).

10. Mitchel (1815–75) died in the land of his birth, Ireland, but lived in America for over

twenty years, sent three sons to the Confederate army and, while editing the pro-South *Enquirer,* served on the army's ambulance committee (*Dictionary of American Biography,* s.v. "Mitchel, John").

11. Pollard (1831–72), though generally pro-Confederacy, bitterly opposed Jefferson Davis (ibid., s.v. "Pollard, Edward Alfred").

12. Domschcke may be confused here. Pollard's *Examiner* asserted the strongest anti-Davis opinions.

13. Prisoners also played cards, checkers, and chess; performed or listened to music; and organized the Libby Prison Minstrels and other groups for amusement (Earle, "In and Out of Libby Prison," 262).

14. Moody, "Life in Confederate Prisons," 352, and Cochran, "Reminiscences of Life in Rebel Prisons," 337, generally agree with Domschcke on the Sawyer-Flynn incident, but disagree with Domschcke—and differ from one another—in a few details. The method of choice was the "Libby Prison Lottery": slips drawn from a basket passed among inmates "ordered into line" (Moody, "Life in Confederate Prisons," 352).

Chapter 5

1. Special exchanges included a variety of forms and much individual variation. See Hesseltine, *Civil War Prisons,* 15–18, 27–28.

2. The "Sanderson controversy" came to a head when, because of Lieutenant Colonel James M. Sanderson's alleged misbehavior, General Neal Dow and Corporal William A. Taylor brought formal charges against him: (1) cruel treatment of prisoners at Belle Island, (2) misappropriation of government stores, (3) betrayal of an escape plot, and (4) disloyalty to the Union. He was dismissed from the army on 8 June 1864. A military commission convened on 14 October 1864, heard witnesses, reversed the dismissal, and reinstated him. He deserved praise, not censure, for his conduct at the Libby, the commission said. Neither the issues nor the air have cleared even now; the controversy remains open (see Hesseltine, ibid., 117–18, 128–29; Sanderson, *My Record,* passim).

3. Rudolph Erich Raspe (1737–94) published a *Narrative of Baron Munchhausen's Marvelous Travels* (1785), purporting to record the exploits of the original baron (1720–97), who, according to Raspe, for example, once shot a stag with a cherry stone and returned later to find the stag alive with a cherry tree growing out of its head. Eulenspiegel, made famous by Richard Strauss's tone poem, was a legendary German peasant, hero of tales—in printed forms since the fifteenth century—of his pranks and practical jokes.

4. "Here [the salutation] is 'Have you got a box?'" The question about a package from the North expressed "the utmost felicity this life affords" (Bartelson, *Letters from Libby Prison,* 58). "When a box is received, there is great joy with the recipient. If it is a dull season for boxes, great crowds [of prisoners] gather around with the most vociferous cries and pass critically on each article received, tickled to death, like a child with a new toy" (ibid., 71).

5. Prison officials often withheld packages, broke into them, rifled the contents, and damaged them in search of forbidden articles hidden there: money, for instance, pressed in butter or baked in bread (Chamberlain, *Scenes in Libby Prison,* 348).

6. *Belle Isle* is another spelling. Domschcke has Belle Island throughout, a spelling used often at his time and since. It signified the prison on the island of the same name in the James River at Richmond: an enclosure around tents, for enlisted men.

7. The councilman meant that he did not want the poorhouse reduced to the same condition.

8. Earle, "In and Out of Libby Prison," 259, claimed that there were "neither barracks, tents, nor shelter of any kind" at Belle Island. Inmates endured privations "no pen can describe."

9. Dow (1804–97), tried and found guilty in the civilian courts of Alabama of stealing furniture, had been released by a court that said it lacked jurisdiction to rule on the matter. Dow's views on temperance, which Domschcke found so interesting, originated years before and continued long after the war. Dow wrote the rigid "Maine Law" on prohibition in 1851 and ran for president on the Prohibition ticket in 1880 (*Dictionary of American Biography,* s.v. "Dow, Neal").

Chapter 6

1. Domschcke seems to anticipate the Ould-Butler correspondence. Butler did not become agent of exchange until 17 December 1863. He and Ould seldom communicated before March 1864. Ould objected to dealing with the "Beast of New Orleans" who labored under Jefferson Davis's declaration of outlawry and was persona non grata to the Confederacy (Hesseltine, *Civil War Prisons*, 210–18). Domschcke may mean the controversy between Ould and Butler's predecessor as exchange agent, General Samuel A. Meredith. They quarreled over exchange in the later months of 1862 (ibid., 102–13).

2. The Dix-Hill cartel—named after the generals who framed it, John A. Dix (Union) and Daniel H. Hill (Confederacy), and ratified on 22 July 1862—provided for parole and exchange, raised prisoners' hopes, and deepened their disappointment when they were not exchanged. See ibid., 32–33, 69–113.

3. Lincoln's government balked at anything, such as negotiation for exchange and exchange itself, that might imply Union recognition of the Confederacy; the 1862 cartel had been "forced" from "the reluctant government of Lincoln" (ibid., 85; see also 32).

4. After probing Lee's defenses since September, and crossing the Rappahannock and the Rapidan in Virginia north of Richmond in November, Meade found Lee too strong and began withdrawing back across the Rapidan and into winter quarters, 1 December 1863 (Long, *Civil War Day by Day*, 401, 431, 439–41).

5. In "the first six months of prison life, an officer[-prisoner] is called a 'fresh fish;' the next four months, a 'sucker;' the next two months, a 'dry cod;' the balance of his time, a 'dried herring;' and after exchange, a 'pickled sardine' " (Glazier, *The Capture*, 115).

6. Four small Confederate boats and a handful of men captured the two warships in "a galling experience for the North" (Long, *Civil War Day by Day*. 400).

7. Alfred Ely, a civilian captured at the First Battle of Bull Run and imprisoned in Castle Thunder, complained of monotony, rough food, and bad conditions, but he received mail and seems to have been no worse off, and may have been better off, than Domschcke's officers in the Libby (Ely, *Journal*, passim).

8. Josef Lanner (1801–43): Austrian violinist and composer of waltzes that laid the foundation for the classical Viennese waltz. Vincenzo Bellini (1801–35): Italian composer of operas.

9. According to Domschcke's description, this must have been Chamberlain's Libby Burlesque Troop: prisoners "blacked as minstrels" who sang and danced as well as satirized and burlesqued the prison, its officials and life in it (Chamberlain, "Scenes in Libby Prison," 353–54).

10. Men danced with men, "ladies being indicated by a handkerchief on the left arm" of men playing the role of women (Fiske, "Involuntary Journey," 521; see also Cavada, *Libby Life,* 126).

11. In checkers and chess the pieces might be of wood and bone carved by prisoners; the religious book, the Bible, the commonest book in prison (Moody, "Life in Confederate Prisons," 357).

12. Each man being responsible for his own cooking now, his utensils included "old oyster and tomato cans, or old pans or cans of other description brought in by friendly darkies" (Starr, "In and Out of Confederate Prisons," 78).

13. According to Joseph Fiske, coffee was hard to get, and few possessed this "luxury unspeakable" (Fiske, "Involuntary Journey," 519).

14. This unclear phrase may allude to the fact that slaves could flee their masters and escape to Union forces in the South. There they would be put to work at the most distasteful tasks and the hardest of labor.

Chapter 7

1. They may have been in what one Libby prisoner called the "Pemberton building." Ordered to North Carolina, they followed a "line of march" along the street in our front [at the Libby], and when they passed under our windows we threw out drawers, shirts, stockings, etc., which they gathered up; and when they raised their pale and emaciated faces

to greet their old commanders there were but few dry eyes in the Libby. Many of them were making their last march" (Hobart, "Libby Prison—The Escape," 398).

2. A raid from Yorktown, ordered by Butler and intended to release prisoners at Richmond, resulted in a skirmish at the bridge on the Chickahominy a few miles northeast of Richmond. Confederate resistance, enough to produce a skirmish, sufficed to turn back the Union raiders (see Long, *Civil War Day by Day*, 463–64).

3. The most dramatic and most successful of many attempts to escape from the Libby (Earle, "In and Out of Libby Prison," 269–72). Other authors, including Wallber in the Appendix below, credit Colonel Thomas E. Rose with this plan to escape.

4. Harrison Hobart, in one of many deviations from other authors on this escape, says that the prisoners threw a dancing party to divert guards' attention (Hobart, "Libby Prison—The Escape," 401). Milton Russell describes an escape noiser, rougher, and more chaotic than Domschcke would have it (Russell, "Reminiscences of Prison Life," 37–38).

5. Five or six yards, fifteen to eighteen feet, seems excessive, but Domschcke says "yards."

6. After his latest series of raids and skirmishes in Kentucky, Indiana, and Ohio, Morgan and 364 men surrendered at Salineville, Ohio, 26 July 1863. He escaped from the Ohio State Penitentiary, 27 November 1863 (Long, *Civil War Day by Day*, 391, 439; Duke, "Morgan in 1864," 422–23).

7. The number of escapees to reach Union lines varies elsewhere from fifty-seven (Hobart, "Libby Prison—The Escape," 409) to fifty-nine (Long, *Civil War Day by Day*, 462) to sixty-five (Russell, "Reminiscences of Prison Life," 38).

Chapter 8

1. This discussion of Confederate monetary and fiscal policy, if essentially correct, oversimplifies this complicated subject. See Yearns, *Confederate Congress*, 203–9.

2. See ibid.

3. See ibid., 116–25.

4. The law of 17 February 1864 did not give Davis this much power. See ibid., 88.

Chapter 9

1. "The abundance of vermin [in the Libby] scarcely permitted us to rest day or night. . . . They lodged in our clothing, in our hair and whiskers, making a continual war upon us; and, in spite of our best efforts, they maintained the mastery" (Harrold, *Libby, Andersonville, Florence,* 34). "Our best efforts" meant "skirmishing," as it was called. The individual stripped to the skin, searched every article of clothing and his body—he ran a finger along every seam and fold of the clothing, and each joint and wrinkle of the body—and crushed the captured vermin between fingernail and thumbnail (Roe, "In a Rebel Prison," 16–17; Starr, "In and Out of Confederate Prisons," 78; Abbott, *Prison Life,* 185).

2. Officers of Negro regiments, almost certainly white, were probably held for special hostility by the Confederates. See Congressional Committee on Treatment of Prisoners Report, 284. Hostages were used as levers to get something from the enemy by threat: either a request was complied with or the hostages would suffer specified obscenities or atrocities. See the Sawyer-Flynn incident, Chapter 4 above; and Moody, "Life in Confederate Prisons," 352.

3. Asa B. Isham remembered sixty-one prisoners and four guards in one car. Prisoners would "spoon in," or sit between one another's legs in rows across the car, like spoons in a drawer. One door, open two feet, gave the only ventilation (Isham, "Experience in Rebel Prisons," 39). If the Society for the Prevention of Cruelty to Animals could see prisoners in cattle cars, it would never complain about cattle in them again (Simpson, "Four Months' Experience," 21–22). Too few guards meant closed cars for days on end and passengers not allowed out for air or exercise: "the sick and well, the wounded and unwounded, from sixty to eighty huddled in each car." They were often put in after cattle had been taken out of uncleaned cars "and the excrement of the beast[s] was the bed of the men" (Congressional Committee on Treatment of Prisoners Report, 25).

4. A reference to Grant's Army of the Potomac, its advance on Richmond during the summer of 1864, and its threat to capture the city in late summer and early fall.

5. No important battlefields were near Danville. The families could have come from any of several at a distance, even Bull Run.

6. Probably war caused this appearance. Danville had been a "tobacco-market town" since the eighteenth century, thriving on the improvement of transportation on the Dan after 1820, and prospering after the introduction of the "auction warehouse system" in 1852. During the war, Danville's idle warehouses were used as hospitals and a prison. Danville was the capital of the expiring Confederacy, 3–10 April 1865 (Writers' Program, *Virginia,* 598).

7. Those enlisted prisoners may have suffered more than Domschcke and his fellow officers because officers possessed or could more readily get money to buy food and other essentials. Guards smuggled them in and charged fabulous prices, such as $15 for a pound of butter (Burrage, "Reminiscences of Prison-Life" 52–53, 56).

8. On 27 January 1864, citizens of Danville petitioned the Confederate secretary of war, James A. Seddon, to remove stench and sickness, especially smallpox, ravaging the 4,000 prisoners and threatening the town (Congressional Committee on Treatment of Prisoners Report, 671–72).

9. In the severe cold the stoves, which burned inferior coal and smoked, had to be cleaned once a day—over the objections of prisoners "so thinly clad that a draught of cold air was even more disagreeable to them than the choking gas" (Burrage, "Reminiscences of Prison-Life" 45).

10. Captain Henry (or Henri) Wirz (1822–65) commanded Andersonville, the worst prison of the war. In twenty-six and a half acres, as many as 33,000 men were confined and 13,000 died in overcrowded conditions that included inadequate sanitation, clothing, shelter, and medical care; polluted water; mosquitoes; bloodhounds; brutality by guards to prisoners and by prisoners to prisoners; and sickness: dysentery, scurvy, and gangrene. Wirz was tried by a military court and hanged for crimes against individual prisoners and conspiring to murder prisoners en masse (Hesseltine, *Civil War Prisons,* 133–58, 237–45).

11. At Danville the prisoners tried to pass the time much as they had at the Libby (Burrage, "Reminiscences of Prison-Life" 53).

Chapter 10

1. Old locomotives were the least of the Confederacy's railroad problems. The Confederate Congress, for safety on ramshackle lines, limited trains to twelve miles an hour (Abbott, *Prison Life,* 44). Worse, the government, respecting states' rights, never seized and coordinated the railroads. Hence, never united, they suffered the shortcomings of disjunction (Abdill, *Civil War Railroads,* 5).

2. With Domschcke, here as elsewhere in the book, "Germans" means German-Americans, in contrast to Anglo-Americans and others of various national origins. Hence these Germans may have been of long residence and were perhaps born in the United States.

3. Rocinante, usually Rosinante in English, was Don Quixote's horse.

4. Description of this and of all prisons vary from author to author. For example, Domschcke's twelve-foot fence is fifteen feet according to Glazier, *The Capture,* 113–14, and twenty feet according to Moody, "Life in Confederate Prisons," 355.

5. Wessels (1809–89) commanded at Plymouth and surrendered 2,800 men and many supplies to the Confederates under Brigadier General Robert Frederick Hoke on 20 April 1864, after three days of fighting that included attack by CSS *Albemarle,* a new ram (Boatner, *Civil War Dictionary,* 901–2; Long, *Civil War Day by Day,* 486–87).

6. Scammon (1816–94) commanded the Third Division when captured in West Virginia in February 1864 (Boatner, *Civil War Dictionary,* 724–25).

7. Captured while recovering from two wounds sustained at Port Hudson, Louisiana, in 1863 and sent to the Libby, Dow was exchanged for William Henry Fitzhugh ("Rooney") Lee, second son of the Confederate commander (ibid., 245).

8. According to George Starr, the number was "upwards of seventeen hundred, all commissioned officers," as of 28 July 1864 (Starr, "In and Out of Confederate Prisons," 89).

9. "When thou does alms, let not thy left hand know what thy right hand doeth" (Matt. 6:3).

10. Inscribed on the coffeepot of a mess at the Libby: "To borrow is human—to return, divine" (Cavada, *Libby Life,* 166).

11. By now the Confederacy's chances were slim. In May, Grant was proceeding toward Richmond, Sherman toward Atlanta. In July, Grant was a few miles from Richmond, and Sherman began the attack on Atlanta. Johnston did nothing but retreat, however skillfully, until relieved by General John Bell Hood on 17 July (Long, *Civil War Day by Day,* 495, 540, 546, 548).

12. Brigadier General Sturgis (1822–89) commanded Federal forces at Brice's Cross Roads, Mississippi, 10 June 1864. Half as many Confederates so routed his Federals that Union authorities called the engagement a disaster. An investigation produced no findings. Sturgis, never reassigned, awaited orders the rest of the war (Boatner, *Civil War Dictionary,* 816; Long, *Civil War Day by Day,* 519).

13. Domschcke himself was soon to suffer the same fate.

14. Probably a reference to Grant's crossing the James on 12–17 June with 100,000 men southwest from Cold Harbor on the way to Richmond. Sherman was by then within fifty miles of Atlanta (Long, *Civil War Day by Day,* 520–24).

15. Domschcke's *liess . . . in den Bock spannen* translates as "stretched in the rack." He probably means "bucked," a favorite among tortures that included the stocks, the chain gang, the spread eagle, the wooden horse, and tying up by the thumbs. Hesseltine, *Civil War Prisons,* 162, says Irich was bucked and gagged. That is, "the prisoner was seated on the ground, his wrists firmly tied together and placed over his knees, and a stick run under his knees and over his arms at the elbow joints. A stick or 'gag' was then placed in his mouth and tied tightly by strings extending back of his head. In this position the sufferer (often a sick man) was kept several hours in the sun. This mode of punishment prevailed at all the prisons, and was inflicted for the most trivial (real or imagined) offenses" (Congressional Committee on Treatment of Prisoners Report, 203). Domschcke could have meant the stocks or the wooden horse. In the stocks the prisoner was tied to a frame and forced to stand or lie painfully for long periods, sometimes days at a stretch, and through rain and heat. The prisoner condemned to the wooden horse was put astride a trestle, gagged, and his legs held apart by ropes from his ankles to stakes in the ground (ibid., 203–4).

16. Or "D——d smart prayer, but it won't answer the purpose" (Glazier, *The Capture,* 122).

17. Alexander Shaler (1827–?) commanded Johnson's Island Military Prison (Ohio) in 1863 and 1864, and the Fourth Brigade, First Division, Sixth Corps, in the Wilderness (April–May 1864), where he was captured (Boatner, *Civil War Dictionary,* 734).

18. At other times, Gibbs commanded the prisons at Salisbury and Andersonville.

19. "Fort McHenry" is probably Fort Henry, Tennessee. Confederates generally were horrified at black men in arms against them: slaves, subhumans, rebelling against their masters—they should be treated as criminals. Hence, stories such as that referred to by Gibbs would spread like wildfire (see Berlin, *Freedom,* 567). Horror, erupting in the South over the North's use of black troops, preceded rumors of their treatment of white prisoners (Cornish, *The Sable Arm,* 157–62).

20. At Andersonville, Commandant Wirz gave a guard, one Scott of the Fourth Georgia Reserves, leave as a reward for shooting Henry Lochmire of a Pennsylvania regiment (Congressional Committee on Treatment of Prisoners Report, 202).

21. Perhaps Thomas Jones Thorp of the Nineteenth New York Cavalry.

22. Glazier, *The Capture,* 129, has:

C.S. MILITARY PRISON,

Special Orders,   MACON, GA.,July 4, 1864
  No. 9

I.Lieutenant Colonel Thorp is relieved from duty as senior officer of prisoners, for a violation of prison rules, and Lieutenant Colonel McCreary will again assume that position.

II.The same order and quiet will be observed on this day as on any other.

III.A disregard of this order may subject offenders to unpleasant consequences.

GEO. C. GIBBS,
CAPTAIN COMMANDING

23. Beginning in April and taking effect by July 1861, the Union blockade was capturing one ship in three approaching Southern ports in 1864. The capture of Fort Pulaski at the entrance to Savannah harbor, 11 April 1862, must have interdicted supplies, including medicine, to Macon. See Long, *Civil War Day by Day*, 103, 198, 454.

24. "Complaints against Union army physicians have been astonishingly numerous. On the one hand, many of the physicians respected the gravity of their assignment and, with meritorious zeal, devoted every movement to the practice of medicine. On the other hand, not a few were as deficient in the healing arts as in good will and in character itself. Let me adduce one of a number of possible examples, this from Davidson's *Fourteen Months in Southern Prisons*. Union soldiers wounded and captured at Chickamauga were brought to a so-called general hospital. Soon, under a flag of truce, 196 Union ambulances, carrying everything the wounded would need, set out for the hospital. But at Rebel lines, the Union drivers had to relinquish their places to Rebels, who drove the ambulances to the hospital. Taking advantage of the situation, the Rebels plundered the ambulances shamelessly, stealing as much as they could. What remained was brought to a tent and put under guard. Every last sentry at the tent, like the prior thieves, stole from the supplies intended for the wounded. Davidson continues: 'We complained to the chief surgeon in charge of the hospital, but he made no effort to have the matter corrected, though he had entire control of the medicines and supplies. He freely offered to the Confederate officers the hospital whiskey and dainties that were designed for the exclusive use of the wounded. It is presumed that he thought by so doing to gain favor with the enemy, and anticipated a little more gentle treatment in return at their hands on his arrival in Richmond, whither he was soon to be sent as a prisoner.' Davidson concludes: 'Such men deserve the condemnation of the whole world, and should receive a dishonorable dismissal from the United States service' [pp. 27–28]" (Domschcke, *Zwanzig Monate*, 132 n).

25. They were sent to Charleston on 10 June, and Domschcke and the others would follow in July, "to be placed under fire of our [Union] siege-guns on Morris Island," as a way to stop the bombardment of the Confederate city by Union artillery (Glazier, *The Capture*, 129).

Chapter 11

1. According to Glazier, a total of 600 prisoners were involved (*The Capture*, 129).

2. The Federal government had built and used these hospitals in Southern coastal cities before the war, when the Confederacy took them over. Domschcke's "United States" in the name would not have pleased the Confederates.

3. "So great is the contrast between our treatment here [Savannah] and at other places, that we cannot but feel that fortune has certainly smiled kindly upon us for once" (Glazier, *The Capture*, 132–33).

4. Joseph Fiske reported more and better food here and at Charleston: plenty of rice and even a little more meat at Charleston than at Savannah (Fiske, "An Involuntary Journey," 518).

5. Some stories say that Jefferson Davis disguised himself as a woman—at least he seems to have been wearing a shawl—when trying to escape the Federal troops who surprised his camp near Irwinville, Georgia, 10 May 1865 (Long, *Civil War Day by Day*, 687).

6. According to Glazier, they were the First Georgia Volunteers (*The Capture*, 133).

7. This is a different evaluation of Wayne than Glazier's: "an unprincipled tyrant" who "would consider it beneath his dignity to confer a Christian favor" (ibid., 138).

8. Probably a reference to Federal attacks on Morris Island near Charleston, South Carolina, in July 1863.

9. According to Glazier, the guards "have been prisoners of war, and have learned what we had a right to expect, from the magnanimous treatment they themselves have received from the Federal government" (*The Capture*, 133).

10. Glazier has it that a cow broke through, fell in, and thereby announced the tunnel to the Rebels (ibid., 136).

11. The fort guarded the sea approach to Savannah, captured by Federals, 11 April 1862 (Long, *Civil War Day by Day*, 198).

12. Confederates favored dogs to track and catch people, using them on prisoners of war as they had on runaway slaves. Union prisoners feared the dogs; memoirs abound with such references. An "Indiana Soldier" claimed that "an officer [a Union prisoner] was torn to pieces by dogs" (Indiana Soldier [Capt. John V. Hadley], *Seven Months a Prisoner*, 59, 70–71).

13. This may have been Ould's letter to the Southern people, saying that he proposed exchanges, published in response to clamor for exchange. Indeed, public opinion on both sides so wanted exchange that Butler published in the *New York Times* a letter in response to Ould's. Exchange resumed in earnest now, to continue till the end of the war (Hesseltine, *Civil War Prisons*, 225–32).

14. Late in December 1863, Butler and Ould renewed exchange at City Point on the James River (Eaton, *A History of the Southern Confederacy*, 105).

15. Probably a reference, not entirely accurate, to Southern political power during the formation and in the early days of the Republic, when the Constitution permitted slavery and when the law of the land included the Fugitive Slave Act.

Chapter 12

1. Morris Island, in Charleston harbor, South Carolina, took part in the bombardment of Fort Sumter, 12 April 1861. Federal troops held it after 7 September 1863, and it became a place of prisoner exchange (Long, *Civil War Day by Day*, 57, 406).

2. In fact, the alligator's snout is broad and stubby, especially when compared to the long and narrow one of the crocodile.

3. According to Domschcke's later references to Negroes, these and other "colored people" seem to have met them here and elsewhere because they favored the Union and sympathized with its soldiers who were now prisoners.

4. The workhouse was "large" and "bastille shaped"; the wall a "massive" sixteen feet of masonry (Glazier, *The Capture*, 144).

5. Things could be bought in most prisons if the prisoner in need had money and plenty of it. Horace Burbank looked at the nine "State of Maine" buttons on his vest, removed six, sold them to a Confederate sergeant, made do with three, and "thus converted brass into bread" (Burbank, "Prison Life," 17).

6. Winder (1800–1865), provost marshal, commander of prisons, and object of controversy, retained support as a capable officer by Jefferson Davis and others (Boatner, *Civil War Dictionary*, 940–41). Domschcke seems to side with those who reviled him as a monster and a brute.

7. Probably a reference to attacks by Federal forces, under Brigadier General Quincy A. Gilmore, on Morris Island, near Charleston, in July 1863. On 18 July 6,000 Federals attacked Battery Wagner on the island. At their head was the Fifth-Fourth Massachusetts Colored Infantry, whose many losses included the death of their colonel and organizer, Robert Gould Shaw (Long, *Civil War Day by Day*, 387).

8. Glazier, *The Capture*, 152, speaks of "Negro melodies" here at Charleston and offers this example by one Sergeant Johnson:

I

When I enlisted in the army,
  Then I thought 'twas grand,
Marching through the streets of Boston
  Behind a regimental band.
When at Wagner I was captured,
  Then my courage failed;
Now I'm lousy, hungry, naked,
  Here in Charleston jail.
CHORUS   Weeping, sad and lonely—
      Oh! how bad I feel;
    Down in Charleston, South Car'lina,
    Praying for a good "square meal."

II

If Jeff. Davis will release me,
    Oh, how glad I'll be;
When I get on Morris Island
    Then I shall be free;
Then I'll tell those conscript soldiers
    How they use us here;
Giving us an old "corn-dodger"—
    They call it prisoner's fare.

III

We are longing, watching, praying,
    But will not repine
Till Jeff. Davis does release us,
    And send us "in our lines."
Then with words of kind affection,
    How they'll greet us there!
Wondering how we could live so long
    Upon the "dodger's fare."
CHORUS— Then we will laugh long and loudly—
    Oh, how glad we'll feel,
    When we arrive on Morris Island
    And eat a good "square meal."

9. In mid-July, Gilmore's Union forces, intent on Charleston, decided to continue siege rather than attack. Artillery on Morris Island was to bombard the city into submission, despite the presence of Union prisoners in the city, put there to stop such bombardment. The island was mostly a swamp where mud more resembled water than earth; but the heavy batteries had included the Swamp Angel, an eight-inch Parrott gun that hurled a two-hundred-pound missle more than 4 miles. After the Angel exploded on its thirty-sixth round, Knox coastal mortars replaced it, three-hundred-pounders, and it is to them that Domschcke refers (Long, *Civil War Day by Day,* 383, 388, 400; Boatner, *Civil War Dictionary,* 621, 822). The Southern press denounced the shelling as barbarous. In retaliation, 600 Union prisoners went "under fire," and in turn, 600 prisoners of the Union went under the fire of Confederate batteries (Moody, "Life in Confederate Prisons," 359).

10. "I must say, I never passed so many happy moments of reflection as during my imprisonment under fire." Everybody seemed to take pride "at being again the victims of this new phase of Southern chivalry." Despite short rations, strong bodies took heart at the thought of sacrificing for the Union (Sabre, *Nineteen Months a Prisoner,* 125).

11. Glazier, *The Capture,* 159, has the parole as follows:

"CHARLESTON, S.C., C.S.A.,
"September—, 1864

We the undersigned, prisoners of war, confined in the city of Charleston, in the Confederate States of America, do pledge our parole, individually, as military men and men of honor, that we will not attempt to pass the lines which shall be established and guarded around our prison-house; nor will we, by letter, word, or sign, hold any intercourse with parties beyond those lines, nor with those who may visit us, without authority. It is understood by us that this parole is voluntary on our part, and given in consideration of privileges secured to us, by lessening the stringency of the guard, of free ingress and egress of the house and appointed grounds during the day, by which we secure a liberty of fresh air and exercise grateful to comfort and health.

Hereby we admit that this our parole binds us in letter and spirit, with no room for doubt or technicality of construction and its violation will be an act of lasting disgrace. Signed.

This seems not to have been a typical parole but one composed ad hoc, as the following examples of typical ones will show by comparison (*Official Records,* 2d ser., 3:9, 10, 299, 305, respectively):

I swear (or affirm) that I will not take up arms against the United States or serve in any military capacity whatsoever against them until regularly discharged according to the usages of war from this obligation.

We and each of us for himself severally pledge our words of honor as officers and gentlemen that we will not again take up arms against the United States nor serve in any military capacity whatsoever against them until regularly discharged according to the usages of war from this obligation.

I beg to state that we have remained on parole of honor ever since————not to serve directly or indirectly against the Southern Confederacy until properly exchanged by said Government of the Confederate States for prisoners of [equal] rank held by the Federal Government that may be agreed upon between the Secretary of War of the Confederate States and of the Federal Government.

Whereas,———— ————, agent for the care and custody of prisoners of war at————, has granted me the undersigned prisoner described on the back hereof permission to return to ————upon condition that I give my parole of honor that I will not enter into any naval, military or other service whatever against the————or any of the dominions thereunto belonging, or against any powers at peace with————until I shall have been regularly exchanged, and that I will surrender myself if required by the agent of the government at such place and at such time as may be appointed in case my exchange shall not be effected. And I will until exchanged give notice from time to time of my place of residence.

Now in consideration of my enlargement I do hereby declare that I have given my parole of honor accordingly and that I will keep it inviolably.

Given under my hand at————this————day of————, in the year of our Lord————.

12. Probably Beaufort, South Carolina, rather than Beaufort, North Carolina, though both were in Federal hands. Pocotaligo was in South Carolina, near *that* Beaufort, to the northwest.

13. That is, probably, he would promise to repay what the person or firm advanced to the broker. "Eastern states" likely refers to the eastern states of the Union. At Andersonville, prisoners themselves carried on the exchange. About $40,000 in greenbacks circulated as Confederate dollars were bought and sold by prisoners as needed. The rate varied: a greenback dollar would bring from five to ten Confederate; a dollar in gold, twenty in Confederate (Weiser, *Nine Months in Rebel Prisons,* 30–32).

14. A version of these money exchanges seems to have existed in every prison. See, for example, Moody, "Life in Confederate Prisons," 362; Phillips, "Experiences in the Libby Prison," 68; and Sabre, *Nineteen Months a Prisoner,* 61. In general, according to A. O. Abbott, the prisoner who wanted money would put in writing that he had borrowed a sum and that it should be paid to the bearer of the note. The speculator, or broker as the money traders were called, would (in person or by agent) give the prisoner a fraction of the sum, then send the note north to be presented and the face value collected (Abbott, *Prison Life in the South,* 161).

15. "The man" was John C. Calhoun (1782–1850), author of the theory of nullification and other theories that prefigured secession.

16. Domschcke refers to the bombardment from Morris Island.

17. John Bell Hood (1831–79) commanded a Confederate corps in the Atlanta campaign.

18. "Captured naval officers" may be ones taken in Union maritime action against Charleston and Charleston harbor in August.

19. That is, the Union ships blockading Charleston harbor, supplying Gilmore's forces, and carrying out some offensive operations in the area.

Chapter 13

1. Crackers were also called hardtack. Usually men of the western armies said "crackers"; men of the eastern, "hardtack" (Billings, *Hardtack and Coffee,* 119–21).

2. Jupiter, the supreme god of Roman mythology, played several roles, including that of the god of rain. In that role he was called Jupiter Pluvius.

3. Reynard is the hero of the French medieval beast epic, *Roman de Renart* (1175–1205), an agreeable rascal who usually wins as he illustrates the work's theme: the triumph of cunning and wit over brute force. Domschcke refers of course to Goethe's free translation, *Reineke Fuchs* (1794).

4. Domschcke does not identify or explain the quotations here and in the next paragraph.

5. The United States Sanitary Commission, which resembled the later Red Cross, was set up on 8 June 1861, to aid the health and comfort of Union soldiers. It concerned itself with hygiene, diet, care of the wounded, and lodging and homes for transient and discharged soldiers (Boatner, *Civil War Dictionary,* 720).

6. In their hunger, prisoners here would pick moldy bread and potato peelings out of the hogshead that held waste "and devour them greedily" (Burbank, "Prison Life," 17). In great hunger, "the moral sense suffered notable perversion" (Isham, "Experience in Rebel Prisons," 32–33), and "starvation would bring to the surface all the animal there is in man" (Chamberlain, "Scenes in Libby Prison," 347), hence the widespread bickering, strife, fighting, and stealing.

7. "The Georgia troops [here the Thirty-second Georgia Volunteers] seemed to be by far the most civil and gentlemanly of the southern army" (Glazier, *The Capture,* 169–70).

8. That is, according to Domschcke, freeing the slaves would destroy the oppressive aristocracy and thus bring freedom and material benefits to the poor whites. Cf. U. S. Grant's discussion of this subject (Grant, "Chattanooga," 689).

9. As to this man, when he came looking for his dogs, "if we had been able to conduct him to their resting place and lay him tenderly by their side, it would have been to us a very satisfactory job" (Moody, "Life in Confederate Prisons," 360).

10. These were the tickets for the 1864 elections on 8 November, Republican and Democratic respectively. Domschcke does not explain the discrepancy in the totals. Such elections occurred in other prisons, too. Confederate officials encouraged them, "for they wanted to know the feelings of the prisoners" (Weiser, *Nine Months in Rebel Prisons,* 44). In Andersonville the voting prisoner dropped a white pea (McClellan) or a black pea (Lincoln, "the nigger President") into a box. Only four prisoners in the group voted for McClellan. They were attacked by other prisoners and beaten (Moore, "Reminiscence," 457–58).

11. Glazier was one. He tells the story in *The Capture,* 197–300.

12. That is, escapes continued as plentifully as before.

13. "Colored" people helped Weiser and his companions in this fashion, and they welcomed "half a ham nicely cooked, some corn bread and a pint of brandy" (Weiser, *Nine Months in Rebel Prisons,* 50; see also Heslin, "Diary," 274). Union prisoners met "universal good-will and sympathy" from Negroes in the Carolinas in 1864 (Sabre, *Nineteen Months a Prisoner,* 78).

14. William Joseph Hardee (1815–73) had been appointed to that command in September 1864. He also led corps at Shiloh, Perryville, Missionary Ridge, and Stones River, and in the Atlanta campaign (Boatner, *Civil War Dictionary,* 374).

15. Andersonville would of course have been worse, but Domschcke probably refers only to prisons for officers.

16. The prisoner able to pander to the Confederate greed for greenbacks could live confortably enough in perhaps every prison (see Sabre, *Nineteen Months a Prisoner,* 59).

17. A. O. Abbott speaks with contempt of the "old gentleman by the name of Potter." The sort of camp follower who prostituted himself to filthy lucre, he followed these Union prisoners from Charleston to Columbia and declared himself "always a Union man" who wanted to help prisoners (Abbott, *Prison Life,* 161).

18. Blockade runners desired greenbacks to use for purchases in the North, but the law forbade Confederate citizens from accepting greenbacks for any sale. So the exchange system flourished in prisons. Money sent south to prisoners would return with runners and pay for goods brought south to Confederate customers (see Chamberlain, "Scenes in Libby Prison," 356–57).

19. The "grand fireworks" were Columbia itself in flames, which began the evening of the day Sherman's forces entered the city, 17 February 1865.

20. A prison of a former fortification in the Delaware River, west of Salem, New Jersey, and dreaded in the South.

21. Confederate prisons of various kinds in Virginia (Belle Island and Richmond), Georgia, North Carolina, and South Carolina, respectively.

Chapter 14

1. That is, Grant told the Southern authorities, and proceeded to act according to his decision, that the North would comply with the exchange agreement reached between agents

of each side in the summer of 1864 (Hesseltine, *Civil War Prisons*, 222–25, 229–31).

2. That is, to protect Richmond with the presence of Union prisoners, which would discourage Union attacks, especially bombardment. See Chapter 12, note 9, above.

3. See Chapter 9, note 3, above.

4. Sherman's march having split the Confederacy, Wilmington was in Union hands and Goldsboro the Union's next objective. Hence, as Domschcke says, "the farthest of Rebel outposts" lay "twelve miles from Wilmington" (see Nevins, *War for the Union,* 4:259–60).

5. "Vulgarity" and "coarseness" convey the sense of *Gemeinheit,* which seems an understatement, given Domschcke's prior claims of brutality and sadism.

6. This anecdote, cryptic here, is equally so in the original.

Appendix
"THE ESCAPE FROM THE LIBBY"

1. "A member of Streight's party, which escaped the Libby on 9 February 1864, [Wallber had been] the adjutant of the Twenty-third Wisconsin. Like the author of these reminiscences [Domschcke], Wallber was captured on 1 July 1863, at Gettysburg" (Domschcke, *Zwanzig Monate,* 213n).

2. Cf. this description with that in Chapter 7 above. According to George Starr, the plot to tunnel out of the Libby was designed and executed under the direction of Colonel Thomas E. Rose, of the Seventy-seventh Pennsylvania Volunteers, and Major A. G. Hamilton of the Twelfth Kentucky Cavalry (Starr, "In and Out of Confederate Prisons," 80).

3. The diggers thought that the two sentries had looked at the hole. One sentry: "I have been hearing a strange noise in the ground here." The other: "Nothing but rats" (Hobart, "Libby Prison—The Escape," 400).

4. Colonel Abel D. Streight "was so stout that he had to take off his clothes and tie them to his feet before he could crawl through the tunnel" (Turner, "War-Time Recollections," 619).

5. Rose seems to have directed the escape and emerged at its start, but had stayed behind and left now with Wallber.

6. "We were often secretly fed by the ever-faithful negroes" in "the swamps and cotton gins" (Glazier, *The Capture,* 197). A Negro rolled up the whites of his eyes and said, "Don't be afraid, massa white man." When the escapees from Andersonville told him that they were hungry, he brought them food (Congressional Committee on Treatment of Prisoners Report, 66). The "colored people of the South" not only helped escapees but also brought food and other aid to prisoners when confined" (ibid., 248). At the Libby, the infamous Turner whipped the one named Ford senseless because he had been smuggling prisoners' letters in and out (ibid., 233).

7. The Union had occupied Williamsburg since capturing it on 6 May 1862, in the Peninsula campaign.

"BELLE ISLAND"

1. "Joseph Arnold, captured at Gettysburg on 1 July 1863, later joined those who spent months on the desolate island in the James River. Mr. Arnold, then a sergeant of Company E, and subsequently a lieutenant (holding those ranks in the Twenty-sixth Wisconsin), kindly let me use his report [on Belle Island]. From it I have drawn the following selection" (Domschcke, *Zwanzig Monate,* 235). Though "Belle Isle" has become frequent in secondary sources, "Belle Island" is typical in this and other primary documents.

2. Prisoners at Belle Island skinned rats and ate them raw (Congressional Committee on Treatment of Prisoners Report, 974).

3. "Cases have been known at Belle Isle of prisoners' vomiting up their breakfast, and this afterward was eaten by others" (Bartleson, *Letters from Libby Prison,* 82).

4. Rats, abundant near the "dead-house" of the hospital here, ate the eyes and faces of Union dead (Congressional Committee on Treatment of Prisoners Report, 973–74).

5. A burial party would search the camp at noon for deaths of the night before. Sleepers and other reclining and motionless forms would be shaken to wake them, and asked: "Hello, there, are you dead yet?" Anybody who did not answer went into a pine box for carting to the graveyard. "No one knows how many of these, by proper treatment, were capable of rescucitation" (Sabre, *Nineteen Months a Prisoner,* 47–48).

Bibliography

Abbott, A. O. *Prison Life in the South*. New York: Harper & Brothers, 1865.

Abdill, George B. *Civil War Railroads*. New York: Bonanza Books, 1961.

Amis, Martin. "Broken Lances." Review of *Don Quixote,* translated by Tobias Smollett. *Harper's,* March 1986, 104–6.

Armstrong, William M. "Cahaba to Charleston: The Prison Odyssey of Lt. Edmund E. Ryan." *Civil War History* 8 (June 1962): 218–27.

Arndt, Karl J. R., and May E. Olson. *German-American Newspapers and Periodicals*. Heidelberg, West Germany: Quelle & Meyer, 1961.

Bartleson, Frederick A. *Letters from Libby Prison*. Edited by Margaret W. Peelle. New York: Greenwich Books, 1956.

Battles and Leaders of the Civil War. See Johnson and Buell.

Berlin, Ira, ed. *Freedom: A Documentary History of Emancipation*. Series 2, *The Black Military Experience*. Cambridge: Cambridge University Press, 1983.

Billings, John D. *Hardtack and Coffee: The Unwritten Story of Army Life*. Edited by Richard Harwell. Chicago: R. R. Donnelley & Sons (Lakeside Press), 1960.

Boatner, Mark Mayo, III. *The Civil War Dictionary*. New York: David McKay Company, 1959.

Boggs, Samuel S. *Eighteen Months a Prisoner.* . . . Lovingston, Ill.: S. S. Boggs, 1887.

Boyd, William. "In Search of the South." *House and Garden,* May 1985, 82–96.

Burbank, Horace H. "My Prison Life." In *War Papers—Maine* (q.v.), 2:11–27.

Burrage, Henry S. "Reminiscences of Prison-Life at Danville, Virginia." In *War Papers— Maine* (q.v.), 3:43–60.

Byers, S. H. M. *What I Saw in Dixie; or, Sixteen Months in Rebel Prisons*. Dansville, N.Y.: Robbins & Poore, 1868.

Byrne, Frank L., ed. "A General behind Bars: Neal Dow in Libby Prison." *Civil War History* 8 (June 1962): 164–83.

———. "Prisons and Prisoners of War." In Nevins, Robertson, and Wiley (q.v.), 185–206.

Catton, Bruce. *Glory Road: The Army of the Potomac*. Garden City, N.Y.: Doubleday, 1952.

Cavada, Frederick Fernandez. *Libby Life: Experiences of a Prisoner of War in Richmond, Va., 1863–64*. 1865. Reprint. Lanham, Md.: University Press of America, 1985.

Chamberlain, J. W. "Scenes in Libby Prison." In *Sketches of War History* (q.v.), 2:342–70.

Chukovsky, Kornei. *A High Art: The Art of Translation*. Translated and edited by Lauren G. Leighton. Knoxville: University of Tennessee Press, 1984.

Civil War Papers Read before the Commandery of the State of Massachusetts, Military Order of the Loyal Legion of the United States. 2 vols., continuously paginated. Boston: Printed for the Commandery, 1900.

Coblentz, Stanton A. *From Arrow to Atom Bomb: The Psychological History of War*. New York: Beechhurst Press, 1953.

Cochran, M. A. "Reminiscences of Life in Rebel Prisons." In *Sketches of War History* (q.v.), 4:334–54.

Commission of Inquiry, U.S. Sanitary Commission. *Narrative of Privations and Sufferings . . . of Prisoners of War . . . a Report . . . with . . . Testimony.* Philadelphia: King & Baird, 1864.

Connnelly, Thomas L. "Civil War." In *The Encyclopedia of Southern History.* Baton Rouge: Louisiana State University Press, 1979.

Cooke, John Esten. *Outlines from the Outpost.* Edited by Richard Harwell. Chicago: R. R. Donnelley & Sons (Lakeside Press), 1961.

Cooper, A[lonzo]. *In and Out of Rebel Prisons.* Oswego, N.Y.: R. J. Oliphant, 1888.

Cornish, Dudley Taylor. *The Sable Arm: Negro Troops in the Union Army, 1861–1865.* New York: Longmans, Green, 1956.

Custance, Reginald. *A Study of War.* 1924. Reprint. Port Washington, N.Y.: Kennikat Press, 1970.

Davidson, Henry M. *Fourteen Months in Southern Prisons.* Milwaukee: Daily Wisconsin Printing House, 1865.

Destler, C. M. "An Andersonville Prison Diary [by Charles Ross of Vermont]." *Georgia Historical Quarterly* 24 (March 1940): 56–76.

Dictionary of American Biography. Edited by Allen Johnson and Dumas Malone. 20 vols. New York: Charles Scribner's Sons, 1927–36.

Dictionary of Wisconsin Biography. Madison: State Historical Society of Wisconsin, 1960.

"Domschke, Bernard [sic]." In *Dictionary of Wisconsin Biography* (q.v.), 105.

"Dow, Neal." *See* Waterman.

Duke, Basil W. "John Morgan in 1864." In Johnson and Buell (q.v.), 4:422–24.

Earle, Charles Warrington. "In and Out of Libby Prison." In *Military Essays* (q.v.), 1:247–92.

Eaton, Clement. *A History of the Southern Confederacy.* New York: Macmillan, 1954.

Ely, Alfred. *Journal of Alfred Ely, a Prisoner of War in Richmond.* Edited by Charles Lanman. New York: D. Appleton, 1862.

Faust, Albert Bernhardt. *The German Element in the United States.* 2 vols. New York: Steuben Society of America, 1927.

Fiske, Joseph E. "An Involuntary Journey through the Confederacy." In *Civil War Papers* (q.v.), 2:513–29.

Freeman, Douglas S. "Jackson, Thomas Jonathon." In *Dictionary of American Biography* (q.v.), 9:556–59.

———. *R. E. Lee: A Biography.* 4 vols. New York: Charles Scribner's Sons, 1935.

Freidel, Frank. *Francis Lieber: Nineteenth-Century Liberal.* Baton Rouge: Louisiana State University Press, 1947.

Furness, Henry B. "A General Account of Prison Life and Prisons in the South . . . Including Statistical Information. . . ." In Isham et al. (q.v.).

Galloupe, Isaac Francis. "Reminiscences of a Prisoner of War." *Civil War Papers* (q.v.), 2:499–510.

Gilmore, James H. *Notes of a Course of Lectures on Vattel's Law of Nations.* Charlottesville, Va.: James Blakey, 1891.

Glazier, Willard W. *The Capture, the Prison Pen, and the Escape.* New York: United States Publishing Company, 1868.

Glimpses of the Nation's Struggle: A Series of Papers Read before the Minnesota Commandery of the Military Order of the Loyal Legion of the United States. St. Paul: St. Paul Book and Stationery Company, 1887.

Grant, Ulysses S. "The Battle of Shiloh." In Johnson and Buell (q.v.), 1:465–86.

———. "Chattanooga." In ibid., 3:679–711.

———. *The Papers of Ulysses S. Grant.* Edited by John Y. Simon. 14 vols to date. Carbondale and Edwardsville: Southern Illinois University Press, 1967–.

Grebner, Constantin. *"Die Neuner": Eine Schilderung der Kriegsjahre des 9ten Regiments Ohio Vol. Infanterie.* Cincinnati: S. Rosenthal, 1897.

Hamilton, J. G. D. "Pollard, Edward Alfred." In *Dictionary of American Biography* (q.v.), 15:47–48.

Harley, Lewis R. *Francis Lieber: His Life and Political Philosophy.* New York: Columbia University Press, 1899.

Harris, William C. *Prison Life in the Tobacco Warehouse at Richmond.* Philadelphia: George W. Childs, 1862.

Harold, John. *Libby, Andersonville, Florence.* . . . Philadelphia: W. B. Selheimer, 1870.

Hartigan, Richard Shelly. *See* Lieber.

Harwell, Richard. *See* Cooke.

Heinrici, Max. *Das Buch der Deutschen in Amerika.* Philadelphia: Walther's Buchdruckerei, 1909.

Henderson, G. F. R. *The Science of War.* London: Longmans, Green, 1913.

Heslin, James J., ed. "The Diary of a Union Soldier in Confederate Prisons." *New York Historical Society Quarterly* 41 (July 1957): 233–78.

Hesseltine, William Best. *Civil War Prisons: A Study in War Psychology.* 1930. Reprint. New York: Frederick Ungar Publishing Company, 1964.

———. "Civil War Prisons—Introduction." *Civil War History* 8 (June 1962): 117–20.

Hobart, Harrison. C. "Libby Prison—The Escape." *War Papers—Wisconsin* (q.v.), 394–409.

Indiana Soldier [Capt. John V. Hadley, Danville, Indiana]. *Seven Months a Prisoner . . . Personal Experience of Prison Life.* Indianapolis: Meikel, 1868.

Isham, Asa B. "Experience in Rebel Prisons for United States Officers at Richmond, Macon, Savannah, Charleston and Columbia." In Isham et al. (q.v.), 1–238.

———, et al. *Prisoners of War.* Cincinnati: Lyman & Cushing, 1890.

"Jackson, Thomas Jonathon." *See* Freeman.

Johnson, Robert Underwood, and Clarence Clough Buell, eds. *Battles and Leaders of the Civil War.* 4 vols. New York: Century Company, 1887.

Jova, Joseph John. Prefatory matter to Cavada, 1985 edition (q.v.), pages not numbered.

Kaufmann, Wilhelm. *Die Deutschen im amerikanischen Bürgerkriege.* Munich and Berlin: R. Oldenbourg, 1911.

Kellogg, Robert H. *Life and Death in Rebel Prisons . . . Principally at Andersonville . . . and Florence.* . . . Hartford, Conn.: L. Stebbins, 1866.

Kniffin, G. C. "The Battle of Stone's River." In Johnson and Buel (q.v.), 3:613–32.

Koss, Rudolph A. *Milwaukee.* Milwaukee: Schnellpressendruck des "Herold," 1871.

Lewis, Lloyd. *Sherman: Fighting Prophet.* New York: Harcourt, Brace and Company, 1932.

Lieber, Francis. *Lieber's Code and the Law of War.* Edited by Richard Shelly Hartigan. Chicago: Precedent Publishing, 1983.

" 'Life in the Wild': Three German Letters from Indiana." [Anonymous]. Edited and translated by Frederic Trautmann. *Indiana Magazine of History* 80 (June 1984): 146–65.

Lincoln, Abraham. *The Collected Works of Abraham Lincoln.* Edited by Roy P. Basler, 8 vols. New Brunswick, N.J.: Rutgers University Press, 1953.

Long, E. B. *The Civil War Day by Day: An Almanac.* Garden City, N.Y.: Doubleday & Company, 1971.

Lonn, Ella. *Foreigners in the Confederacy.* 1940. Reprint. Gloucester, Mass.: Peter Smith, 1965.

———. *Foreigners in the Union Army and Navy.* Baton Rouge: Louisiana State University Press, 1951.

Love, William DeLoss. *Wisconsin in the War of the Rebellion: A History of All Regiments and Batteries.* Chicago: Church and Goodman, 1866.

Luttwak, Edward. *A Dictionary of Modern War.* New York: Harper & Row, 1971.

MacCauley, Clay. "From Chancellorsville to Libby Prison." In *Glimpses of the Nation's Struggle* (q.v.), 179–201.

McElwee, William. *The Art of War: Waterloo to Mons.* Bloomington: Indiana University Press, 1974.

Mattocks, Charles P. "In Six Prisons." *War Papers—Maine* (q.v.), 1:161–80.

Melville, Herman. *Billy Budd, Sailor.* Edited by Harrison Hayford and Merton M. Smealts, Jr. Chicago: University of Chicago Press, 1962.

Military Essays and Recollections: Papers Read before the Commandery of the State of Illinois, Military Order of the Loyal Legion of the United States. 3 vols. Chicago: A. C. McClurg and Company, 1891.

Miller, Francis Trevelyan, ed. *Photographic History of the Civil War.* 10 vols. New York: Review of Reviews Company, 1912.

Milton, George Fort. *Conflict: The American Civil War.* New York: Coward-McCann, 1941.

"Mitchel, John." *See* Monoghan.

Monaghan, Frank. "Mitchel, John." In *Dictionary of American Biography* (q.v.), 8:35–36.

Montesquieu, baron de la Brede. *Spirit of the Laws.* Translated by Thomas Nugent. Rev. ed. 2 vols. New York: Colonial Press, 1900.

Montross, Lynn. *War through the Ages.* New York: Harper & Brothers, 1944.

Moody, Joseph E. "Life in Confederate Prisons." In *Civil War Papers* (q.v.), 2:351–69.

Moore, Hugh. "A Reminiscence of Confederate Prison Life." *Journal of the Illinois State Historical Society* 65 (Winter 1972): 451–61.

Murphy, James B., ed. "A Confederate Soldier [William Speer]'s View of Johnson's Island Prison." *Ohio History* 79 (Spring 1970): 101–11.

Nevins, Allan. *The War for the Union.* 4 vols. New York: Charles Scribner's Sons, 1959–71.

———. James I. Robertson, Jr., and Bell I. Wiley. *Civil War Books: A Bibliography.* 2 vols. Baton Rouge: Louisiana State University Press, 1967–69.

Nussbaum, Arthur. *A Concise History of the Law of Nations.* Rev. ed. New York: Macmillan Company, 1954.

Official Records. See U.S. War Department.

Perry-Mosher, Kate E. "The Rock Island P.O.W. Camp." *Civil War Times Illustrated* 8 (July 1969): 28–36.

Personal Narratives: Soldiers and Sailors Historical Society of Rhode Island. 7 series. Providence: Published by the Society, 1891–98.

Personal Recollections of the War of the Rebellion: Addresses before the Commandery of the State of New York, Military Order of the Loyal Legion of the United States. 4 series. New York: G. P. Putnam's Sons, 1891–1912.

Phillips, John W. "Experiences in the Libby Prison." *War Papers—Missouri* (q.v.), 54–73.

Photographic History of the Civil War. See Miller.

"Pollard, Edward Alfred." *See* Hamilton.

Porch, Douglas. Review of *On Writing and Politics, 1967–1983,* by Gunther Grass. *Washington Post Book World,* 11 August 1985.

Powell, Jody. "An Old Dispute." *Philadelphia Inquirer,* 10 July 1985.

Putnam, George Haven. "An Experience in Virginia Prisons during the Last Year of the War." *Personal Recollections* (q.v.), 4:208–48.

Quiner, Edwin B. *The Military History of Wisconsin.* . . . Chicago: Clarke, 1866.

Robbins, Nathaniel A. "Life in Rebel Prisons." *War Papers—District of Columbia* (q.v.), 3:1–12.

Robertson, James I., Jr. "The Scourge of Elmira." *Civil War History* 8 (June 1962): 184–201.

Roe, Alfred S. "In a Rebel Prison; or, Experiences in Danville, Va." *Personal Narratives* (q.v.), 4:5–42.

Ropp, Theodore. *War in the Modern World*. Durham, N.C.: Duke University Press, 1959.

Rosengarten, J. G. *The German Soldier in the Wars of the United States*. 2d ed. Philadelphia: Lippincott, 1890.

Rousseau, Jean Jacques. *Political Writings*. Translated and edited by Frederick Watkins. New York: Thomas Nelson and Sons, 1953.

Ruddy, Francis Stephen. *International Law in the Enlightenment: The Background of Emmerich de Vattel's "Le droit des gens."* Dobbs Ferry, N.Y.: Oceana Publications, 1975.

Russell, Milton. "Reminiscences of Prison Life and Escape." *War Sketches* (q.v.), 1:25–29.

Sabre, G.E. *Nineteen Months a Prisoner of War*. New York: American News Company, 1865.

Sanderson, James M. *My Record in Rebeldom, as Written by Friend and Foe . . . the Official Charges and Evidence before the Military Commission in Washington . . .* [and] *the Report and Finding of the Court*. New York: W. E. Sibell, 1865.

Schlicher, J. J. "Bernhard Domschcke." *Wisconsin Magazine of History* 29 (March/June 1946): 319–32, 435–56.

Scott, H[enry] L. *Military Dictionary*. 1861. Reprint. New York: Greenwood Press, 1968.

Shewmon, Joe. "An Amazing Ordeal." *Civil War Times Illustrated* 1 (April 1962): 45–50, (May 1962): 48–50.

Simpson, Thomas. "My Four Months' Experience as a Prisoner of War." *Personal Narratives* (q.v.), 3:3–40.

Sketches of War History, 1861–1865: Papers Read before the Ohio Commandery of the Military Order of the Loyal Legion of the United States. 4 vols. Cincinnati: Robert Clarke, 1888–96.

Starr, George H. "In and Out of Confederate Prisons." *Personal Recollections* (q.v.), 2:64–103.

Sturgis, Thomas. "Prisoners of War." In ibid. 4:266–328.

Sweet, William Warren. *The Story of Religions in America*. New York: Harper & Brothers, 1930.

Thompson,Holland. *Prisons and Hospitals.*Vol.7 of Miller (q.v.).

Thompson, William Candace. "From the Defense of Atlanta to a Federal Prison Camp: A First-Person Account." *Civil War Times Illustrated* 3 (February 1965): 40–44.

Trefousse, Hans L. *Carl Schurz: A Biography*. Knoxville: University of Tennessee Press, 1982.

Tribe, Keith. "Notes on Translation and Terminology." In Reinhart Koselleck, *Futures Past: On the Semantics of Historical Time,* trans. Keith Tribe. Cambridge: MIT Press, 1985.

Turner, William Dandridge. "Some War-Time Recollections: The Story of a Confederate Officer Who Was at First One of Those in Charge of and Later a Captive in Libby Prison." *American Pocket Magazine* [formerly *American Magazine* and then *Frank Leslie's Popular Monthly*] 70 (September 1910): 619–31.

U.S. Congress. House. Committee on the Treatment of Prisoners of War and Union Citizens. *The Treatment of Prisoners of War, by the Rebel Authorities, during the War of the Rebellion*. . . . 40th Cong., 3d sess., 1869. H. Rept. 45, vol. 4, no. 139.

U.S. War Department. *The Official Atlas of the Civil War*. New York: T. Yoseloff, 1958. Originally 3 vols. of U.S. War Department. *The War of the Rebellion . . . the Official Records* (q.v.).

———. *The War of the Rebellion . . . the Official Records of the Union and Confederate Armies*. 128 vols. Washington: Government Printing Office, 1880–1901.

Vizinczey, Stephen. "Engineers of a Sham: How Literature Lies about Power." *Harper's,* June 1986, 69–73.

Walker, Thomas Alfred. *A History of the Law of Nations*. 2 vols. Cambridge: Cambridge University Press, 1899.

War Papers, Commandery of the District of Columbia, Military Order of the Loyal Legion of the United States. 5 vols. N.p., 1887–1918.

War Papers and Personal Reminiscences, 1861–1865, Read before the Commandery of the State of Missouri, Military Order of the Loyal Legion of the United States. St. Louis: Becktold, 1892.

War Papers Read before the Commandery of the State of Maine, Military Order of the Loyal Legion of the United States. 4 vols. Portland: Lefavor-Tower, 1908.

War Papers Read before the Commandery of the State of Wisconsin, Military Order of the Loyal Legion of the United States. Milwaukee: Burdick, Armitage & Allen, 1891.

War Sketches and Incidents as Related by Companions of the Iowa Commandery, Military Order of the Loyal Legion of the United States. 2 vols. Des Moines: Press of P. C. Kenyon, 1893.

Waterman, W. Randall. "Dow, Neal." In *Dictionary of American Biography* (q.v.), 5:411–12.

Weiser, George. *Nine Months in Rebel Prisons.* Philadelphia: J. N. Reeve, 1890.

Wilde, Oscar. *The Letters of Oscar Wilde.* Edited by Rupert Hart-Davis. London: Rupert Hart-Davis, 1962.

Winston, Robert W. *Robert E. Lee: A Biography.* New York: William Morrow, 1934.

Wittke, Carl Frederick. *The German-Language Press in America.* Lexington: University of Kentucky Press, 1957.

Wright, Quincy. *A Study of War.* Abridged by Louise Leonard Wright. Chicago: University of Chicago Press, 1964.

Writers' Program, Work Projects Administration. American Guide Series. *Virginia: A Guide to the Old Dominion.* New York: Oxford University Press, 1940.

Yearns, Wilfred Buck. *The Confederate Congress.* Athens: University of Georgia Press, 1960.

Zimmermann, G. A. *Deutsch in Amerika: Beiträge zur Geschichte der Deutsch-Amerikanischen Literatur.* 2d ed. 2 vols. Chicago: Eyller, 1894.

Index

(*See also* the roster of officers above, pp. 138–42.)